An Historical Survey of the

DIDCOT, NEWBURY AND SOUTHAMPTON RAILWAY

TRACK LAYOUTS AND ILLUSTRATIONS

by
C.W.Judge

Oxford Publishing Co.

Public Records Office Kew:

File reference numbers to information used in the research.

Didcot - Junction - MPR140/1   (GEN 3/127)

Didcot - Improvements - GEN   3/133 (GEN 3/127)

Electric Train Staff - 1907 - MPR 140/5

Signalling - Rail 250 - Nos. 556, 557, 558, 559, 560, 717

Siding Mr Riches 1907 MP4 144/20

Traffic and Board Meetings - Rail 156, Nos. 9, 16, 17, and 18

Didcot Survey - (1875) GW 3/83

Didcot Timetables 1900-1914 TT26/7 (61/63 65-67)   1895   TT3/38/9 (60 or 64)

Didcot, Newbury and Southampton Railway -

Winchester Section opening MPR 134/1

Construction of MPR 134/2

Board of Trade reports MPR 134/3

Land ownership MPR 135

Shareholders MPR 136

Traffic Managers MPR 137

Doubling in Wartime MPR 140/3 and MPR 144/21

Additional Sidings 1906 MPR 140/2

Amalgamation Papers 1922 Rail 253 - No. 746

List of Weighbridges Rail 253 - No. 289

Railway Circulars Rail 253 - No. 510

Shawford Junction

Shawford Junction Railway Magazine 1954, page 591

Shawford Junction Electric Train Staff Installation MPR 141/7

Shawford Junction Construction of - MPR 141/6

Didcot, Newbury and Southampton Circulars (1877-1909) - Rail 253 - Nos. GW4/515

Whitchurch Station MPR 146/17

Further files MPR 1057 and 1058

Timetables Rail 981 - Nos. 60, 63, 67

Didcot, Newbury and Southampton Railway - Rail 1057

783 - Historical
784 - Construction
810 - Didcot Plan
811 - Newbury
814 - Electric Staff Operation
812 - Didcot Doubling
823 - Shawford
829 - Light Railway
827 - Light Railway
828 - Light Railway
832 - Sutton Scotney Cottage
839 - King's Worthy
843 - Whitchurch
845 - Plans
848 - Woodhay
853 - Woodhay
854 - Compton
856 - Winchester
857 - Sutton Scotney
860 - Winchester
861 - Burghclere
862 - Winchester
864 - Upton
871 - Winnall Sidings
872 - Enborne
875 - Compton
881 - Station lights
887 - Hampstead Norris
889 - Hermitage
892 - King's Worthy
898 - Pinewood
900 - Sutton Scotney
918 - Churn
923 - King's Worthy

Didcot, Newbury and Southampton Signalling Diagrams - Rail 282 Nos. 67-74

Didcot, Newbury and Southampton Surveys - Rail 274 Nos. 97 and 99

Didcot, Newbury and Southampton Financial Story - Rail 1014/13

Typesetting by:
Aquarius Typesetting Services, New Milton, Hants.

Printed in Great Britain by:
Balding + Mansell Ltd., Wisbech, Cambs.

Published by:
Oxford Publishing Co.
Link House
West Street
POOLE, Dorset

Plate 1:   The Didcot, Newbury and Southampton Railway's office at 11 Oxford Street, Southampton, on 17th April 1923, reported to have been a very busy office indeed in the 1920s.

British Rail

Acknowledgements

I gratefully acknowledge the help and patience of the following people and organizations that have helped in the preparation of this book. British Railways (Southern and Western Region), H. C. Casserley, W. Camwell, L. Elsey, J. N. Faulkner, C. Gammell, The Public Records Office Kew, Michael Hale, R. Kirkland, Ian Kennedy, Lens of Sutton, B. Moody, J.P. Morris, C. J. Marsden, The Newbury News, L. N. Owen, The Oxford Reference Library, C. R. Potts, G. Pryer, Stanley Rhodes of Real Photographs, R. C. Riley, The South Devon Railway Museum, G. Wareham, and Lynda for the hours she spent trying to read my writing and typing the manuscript.

Plate 2: This rather nostalgic photograph shows three pensioners who have returned to service with the Great Western Railway for the duration of World War I, to allow the younger men to serve their nation. It shows the nameboard for the Didcot end of the DN&SR and also the old Didcot GWR engine shed in the background.

British Rail

Introduction

The Didcot, Newbury and Southampton Railways was, and still could have been, a very important rail link between the north and south. In researching material for this book I realized just how much traffic had been carried over these lines, especially in World War I, and particularly in World War II. It was during World War II that the Railway Executive became aware of the importance of the route and, therefore, in eight months, improved, at great expense, the line's capacity. I have included here an extract from the Great Western Railway magazine of the time, setting out the work. It was interesting to note that the actual route and station names were not given in the magazine article at the time, for security reasons.

The work consisted of the improvement of a single track connecting route, part of which has been double tracked, and the remainder increased in capacity by the lengthening of loops, the provision of three additional loops, and the installation of improved signalling and point operation. With the major portion that was double tracked there is nothing which may be recorded at the present time, and the following notes concern the 25 mile length of single track of which the capacity has been increased by various improvements. Although the line connects two important main routes, it did not carry a heavy traffic. There were eight small stations on the route, dealing mostly with passengers, parcels and rural goods, and, to permit trains travelling in the opposite directions to pass, short crossing loops were provided at six of these stations.

When the line was built, some 60 years ago, the formation and bridges were made sufficiently wide to accommodate double tracks, although a single track only was laid, but since then weathering of the banks has taken place and due to the accumulation of consequent deposits has become overgrown. From time to time the track has been slewed towards the centre of the formation to obtain the clearances required by new standards, particularly under arched overbridges. It would not have been possible, therefore, to lay an additional track throughout the entire length without considerable adjustment of formation. Accordingly, it was decided to allow the line to remain as single track and to increase its carrying capacity by additional crossing facilities, and other improvements.

All the existing loops were 300yds. long. These have been lengthened to 550yds. which, in effect, allows an extra engine and 20 wagons to use them. Three additional loops, of similar length, have also been constructed; one of these is mid-way between two stations. The loops have been planned so that the new distance between them is nowhere more than about 2½ miles. In addition, the line from the junction at one end has been doubled for a length of two miles, and, near the other end, an entirely new connection has been made with the main line of another railway company where the latter crosses the GWR line on an overbridge. The new connecting line of about a mile in length runs through a large new cutting, over a new embankment, and over a new bridge.

So that the length of time required to execute the works might be reduced to a minimum, all daytime traffic working, apart from that connected with the works, was suspended. Through trains ordinarily passing over the line were diverted, goods traffic was passed during the night only, and passengers and parcels were catered for by a special arrangement of station-to-station bus services with no intermediate stopping places.

The work was arranged so that excavation and tipping were almost balanced, and, in all, some 60,000 cu.yards. of earth was moved. For the bottom ballast, 11,000 cu.yds. of ashes was used, and for top ballast 8,000 cu.yds. of crushed stone. About 6 miles of track have been laid and 2 miles of existing track slewed; 52 new single connections and 15 runaway catch points were laid-in and 22 superseded fittings taken out. Additional water supply for engines has been provided by installing two water columns half-way through the route, fed from a 11,500 galion tank connected to council mains.

The old signal boxes were sited in the middle of the stations, and operated the loop points mechanically. As the lengthened loops made this method of operation impracticable,, the boxes were abolished, and new ones erected at the ends of the loops nearest to the station sidings, the points of which are still mechanically operated. The other ends of the loops have been track-circuited and their fittings operated by electrically-worked motors, actuated from the signal boxes. The line is operated on the 'token' system, and a special feature is the installation of auxiliary token instruments at the ends of the loops furthest from the signal boxes. These auxiliary token instrument boxes are connected directly to the signal boxes by telephone. The works were completed within eight months.

To supplement this article I have been fortunate enough to locate and reproduce the plans of all the wartime track alterations and, therefore, these make good comparisons to the main track diagrams of the original survey of 1908 which was obtained from the British Railways Civil Engineer's office.

To try and delve into the early history of the line was not the object of this book, and therefore the books listed in the bibliography on *page 5* allow the reader to research deeper into the Parliamentary Acts, the railway finances and similar problems that beset this railway. I did feel however, that an extract from an early account of the railway in the *Railway Magazine* did set the scene and reason for the DN&SR to be constructed:

This line, though at present comparatively little known to the travelling public, forms, nevertheless, the shortest route, by a good many miles, from the Midlands and North of England to the great arsenal and dockyard of Portsmouth and the seaside resort of 'Sunny Southsea', to the Isle of Wight, and the very important and rapidly-increasing port of Southampton; and is probably destined, in the not too distant

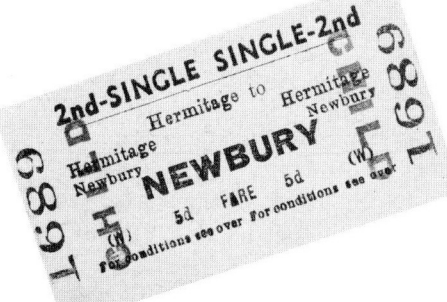

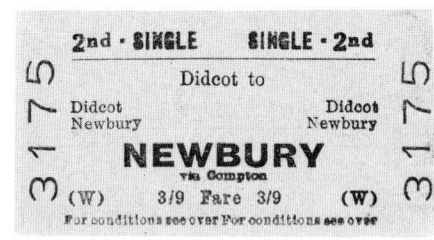

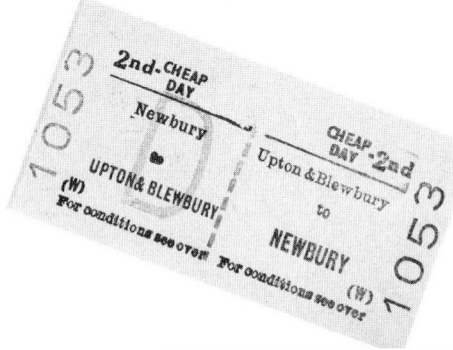

future, to take its proper place as what, in fact, it is, namely, a connecting link in one of the main railway highways of the country.

The railway was originally authorized by an Act of 1873 as a line from Didcot to join the London & South Western Railway north of Micheldever Station, with, in addition, a junction with the Basingstoke and Exeter line. Sundry extensions of time and changes of plan, involving various further Acts, followed, the most important of which was one for an independent line right through from Didcot to Southampton, the Act for which was obtained in 1882, after a severe Parliamentary fight.

To help the reader, I have included a brief route description to identify the positions of various stations and junctions down the line.

The line from Didcot to Newbury was opened on 13th April 1882 and, from there to Winchester, in July 1885. The final section from Winchester to Southampton was partially constructed but, due to the very large cost and heavy earthworks, it was abandoned, in 1889, in favour of a junction at Shawford and agreed running powers with the South Western Railway Company. It was finally absorbed into the GWR in 1923.

The line started at a very important junction on the Great Western Railway at Didcot in Berkshire. This junction afforded connections with the north and thus with all important cities, including Manchester, Liverpool, Chester, Birmingham, Worcester, Cheltenham, Gloucester and even South Wales.

After leaving Didcot Station, the line curved away south and on to Upton (the first station). From there it proceeded to Churn, which was only really used on occasions for the military camps and rifle ranges. Near Churn, the railway crossed The Ridgeway, one of the four Great Roman Roads. Compton was the next station, which served East Ilsley (over two miles away). This village was well known for its sheep fairs and racehorse training, and so the railway transported and benefited from both of these activities. Hampstead Norris is then passed, the route continuing through Pinewood Halt and then on to Hermitage. After crossing the Kennet

and Lambourn rivers, the line runs into Newbury, where the Great Western's Berks & Hants main line runs; an important junction and connection for the DN&SR. Leaving the market town of Newbury, the line is soon at Enbourne Junction where it turns left in the Valley of Enbourne. It was once proposed to flood this valley and form a new reservoir for London. The first stop on this section is Woodhay and, as quoted by a traveller, 'surely the designers of toy railway stations must have passed this way - station house with small windows, lace curtains, potted geraniums and the inevitable saw-tooth edging to the veranda and roof eaves.' At this station the line embarks on a 23 mile journey to Winchester.

The line then passes through Highclere and Burghclere stations where some confusion arose as to which station passengers would alight for Highclere or Burghclere villages, and again a quotation from a traveller probably sums up the atmosphere of these stations. 'The natives certainly think that the stations are not where they ought to be. The lighting at these stations is a mixture of oil lamps, Tilley lamps and electricity. Burghclere has Tilley lamps for the office, hurricane lamps on the platform. I came to Burghclere one dark night and it might well have been the setting for the 'Ghost train'. It is one of the most lonely stations.'

Litchfield is next, serving its tiny hamlet, and the line then continues to Whitchurch in the valley of the River Test. The station of Sutton Scotney had a reputation for clipped box trees on the platform and, during its operative days, caused discussion between the passengers as to what the trees represented. Through Worthy Down and on to King's Worthy, in the valley of the River Itchen, the route continues and then on into Winchester (Cheesehill) Station, the last station on the DN&SR. After leaving Winchester the line joined the London & South Western Railway at Shawford Junction and then ran into Southampton.

I hope you enjoy the photographs, drawings and appendices depicting the railway history of one of the last and important through cross-country routes.

C. W. Judge
March 1984

Bibliography

The Didcot, Newbury and Southampton Railway by P. Karau, M. Parsons and K. Robertson - Wild Swan Publications
History of Newbury by Money
The Didcot, Newbury and Southampton Railway by T. Sands - Oakwood Press
Various Public and Working tometables of the DN&SR, GWR and BR (Western Region)
The Railway Magazine (various issues)
British Rail Magazine (Western Region) April 1949
A Pictorial Record of GWR Architecture by A. Vaughan - Oxford Publishing Company
GWR Magazine (various issues)
History of the Great Western Railway by E. T. MacDermot - GWR 1922
R. A. Cooke's Track Plans of the GWR (Berkshire Section) by R. A. Cooke
Regional History of the Railways of Great Britain (Volume Two) Southern England - David & Charles

Plate 3: At Southampton Terminus, a Didcot, Newbury and Southampton Railway train prepares to leave, hauled by GWR locomotive No. 3440 *City of Truro* on 23rd May 1957. Alongside, a Southern Railway engine, No. 30285 simmers away awaiting its next duty.

H. C. *Casserley*

Plate 4:   A fine view of GWR locomotive No. 3440 *City of Truro*, after overhaul at Swindon Works, waiting in the south bay of Newbury Station with the branch train for Winchester in 1957. The Lambourn Valley branch train can be seen in the background with a GWR pannier tank in charge. *City of Truro* was beautifully restored and often used on the DN&SR.

GRADIENT PROFILE
& DISTANCE MAP

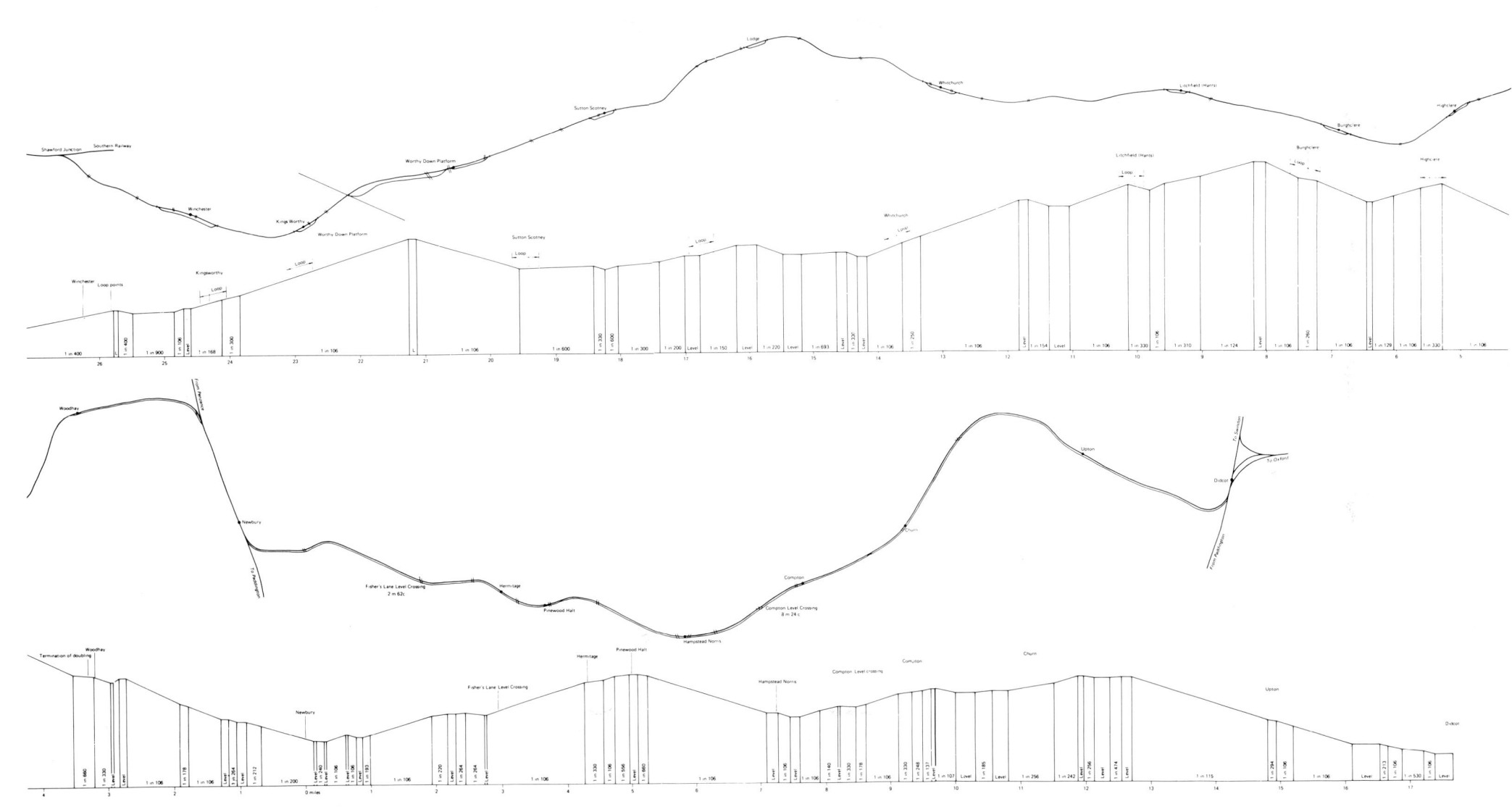

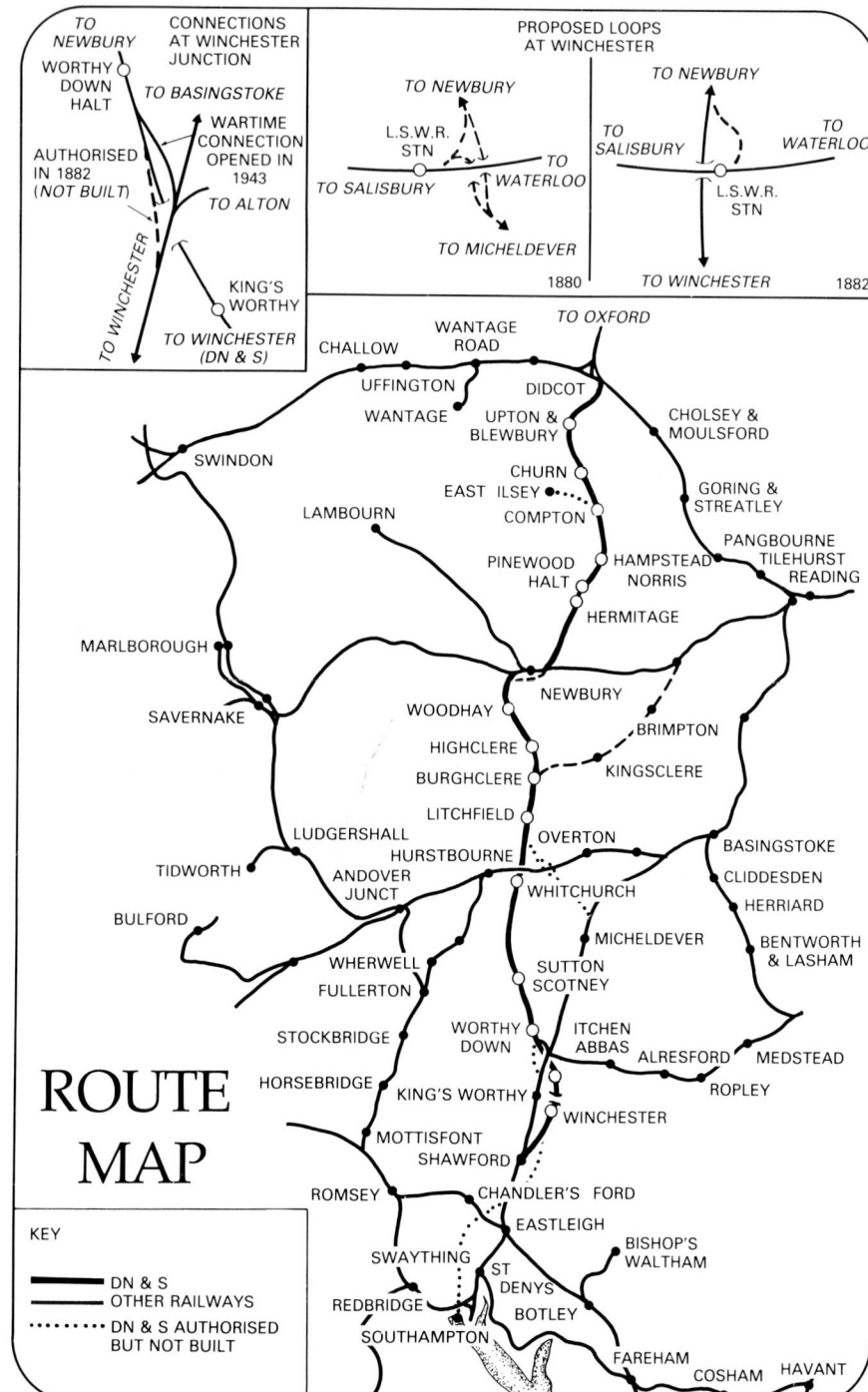

ROUTE MAP

KEY
— DN & S
— OTHER RAILWAYS
⋯ DN & S AUTHORISED BUT NOT BUILT

Didcot, Newbury & Southampton Railway

Record of Mileage in 1947
Double line from Didcot to Woodhay. Single line (worked by electric train token) Woodhay to Winchester (Chesil). Single line (worked by Tyer's electric tablet) Winchester to Shawford Junction.

Mile post distance		Distance from Didcot		
Miles	Chains	Miles	Chains	
				Didcot (Western Region)
17	27		22	Didcot East Junction
14	54	2	75	Upton & Blewbury
11	66	5	63 ('Down')	Ilsley Signals (intermediate home
12	33	5	16 ('Up')	and distant signals, installed 1943)
10	79	6	50	Churn
9	14	8	35	Compton
7	7	10	42	Hampstead Norris
4	69	12	60	Pinewood Halt
4	13	13	36	Hermitage
0		17	49	Newbury East Junction
		17	77	Newbury (Western Region)
0		19	7	Enbourne Junction
2	18	21	25	Woodhay
4	38	23	45	Highclere
6	33	25	40	Burghclere
9	2	28	9	Litchfield
12	57	31	64	Whitchurch
15	77	35	4	Lodge Bridge Loop (opened 28th March 1943; closed 7th March 1950)
18	33	37	40	Sutton Scotney
21	19	40	26	Worthy Down
23	24	42	31	King's Worthy
25	20	44	27	Winchester (Chesil)
25	53	44	60	Winchester (Bar End Goods Sidings)
27	35	46	42	Shawford Junction (Southern Region)

Some of the official Acts relating to the Didcot, Newbury and Southampton Railway.

STATUTORY RULES AND ORDERS 1923, No. 445.
GREAT WESTERN RAILWAY (WESTERN GROUP) PRELIMINARY ABSORPTION SCHEME (No. 4) 1922; Dated March, 27th 1923.

Absorbing:-
Didcot, Newbury and Southampton Railway Company, into Great Western Railway Company.

Great Western Railway and Didcot, Newbury and Southampton Ry. Co., 4/5/82; D. N. & S. Ry Act 1882, S.65.

Didcot, Newbury and Southampton Ry. D. N. & S. Jcn.Ry. Act 1873, S.S. 45-54.

Didcot, Newbury and Southampton Junction Railway Act: 1873, 1876, and 1880.
Didcot, Newbury and Southampton Railway Act: 1883.
Didcot, Newbury and Southampton Railway (Money) Act: 1885.
Didcot, Newbury and Southampton Railway (Extension of Time) Act: 1885, 1887, 1889, 1891, 1897 and 1903.

Change of name. 'Didcot, Newbury and Southampton Junction Railway Co.' to 'Didcot, Newbury and Southampton Railway Co.'; DN&S Ry. Act 1883, S.21.

Didcot

Plate 5: A fine panoramic view of Didcot Station looking west, taken by the official GWR photographer in the 1930s. The DN&SR Bay platform is seen on the far left with the main 'up' and 'down' running lines adjoining it. The two lines in the centre of the picture are the slow, 'up' and 'down' running lines with the goods and engine shed lines on the right. On the far right of the photograph are the through lines to Oxford and the North. The new engine shed is clearly visible and the yard is certainly very active, with no fewer than five locomotives engaged in shunting.

British Rail

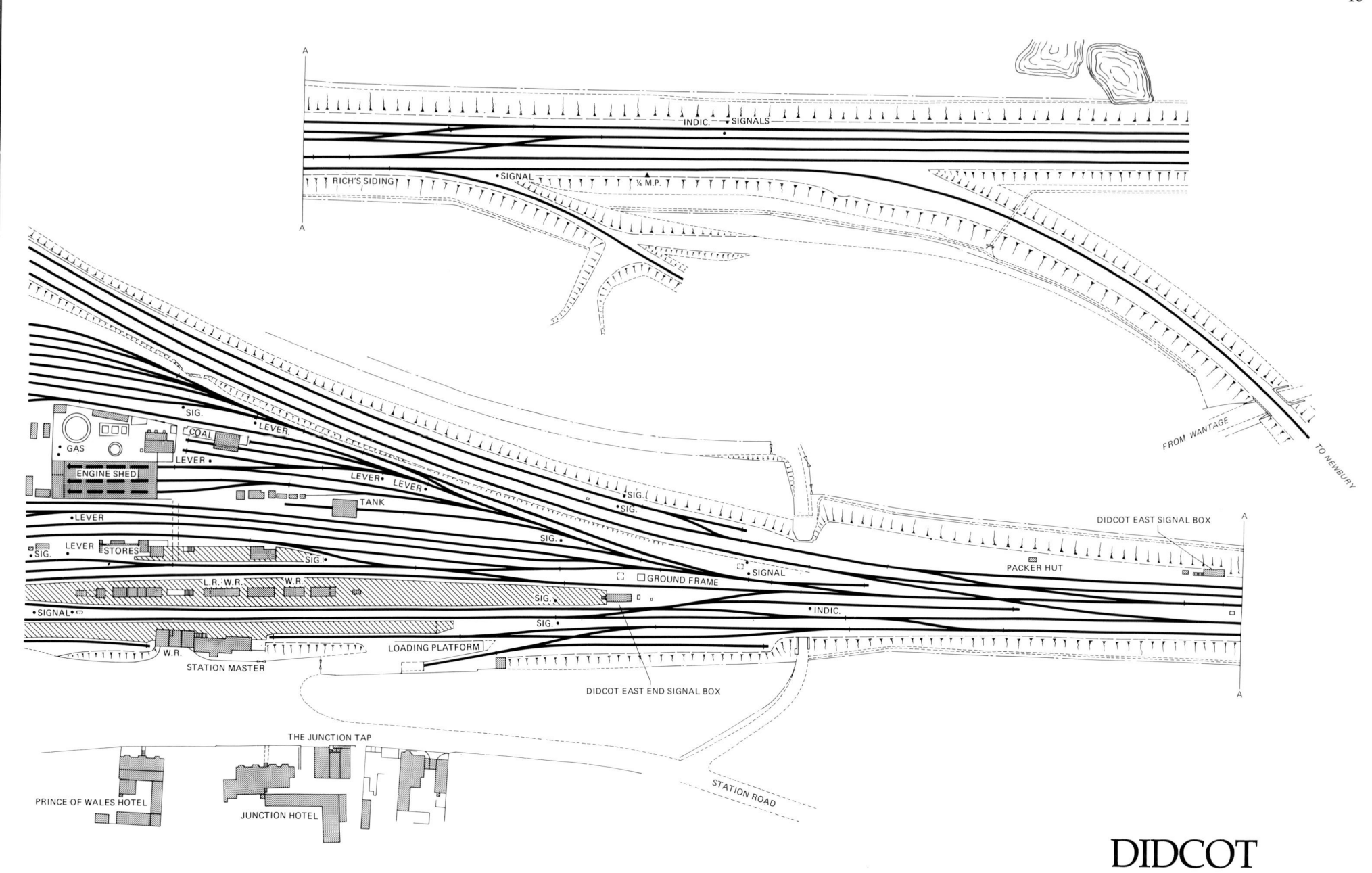

A

A

INDIC. • SIGNALS

RICH'S SIDING

• SIGNAL

¼ M.P.

FROM WANTAGE

TO NEWBURY

SIG. • LEVER.

COAL

GAS

LEVER

ENGINE SHED

LEVER• LEVER •

TANK

LEVER

SIG. •

SIG. •

DIDCOT EAST SIGNAL BOX

LEVER

STORES

SIG. •

SIG. •

SIG. •

PACKER HUT

GROUND FRAME

SIGNAL

L.R. W.R.

W.R.

SIG. •

SIG. •

• SIGNAL •

INDIC.

W.R.

LOADING PLATFORM

A

STATION MASTER

DIDCOT EAST END SIGNAL BOX

A

THE JUNCTION TAP

STATION ROAD

PRINCE OF WALES HOTEL

JUNCTION HOTEL

DIDCOT

Didcot

Didcot Station was first opened to passenger traffic in 1844 when it was a junction for the Oxford branch, between the broad gauge and the main line. The station's appearance at that date can be clearly seen in the woodcut on the title page of this book. The then five platforms (very narrow) were covered by a very ornate roof, and the passenger entrance situated below rail level was reported to be unique in 1844. The station was reconstructed in the distinct GWR style after a tragic fire in 1866, which totally destroyed the 'down' side buildings.

The Didcot, Newbury and Southampton Railway's starting point was the bay at the east end of the 'down' platform which was controlled by a home starting signal. The line ran alongside the GWR main line for about 20 chains with only one point going off to the right into a private siding, known as Rich's Siding.

The track plan (above) of Didcot Station (as with all the surveys throughout this book) was taken from the official 1908 survey held at the Civil Engineer's Office at Paddington. This track plan shows the old engine shed and the platform layouts before reconstruction. The Didcot East End signal box at the end of the 'up' platform is of particular interest. This plan differs from other published plans but has been carefully copied from the official plan and does bear comparison with photographic records. In comparison with the official 1938 track plan over the page, one can see the vast changes in modernization that have taken place. The plan of 1938 has been deliberately included without redrawing, as again it clearly shows discrepancies with other published track plans of Didcot Station, and it is hoped that this plan will put the history books right. On the DN&SR bay, it clearly shows the addition of run-round facilities with a revised horse loading dock. The 1938 layout shows how the engine shed has been moved from behind the station and reconstructed as a new four road shed with a coaling tower and turntable. The supporting photograph clearly shows the buildings just after construction. The new engine shed was 210ft. x 67ft., and could accommodate sixteen engines and was constructed during 1931 and 1932. The complex also contained a new lifting shop, complete with a 50 ton engine hoist, together with a coaling stage and overhead water tank, 44ft. x 36ft. with a capacity of 74,250 gallons. Also installed were a new boiler washing, and sand calcinating plant.

On the operation of the DN&SR line, it was common for the last train of the day into Didcot to use the main line platform, and then the station pilot would remove and shunt the coaches into the DN&SR bay platform ready for the first train out in the morning. All the motive power normally used on the DN&SR line was shedded at the GWR Didcot Shed. The small insert shows, diagrammatically, the layout of the station complex at Didcot and its importance as a junction with the DN&SR.

Plate 6: This photograph shows the new four road engine shed at the commencement of its use in 1932.

British Rail

11

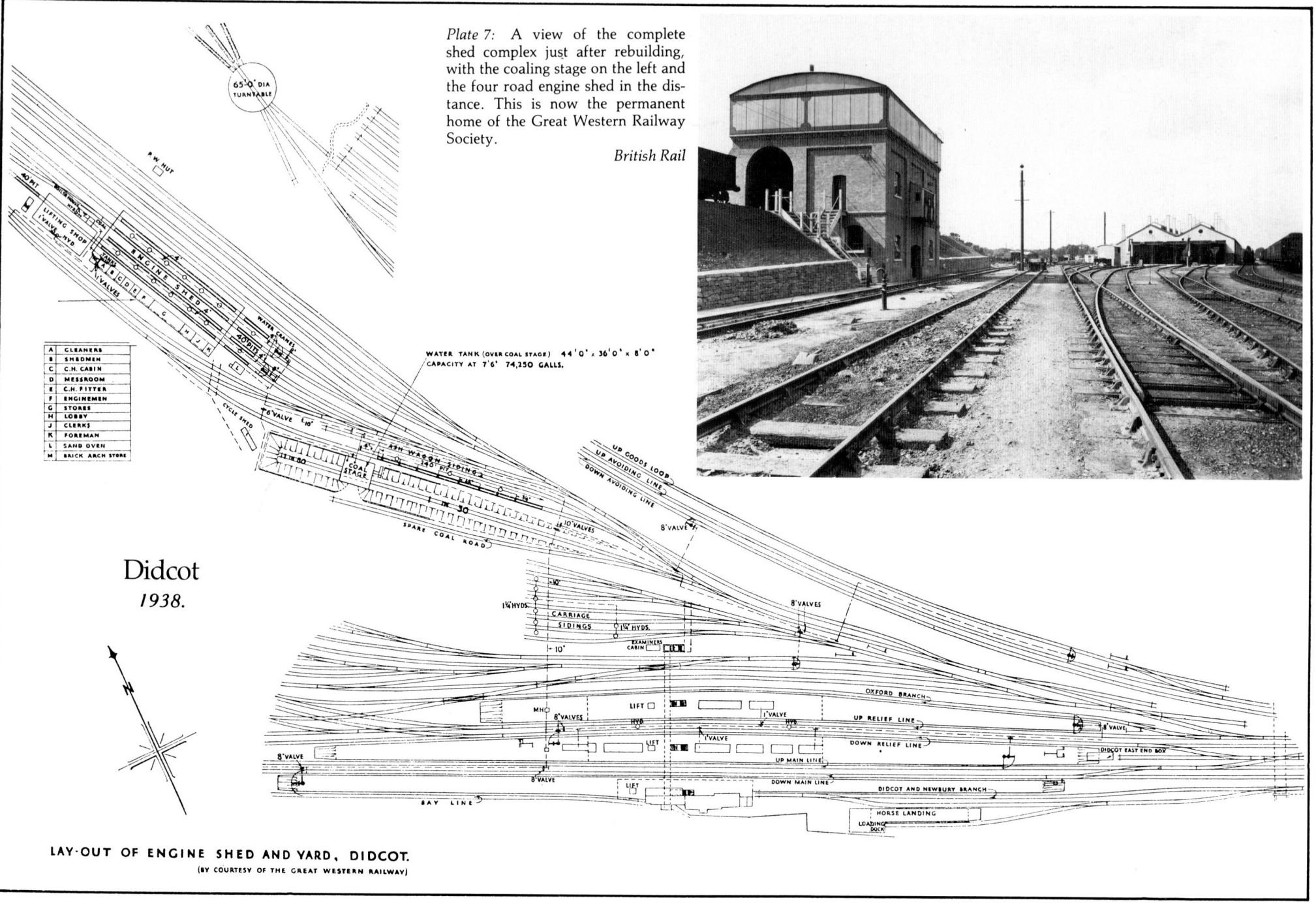

Plate 7: A view of the complete shed complex just after rebuilding, with the coaling stage on the left and the four road engine shed in the distance. This is now the permanent home of the Great Western Railway Society.

British Rail

65'0" DIA TURNTABLE

P. W. HUT

LIFTING SHOP

ENGINE SHED

WATER CRANES

A	CLEANERS
B	SHEDMEN
C	C.H. CABIN
D	MESSROOM
E	C.H. FITTER
F	ENGINEMEN
G	STORES
H	LOBBY
J	CLERKS
K	FOREMAN
L	SAND OVEN
M	BRICK ARCH STORE

WATER TANK (OVER COAL STAGE) 44'0" x 36'0" x 8'0"
CAPACITY AT 7'6" 74,250 GALLS.

CYCLE SHED

ASH WAGGON SIDING

COAL STAGE

SPARE COAL ROAD

UP GOODS LOOP
UP AVOIDING LINE
DOWN AVOIDING LINE

8' VALVE

Didcot
1938.

CARRIAGE SIDINGS

EXAMINERS CABIN

8' VALVES

8' VALVES

MH

LIFT

OXFORD BRANCH

UP RELIEF LINE

DOWN RELIEF LINE

LIFT

I' VALVE

8' VALVE

DIDCOT EAST END BOX

8' VALVE

UP MAIN LINE

DOWN MAIN LINE

DIDCOT AND NEWBURY BRANCH

LIFT

BAY LINE

HORSE LANDING

LOADING DOCK

LAY-OUT OF ENGINE SHED AND YARD, DIDCOT.
(BY COURTESY OF THE GREAT WESTERN RAILWAY)

Plate 8: Didcot Station, in the spring of 1934, after the modernization programme, looking towards London. The DN&SR bay platform is on the right, past the station buildings. The new lift towers stand out well, as do the ornate electric lamps. The bay on the right was the starting place for the local stopping service to Swindon. The lines on the left curve away to Oxford and the North.

British Rail

Plate 9: This photograph, taken in the 1930s, shows, in close-up, the bay platform of the Didcot, Newbury and Southampton Railway. The photograph shows the platform extension with the new edging, and the new horse loading dock and double track allowing run-round facilities for DN&SR trains. The huge telegraph poles are worthy of a glance as they are now a vision of the past in the railway landscape.

British Rail

Plate 10: Standing on this platform (No. 2) the traveller would await the arrival of the fast trains to London. The DN&SR bay can be seen on the right of the picture, just beyond the station buildings. The horse loading bay is clearly visible. Note the fire buckets and that the main poster hoardings seem to be owned by other railway companies in this 1930s' photograph.

British Rail

Plate 11: Having walked down and under the subway, one is now standing on the 'down' main platform looking at the spot where we stood in *Plate 10*. In the distance, in this 1930s' view, can be seen the Didcot Middle signal box and the GWR provender sidings which was the base for the horse-feeding stores of the GWR. Note the little windows in the roof of the station allowing light into the attic roofs of the buildings.

British Rail

Plate 12: This is an early view of the main 'down' platform reconstruction, with the new lifts being installed and the old gas lamps still visible. It clearly shows the old platform layout with the Middle box in the distance. Note the water crane and signals, which disappeared in the reconstruction. The bay platform in the distance is for the local Swindon stopping trains.

British Rail

Plate 13: This photograph, taken in December 1962, covers the same part of the 'down' platform as that shown in *Plate 12*, but now shows the lift and lift towers complete. Bay platform No. 1 is the DN&SR platform, and No. 2 bay platform is for Swindon stopping trains. It is interesting to note the early type of British Railways station signs.

British Rail

Didcot East Junction

The signalling diagram of the east end of Didcot Station, showing all the signalling of the DN&SR bay and running lines after 1942. Note the run-round points in the bay platform are worked by a ground frame, making the train movements independent of the GWR running lines.

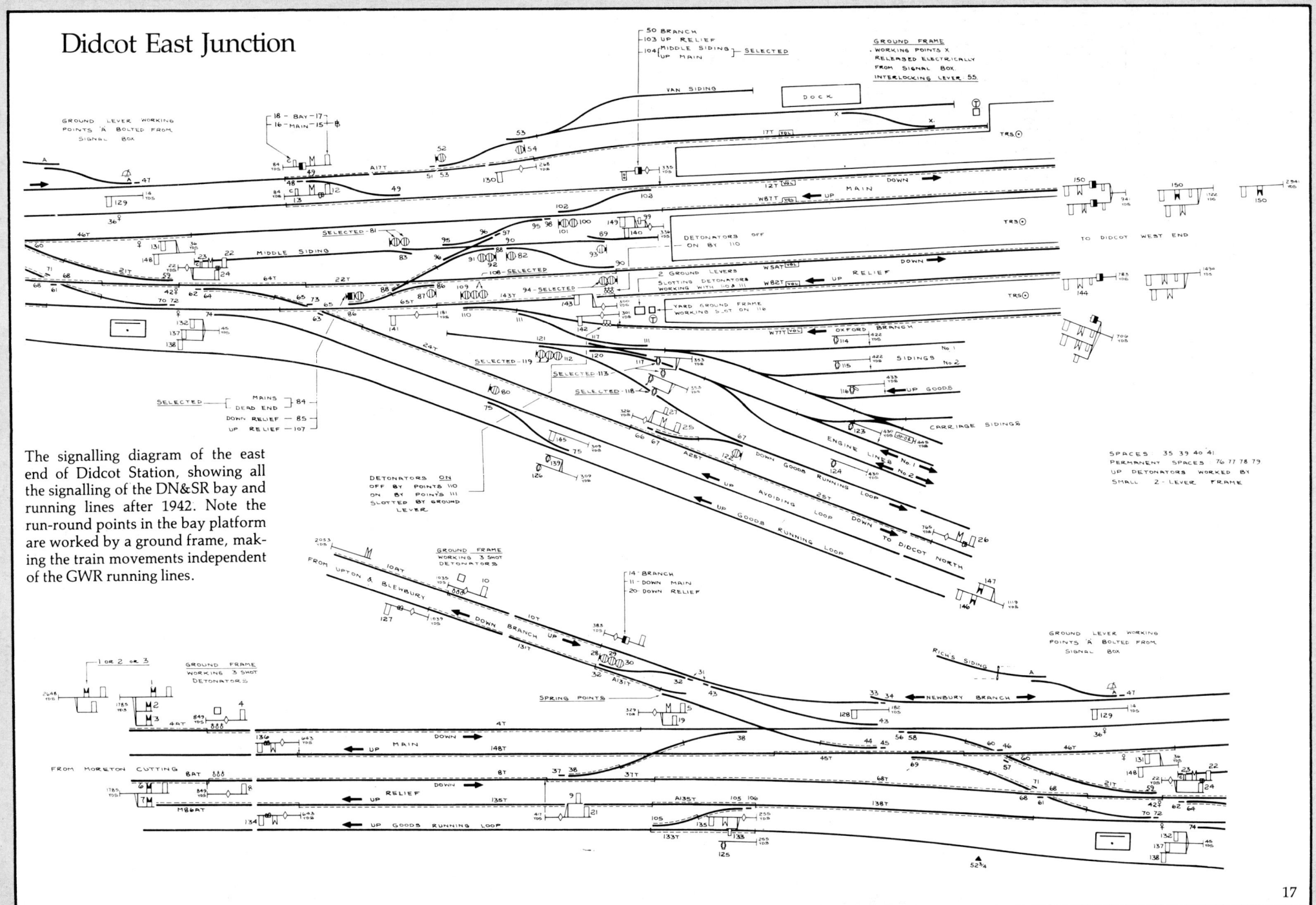

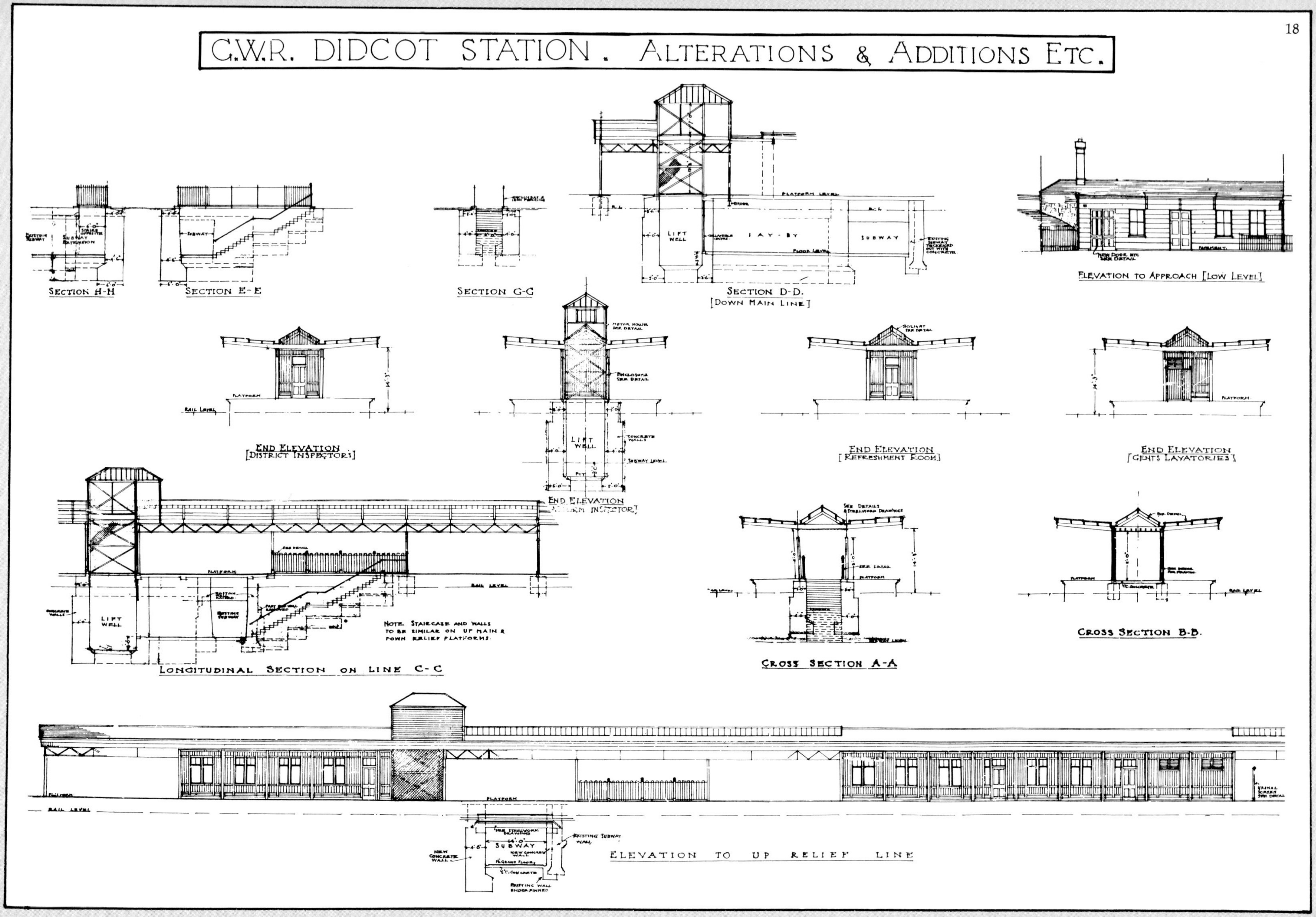

G.W.R. DIDCOT STATION. ALTERATIONS & ADDITIONS ETC.
SECTION H-H
SECTION E-E
SECTION G-G
SECTION D-D. [DOWN MAIN LINE]
LIFT WELL
LAY-BY
SUBWAY
ELEVATION TO APPROACH [LOW LEVEL]
END ELEVATION [DISTRICT INSPECTORS]
END ELEVATION [PLATFORM INSPECTOR]
END ELEVATION [REFRESHMENT ROOM]
END ELEVATION [GENTS LAVATORIES]
CROSS SECTION A-A
CROSS SECTION B-B.
NOTE. STAIRCASE AND WALLS TO BE SIMILAR ON UP MAIN & DOWN RELIEF PLATFORMS.
LONGITUDINAL SECTION ON LINE C-C
ELEVATION TO UP RELIEF LINE

The official drawing on the above page clearly shows the type of buildings at Didcot Station. The location and position of the unusual subway and lifts to each platform are clearly shown. The construction of the buildings consists of a stout timber frame, enclosed by a double wall of plankings, sealed by narrow strips, giving a 'texture' look to the walls. In *Plate 11*, it is easy to see the dark brown and cream stone colour of the paintwork. The valance boards extend (with a dihedral effect of aircraft wings) over the platform and give that 'GWR' appearance.

Plate 14 (top left): This view helps to show the ornate valancing and style of the end of the buildings.

British Rail

Plate 15 (top right): This photograph shows the top of the subway stairs on No. 3 'down' main platform, with signs to the east and west bays..The east bay is the DN&SR platform.

British Rail

Plate 16 (left): This view has been photographed further along the platform and shows virtually the buffer end (*left of picture*) of the DN&SR bay (No. 1 platform).

British Rail

Plate 17: A further platform view helps the reader to appreciate the roof awning supports and the panel board effect, with the narrow strips covering the joints. One can also see in this photograph the colour usage on this type of building.

British Rail

Plate 18: The last of the Didcot Station photographs clearly shows the panel effect and door panel shapes of a GWR station. The unusual telegraph pole is worthy of a glance.

British Rail

Plate 19: On 22nd August 1960, a fast 'up' train, headed by GWR 'Castle' class locomotive No. 7000 *Viscount Portal*, is seen passing a DN&SR stopping train hauled by No. 6164, which awaits the 'off' to Newbury at 11.14.

Michael Hale

Plate 20: A further view of the DN&SR bay platform, with another type of motive power used on the line, ex-GWR locomotive No. 2252, with the usual three coach train of the period. It stands with the 10.50 to Eastleigh, on 14th September 1959. The 'up' express is headed by 'Castle' class No. 7024 *Powis Castle* and is the 08.15 Cardiff to Paddington through service.

J. N. Faulkner

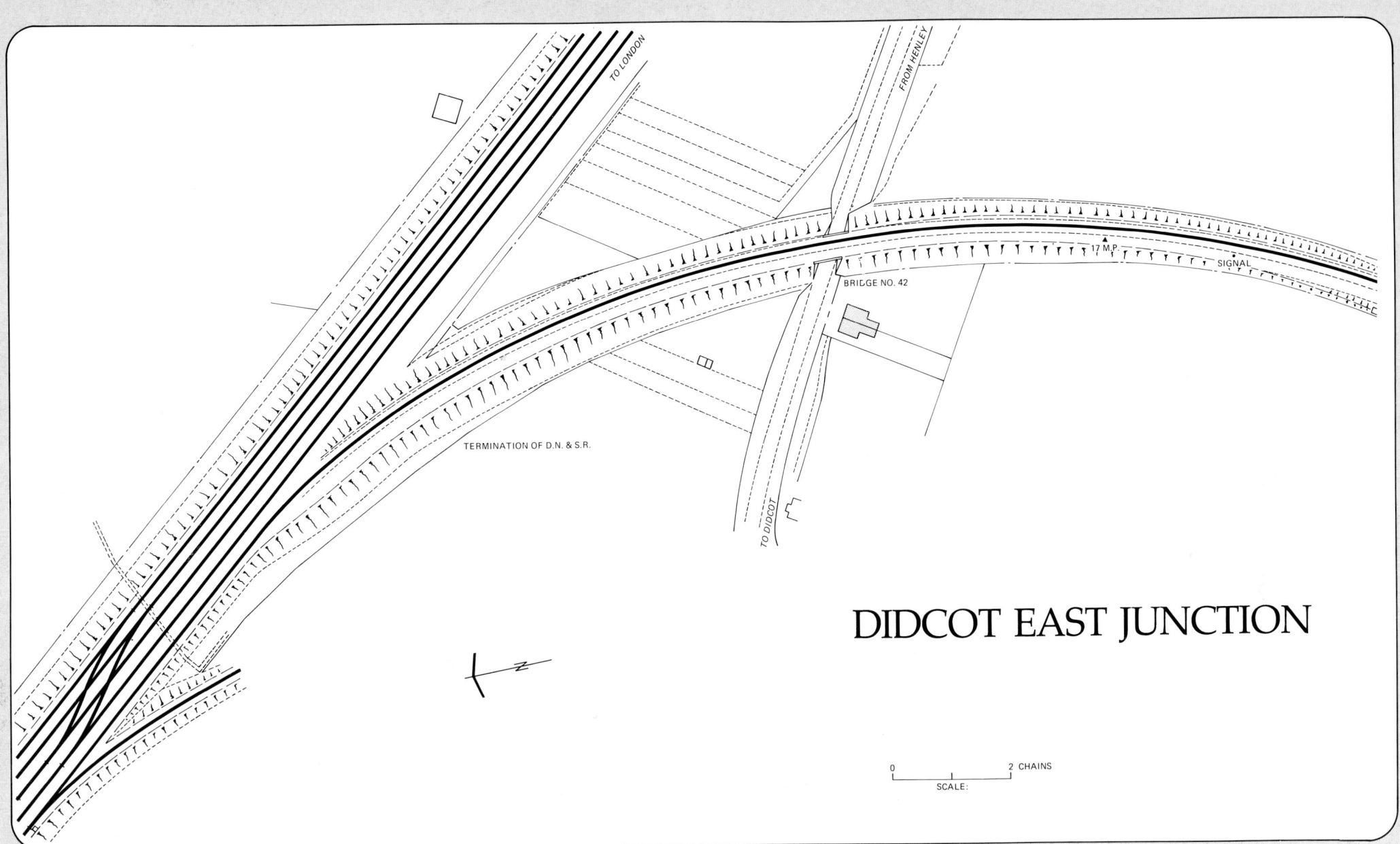

TO LONDON

FROM HENLEY

BRIDGE NO. 42

17 M.P.

SIGNAL

TERMINATION OF D.N. & S.R.

TO DIDCOT

DIDCOT EAST JUNCTION

0   1   2 CHAINS

SCALE:

The track plan of 1908 shows the single line diverging to the south at the start of the DN&SR, with Rich's Siding shown in the bottom left of the plan.

21

DIDCOT EAST JUNCTION

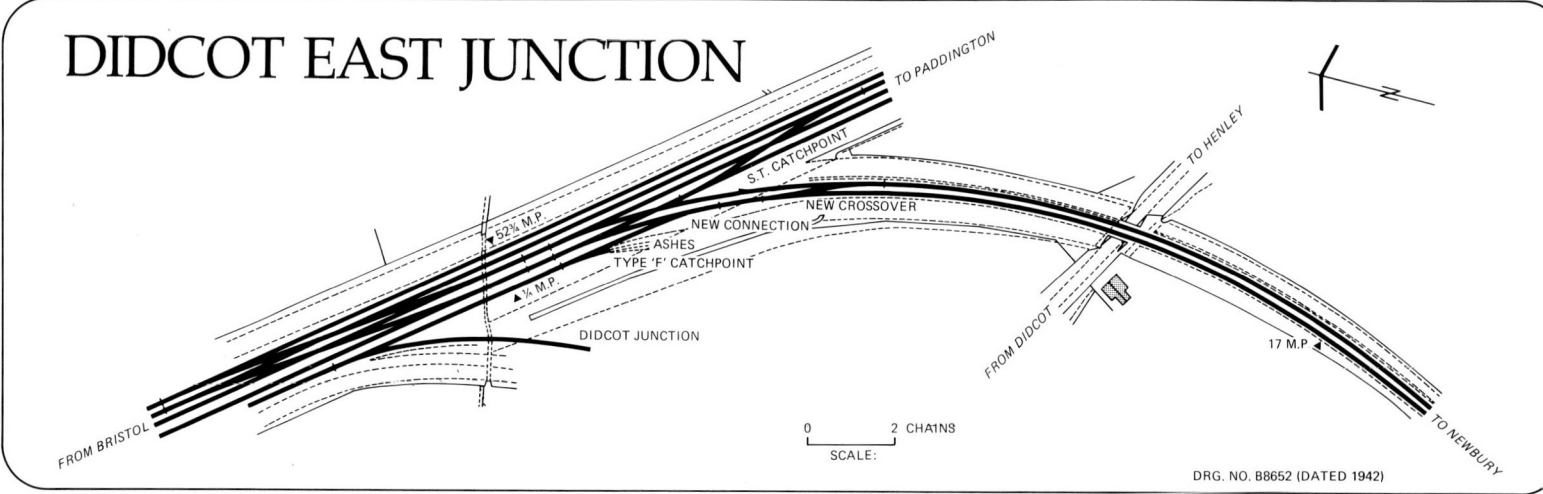

TO PADDINGTON

S.T. CATCHPOINT

NEW CROSSOVER

TO HENLEY

NEW CONNECTION

52¾ M.P.

ASHES

TYPE 'F' CATCHPOINT

¼ M.P.

DIDCOT JUNCTION

FROM DIDCOT

17 M.P.

FROM BRISTOL

0   2 CHAINS

SCALE:

DRG. NO. B8652 (DATED 1942)

TO NEWBURY

Plate 21 (left): This shows the new East Junction signal box completed in February 1932 when all the modernization was carried out at Didcot. The new engine shed can be seen in the background.

British Rail

Plate 22 (above): The single line token apparatus, with a token awaiting collection for the Didcot to Newbury line.

British Rail

The track plan of 1942 *(left)* shows the doubling of the trackwork. It allows trains to travel direct from the DN&SR on to Oxford and the North. The branch is protected by a catch point.

Plate 23: The new style of signal box under construction at Didcot, showing its enormous size and utility form of construction.

British Rail

Plate 24: The rear view of the signal box, as shown in *Plate 23* showing the supports embedded in the steep bank.

British Rail

Plate 25: This final view of Didcot shows the wartime (1942) construction work of laying the double line and the new crossover. This photograph was taken from the bridge over the Didcot to Henley Road.

British Rail

Upton & Blewbury

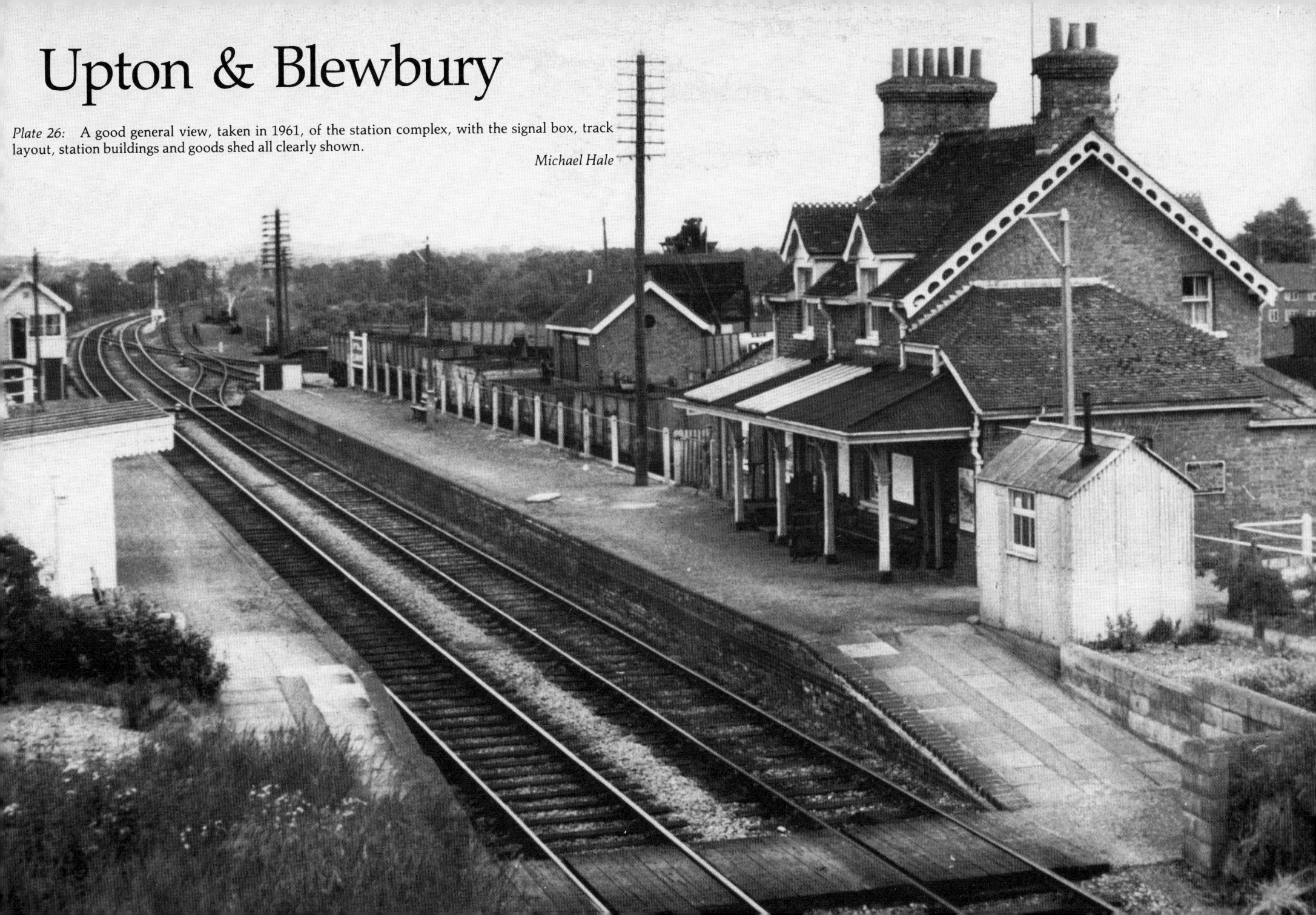

Plate 26:   A good general view, taken in 1961, of the station complex, with the signal box, track layout, station buildings and goods shed all clearly shown.

Michael Hale

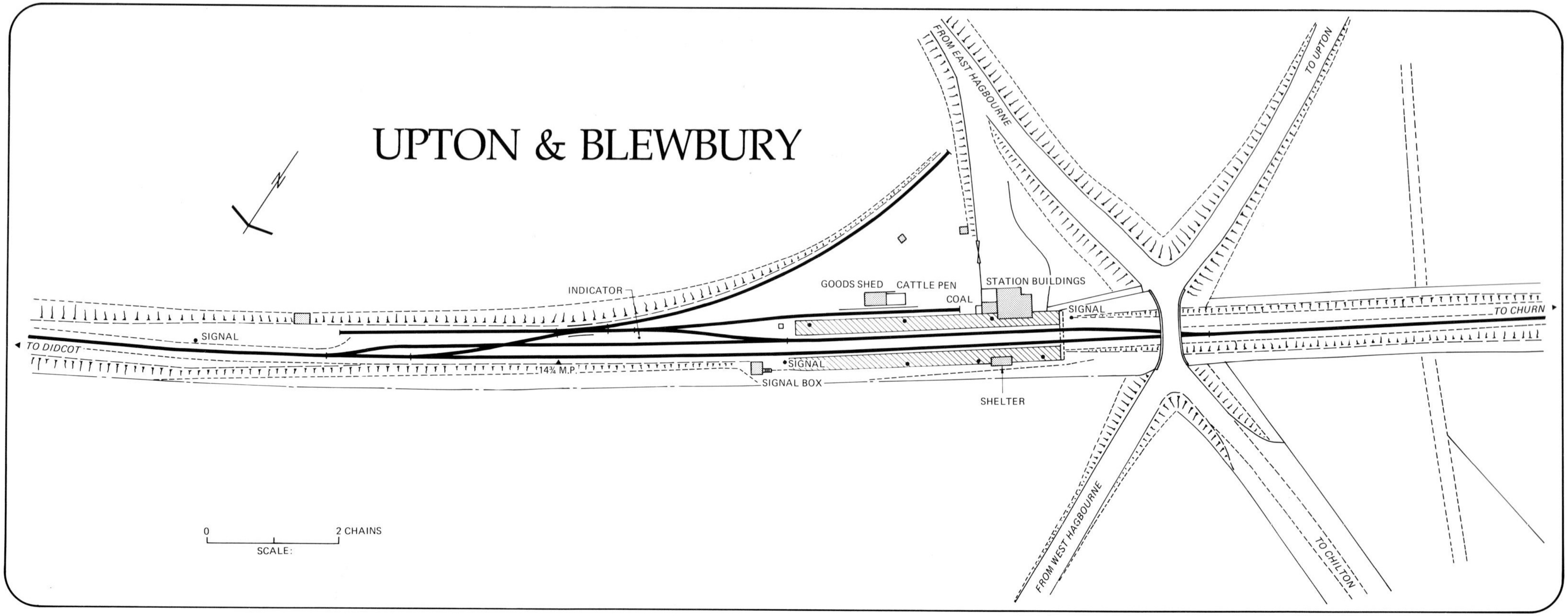

UPTON & BLEWBURY

FROM EAST HAGBOURNE

TO UPTON

INDICATOR

GOODS SHED CATTLE PEN

COAL

STATION BUILDINGS

SIGNAL

TO CHURN

SIGNAL

TO DIDCOT

SIGNAL

14¾ M.P.

SIGNAL BOX

SIGNAL

SHELTER

FROM WEST HAGBOURNE

TO CHILTON

0   2 CHAINS

SCALE:

Plate 27:   This view of the station also shows the goods shed and crane. The decorative weather boards on the eaves of the roof are rather distinctive.   *H. C. Casserley*

Upton & Blewbury

Opened: 13th April 1882
Closed to passenger traffic: 10th September 1962
Closed to goods traffic: 10th August 1964

Situated at only 2¼ miles from Didcot East Junction and at the 14¾ mile post was Upton and Blewbury. This station was originally called Upton, but was renamed Upton and Blewbury in 1911 and was the first station on the line. It was situated on the easy 'up' gradient after a hard climb of 1 in 106 over the Berkshire Downs. The station not only served the villages of Upton and Blewbury but also those of West Hagbourne, Harwell and Chilton. The line curved to the west after leaving the station, before taking a left-hand 90 degree curve and passing through the chalk cutting. The station buildings were typical of the line with the 'down' platform having the main buildings and the 'up' platform the small open passenger shelter. The main building consisted of an office, ladies' waiting-room and toilet, gentlemen's toilet, general waiting-room, booking hall and stationmaster's office. The canopy on this station was supported by ornate timber pillars and early photographs (*Plate 28*) show the roof of the canopy to be tiled and rather bulky. This was altered in the early 1940s to the style seen in *Plate 27*. The original signal box was situated at the end of the 'up' platform. The small goods shed was of a standard design to the line, as shown on the left of *Plate 27*. Cattle pens and a one ton yard crane were also provided and, in the 1930s, a further loading bay was constructed alongside the headshunt, this being mainly used for the loading of racehorses. Crossing the line for passengers was by means of the sleeper crossing at the south end of the station near the red brick road bridge.

Plate 28: An early 1900s postcard view taken from the red road bridge, looking north, showing the early canopy and just a part of a wagon on the extreme right, which is positioned on the long siding. The passenger walkway to the road is also clearly shown. The station carried the nameboards 'Upton' only.

Lens of Sutton

Plate 30: A photograph full of detail. The single line token apparatus can be seen just in front of the engine and a grounded horse-box can be seen near the starter signal, not recorded in later photographs. The station looks extremely busy on this wet day.

Lens of Sutton

Plate 29: This view was taken in 1960 from the main platform, and shows the signal box and lamp hut. The crane jib and end of the goods shed can be seen on the extreme right of the picture.

Author's Collection

Plate 31: A further view, taken at the same time as that in *Plate 30* showing the passenger crossing walkway and single token apparatus.

Lens of Sutton

UPTON & BLEWBURY

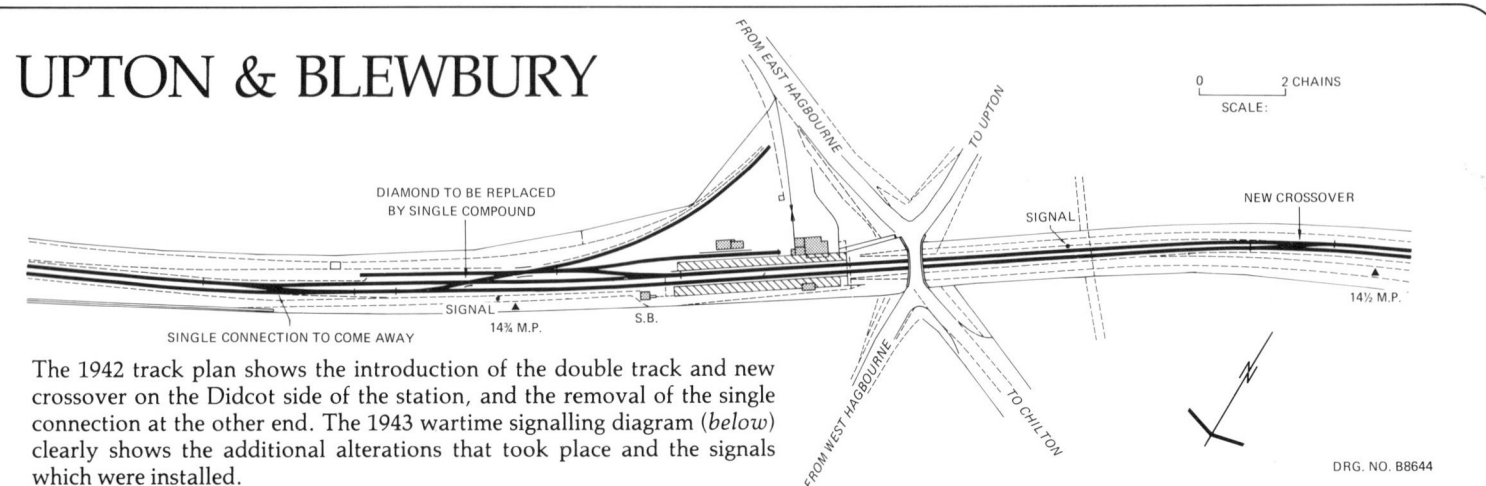

DIAMOND TO BE REPLACED BY SINGLE COMPOUND

SINGLE CONNECTION TO COME AWAY

SIGNAL

14¾ M.P.

S.B.

FROM EAST HAGBOURNE

TO UPTON

FROM WEST HAGBOURNE

TO CHILTON

0   2 CHAINS
SCALE:

SIGNAL

NEW CROSSOVER

14½ M.P.

DRG. NO. B8644

The 1942 track plan shows the introduction of the double track and new crossover on the Didcot side of the station, and the removal of the single connection at the other end. The 1943 wartime signalling diagram (*below*) clearly shows the additional alterations that took place and the signals which were installed.

Plate 32 (top right): A view of the road bridge, passenger steps to the road and the start home signal, taken in July 1960.

Author's Collection

Plate 33 (left): A general view of the station area, taken from the road bridge.

Lens of Sutton

Plate 34 (left): A different view looking towards the red brick road bridge, but this time showing the small open waiting shelter on the 'up' platform. The nameboard now shows the 'Upton and Blewbury' name.

Lens of Sutton

The 1908 track plan shows the single siding to the horse and cattle loading dock, the signal box and the original station buildings.

Upton & Blewbury
1943

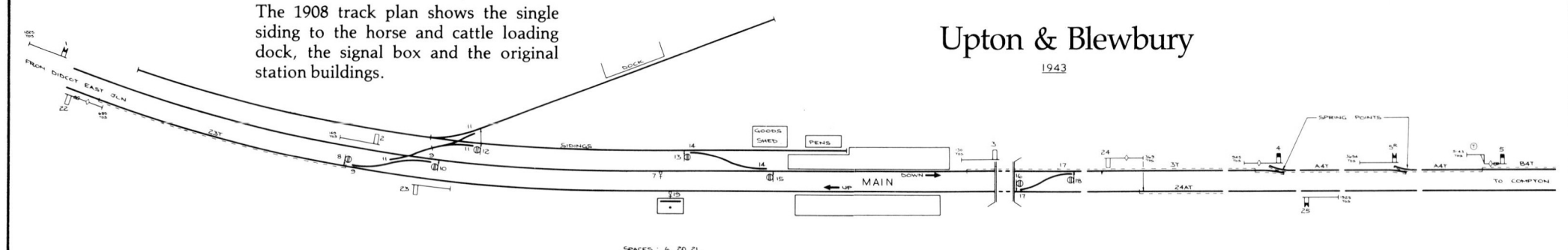

Churn

Plate 35: This shows a general view of this bleak outpost on the DN&SR.

OPC Collection

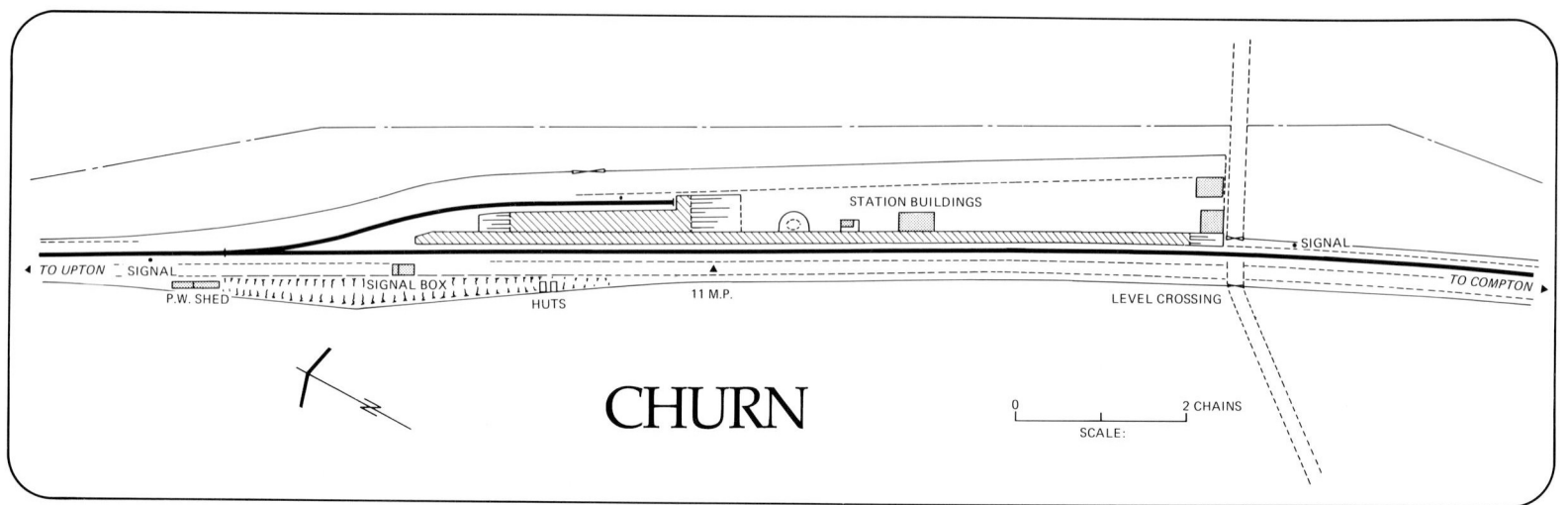

TO UPTON ◄ — SIGNAL
P.W. SHED
SIGNAL BOX
HUTS
11 M.P.
STATION BUILDINGS
SIGNAL
LEVEL CROSSING
TO COMPTON ►

CHURN

0 _____ 2 CHAINS
SCALE:

Plate 36: This view shows the vast expanse of platform area, seldom used, and the road bridge in the distance.

Author's Collection

Churn

Opened: 6th July 1888
Closed to passenger traffic: 10th September 1962
Closed to goods traffic: 14th April 1943 (goods traffic was only accepted when the military camps were open)

From the summit of Churn Down (379ft.) and north of the station, the line descends into Churn Station, which merely consisted of one long bleak platform and just one simple siding. The name of the station derived from the nearby farm. The station appeared to have no visible access by road, laying in a vast ploughed field on the Berkshire Downs. It served the rifle ranges of the military and was the pre-Bisley National range. In fact, an extract from the local council reports said: 'In the year 1888, a spirited endeavour was made by the Newbury Councillors, under the auspices of the late Lord Wantage to establish the National Rifle Association to adopt Churn (two miles north of Compton Station) as a site for the 'New Wimbledon'. The Rifle Association found the railway facilities insufficient, and so the plan was dropped in favour of Bisley in Surrey'.

It was pressed into use for the annual camps and handled vast amounts of servicemen and horses for short periods of time.

In 1905, it appeared as a conditional stop, but with a 24 hour notice of using the facilities. In April 1943, the siding (originally put in for traffic for Churn Farm) and ground frame were removed and the wartime doubling was carried out. This took the form of shortening the platform by about 300ft. at both ends and the making of an island platform. A small occupation crossing appeared at the north end. The original ground frame had been superseded by a signal box which was demolished around 1919. From the photograph it can be seen that passenger comforts were provided by a simple back to back shelter, which must have been bleak in winter.

This wartime track plan shows the shortening of the platform and the removal of the siding.

Plate 37: The bleakness of the station is well portrayed in this photograph taken in May 1961. It shows ex-SR locomotive No. 33021 on a northbound freight passing Churn Halt.

Michael Hale

Plate 38: On the same day, 26th May 1961, an ex-GWR 2-8-0, No. 3839, heads a southbound cattle train out of Churn Halt.

Michael Hale

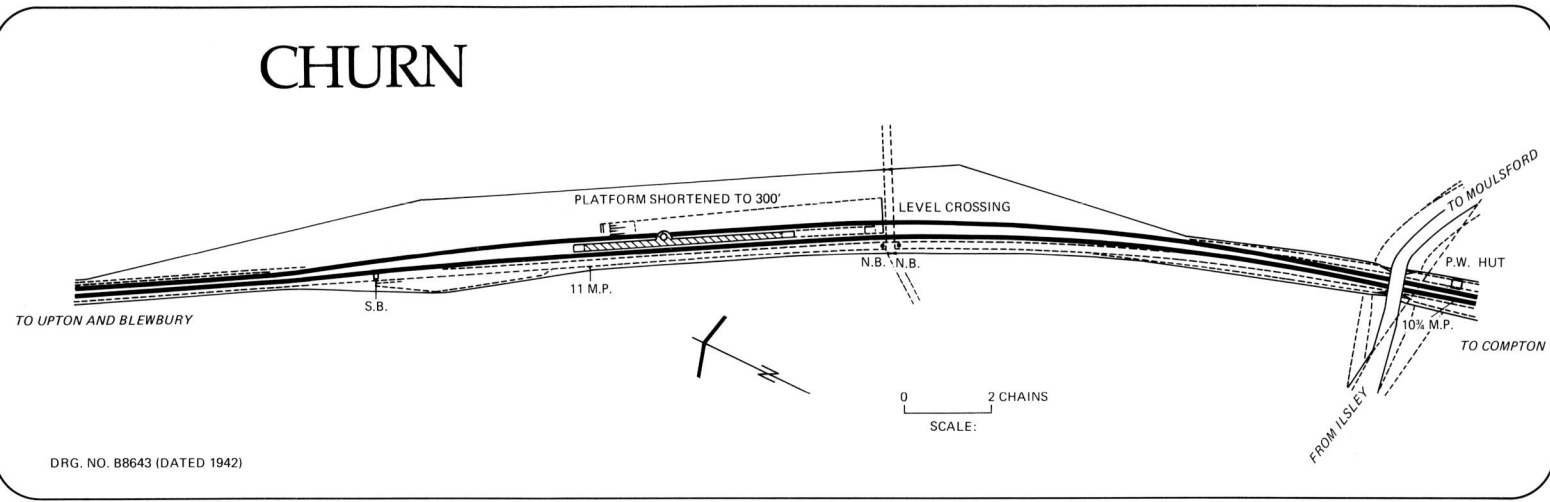

CHURN

PLATFORM SHORTENED TO 300'

LEVEL CROSSING

TO MOULSFORD

P.W. HUT

N.B. N.B.

10¾ M.P.

11 M.P.

TO COMPTON

S.B.

TO UPTON AND BLEWBURY

FROM ILSLEY

0   2 CHAINS

SCALE:

DRG. NO. B8643 (DATED 1942)

During the wartime doubling, it was proposed to erect a new 14 lever signal box which would have controlled an additional block section between Upton and Compton. It was to be named West Ilsley signal box. This was not carried out and eventually only signals were provided, these being known as the 'Ilsley Signals'. The diagram shows their exact positioning, and the signals were powered by electric motors which were controlled from the preceding signal box.

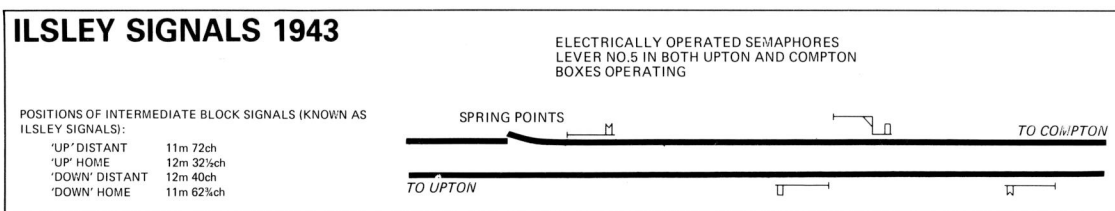

ILSLEY SIGNALS 1943

ELECTRICALLY OPERATED SEMAPHORES LEVER NO.5 IN BOTH UPTON AND COMPTON BOXES OPERATING

POSITIONS OF INTERMEDIATE BLOCK SIGNALS (KNOWN AS ILSLEY SIGNALS):

'UP' DISTANT	11m 72ch
'UP' HOME	12m 32½ch
'DOWN' DISTANT	12m 40ch
'DOWN' HOME	11m 62¾ch

SPRING POINTS

TO COMPTON

TO UPTON

Plate 39: A view from the footbridge in the early 1900s, showing the goods shed, signal box and extensive goods sidings (rather full). On the right of the picture the platform shelter can be seen.

Real Photographs

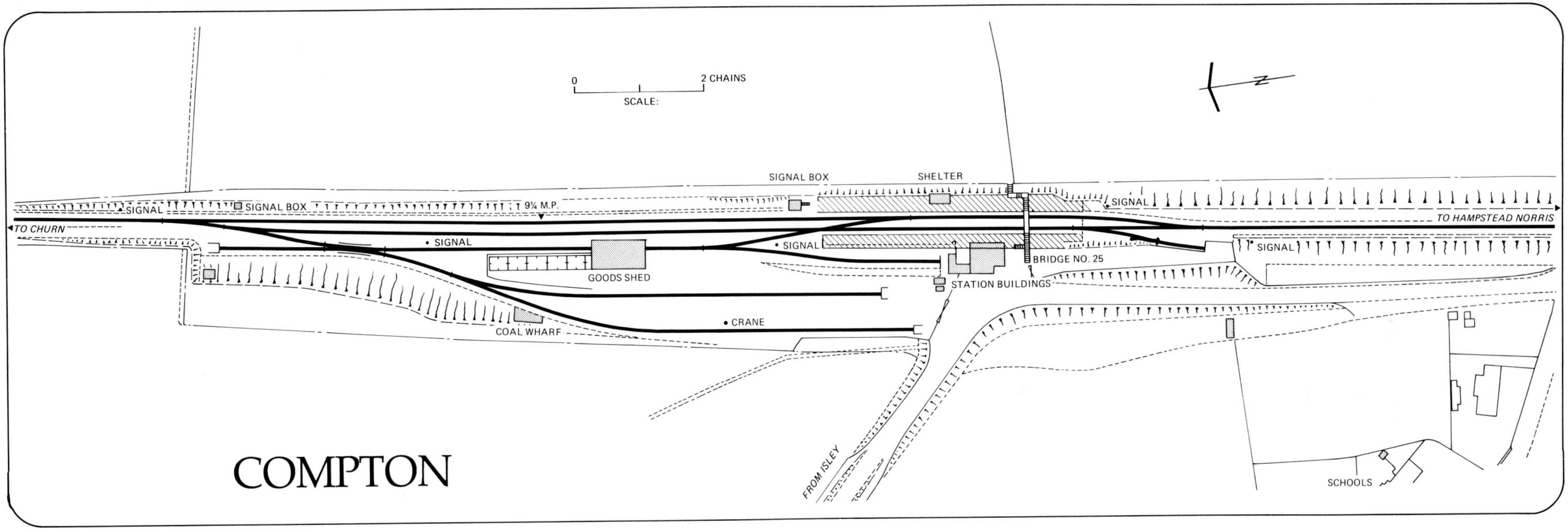

![COMPTON track diagram](scale: 0 to 2 CHAINS)

COMPTON

Labels on diagram: SIGNAL BOX, SHELTER, SIGNAL BOX, 9¼ M.P., SIGNAL, TO CHURN, TO HAMPSTEAD NORRIS, SIGNAL, SIGNAL, GOODS SHED, SIGNAL, BRIDGE NO. 25, STATION BUILDINGS, CRANE, COAL WHARF, FROM ILSLEY, SIGNAL, SCHOOLS

Plate 40: This photograph shows the single slip that replaced the diamond crossover during the wartime doubling. The unique footbridge and stark passenger facilities can clearly be seen.

Author's Collection

Compton

Opened: 13th April 1882
Closed to passenger traffic: 10th September 1962
Closed to goods traffic: 10th August 1964

Being probably the most significant station on the northern section of the DN&SR, Compton, situated at the 9¼ mile post, served the three main villages around; namely Compton, Aldworth and East Ilsley. The station itself was on a level site but the goods yard was in a cutting, whilst to the southern end, the track left the station on a high embankment. This station was originally constructed as a double platform station, (with a long passing loop of 822ft.) to handle the extensive horse-box traffic, which came from the famous surrounding racing stables on the Berkshire Downs. The station layout had three sidings, a head-shunt and a goods shed (which was larger than usual for the line). At the southern end was a further bay, protected by a catch point, for the loading of horses which, during the 1920s, was almost daily. The passenger trains would collect the horse-boxes from the siding or drop them off as necessary. The yard also had a 3 ton crane, at one time constructed of wood, but later of a girder steel construction. The station buildings were situated on the 'up' platform, whilst the 'down' platform was equipped with a small wooden open-fronted waiting shelter for passengers (with hard wooden seat). Alongside the main station buildings, built in the early part of the 1900s, was a corrugated parcels hut, constructed to handle the increase in traffic, and also another larger building (near the footbridge on the same platform) to handle the large amount of milk traffic passing through the station. The signal box was at the northern end of the 'down' platform and was fitted, in the 1920s, with a new GWR standard frame. All the points and interlocking systems had been renewed earlier, in October 1914, at a cost of £711. The station also boasted a footbridge which was put up to maintain a public right of way across the running lines, and connected the church to the village. The early footbridge was an open steel and wood bridge, but this was later replaced by a pre-stressed concrete structure. A weighbridge (No. 4625) was installed in 1914, capable of a 12 ton capacity, and was similar to the one at Sutton Scotney, having a base size of 12ft. x 8ft.

COMPTON

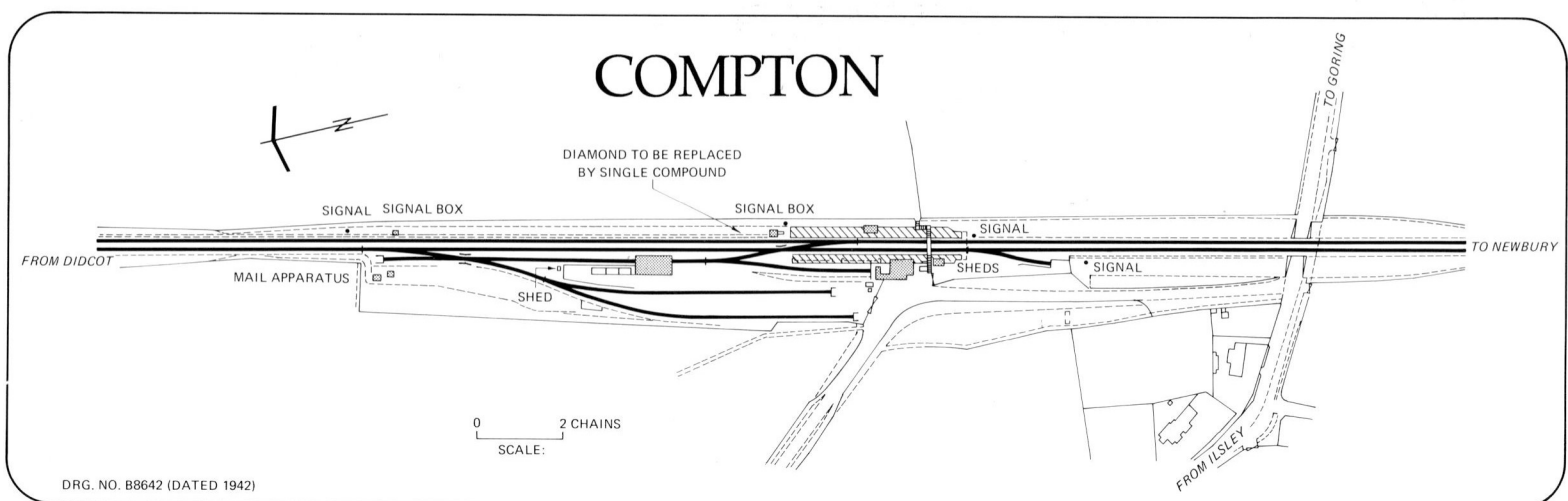

DIAMOND TO BE REPLACED
BY SINGLE COMPOUND

SIGNAL SIGNAL BOX   SIGNAL BOX

FROM DIDCOT   TO NEWBURY

MAIL APPARATUS   SHEDS   SIGNAL

SHED   SIGNAL

TO GORING

FROM ILSLEY

0   2 CHAINS

SCALE:

DRG. NO. B8642 (DATED 1942)

This 1942 revised wartime track plan shows the double lines. The removal of both points at the north and south allowed only one crossover in the station and the diamond was replaced by a single slip.

Plate 41: A general view of Compton Station and buildings, looking south towards Newbury, with a northbound freight passing through in May 1961.

Michael Hale

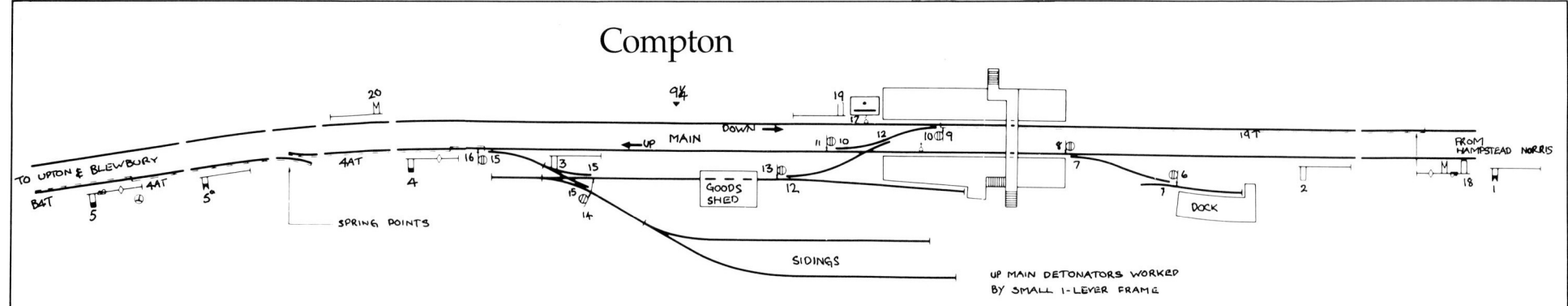

Compton

TO UPTON & BLEWBURY

BAT

SPRING POINTS

GOODS SHED

SIDINGS

UP MAIN DETONATORS WORKED
BY SMALL 1-LEVER FRAME

DOCK

FROM HAMPSTEAD NORRIS

Plate 42: In this view, the corrugated iron parcels hut can be clearly seen, as ex-SR locomotive No. 30117 heads a three coach stopping train out of the station.

Lens of Sutton

Plate 43: Another view of the same train entering the station. This view shows the goods shed, signal box and lamp hut, in addition to the crossover at the north end of the station.

Lens of Sutton

35

Hampstead Norris

Plate 44: A general view, looking south, giving a good overall view of the footbridge, station buildings, signal box and goods yard.

OPC Collection

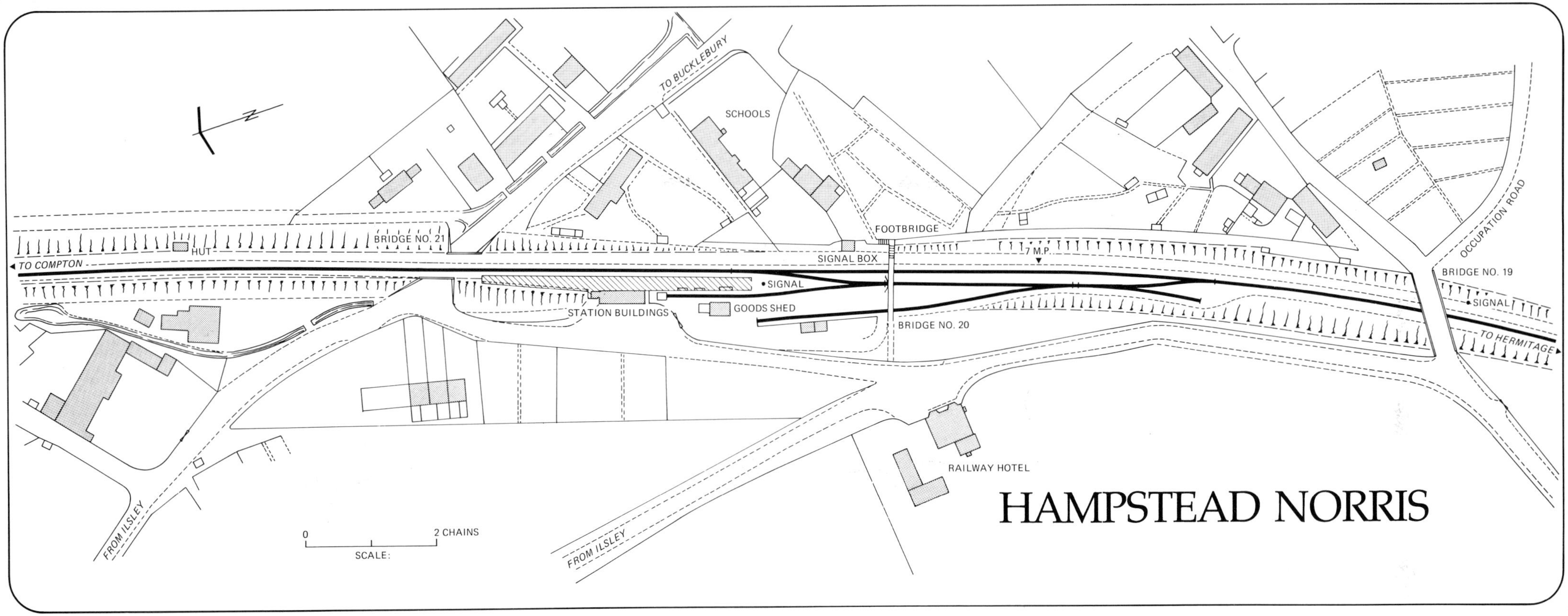

The map shows Hampstead Norris station with labels: TO BUCKLEBURY, SCHOOLS, FOOTBRIDGE, SIGNAL BOX, 7 M.P., OCCUPATION ROAD, BRIDGE NO. 21, HUT, TO COMPTON, SIGNAL, BRIDGE NO. 19, STATION BUILDINGS, GOODS SHED, BRIDGE NO. 20, SIGNAL, TO HERMITAGE, RAILWAY HOTEL, FROM ILSLEY, FROM ILSLEY, HAMPSTEAD NORRIS

0 ___ 2 CHAINS
SCALE:

Hampstead Norris

Opened: 13th April 1882
Closed to passenger traffic: 10th September 1962
Closed to goods traffic: 10th August 1964

This station overlooked the main road in the village which was an attractive thoroughfare. When built, the station had a single line and, although an area was clearly left for a double line, and passing loop and all the earthworks were provided, it was clear that the DN&SR considered the revenue from the station insufficient to warrant the expense. The standard house on the platform was even reduced to a single storey construction and was of a unique design to this railway.

The original plans and reports suggest that a passing loop was considered, but the signals were removed and the signalling equipment was controlled by a ground frame released by the enginemen themselves. The facilities were simple, comprising a small goods shed and cattle dock. The yard crane was added in 1885 and had a capacity of 3 tons. The main alterations were effected in 1943 when the wartime doubling was carried out. A new 'down' platform was erected constructed of reinforced concrete, with many supports to hold the platform, as this was situated on the side of the embankment. The flimsy and sparse passenger waiting shelter was also added and a new wartime-designed signal box was built almost on the site of the original signal box.

Plate 45: This view of the station, looking towards Didcot, was taken in May 1961 and shows the modified amenities at this station. The old signal box was being used as a parcels office and the sparse waiting shelter can be clearly seen.

Michael Hale

Plate 46: This view, looking towards Newbury, was photographed by the GWR just before the wartime doubling in 1943. It helps to show the embankment height above the village and also the width for the double track which the DN&SR never put into place. It was obviously a finely balanced decision as even the point rodding on early photographs was clearly placed to allow for the passing loop. The bridge in the background was not for passenger use but was an occupation footbridge.

British Rail

Plates 47 & 48: Two official Great Western Railway photographs taken after the completion of the new 'down' platform in May 1943. This was before the nameboard and waiting shelter were added. These views again show the many features of the stations: e.g. its height above the picturesque village, the ARP type signal box and the open structure of the footbridge.

British Rail

HAMPSTEAD NORRIS

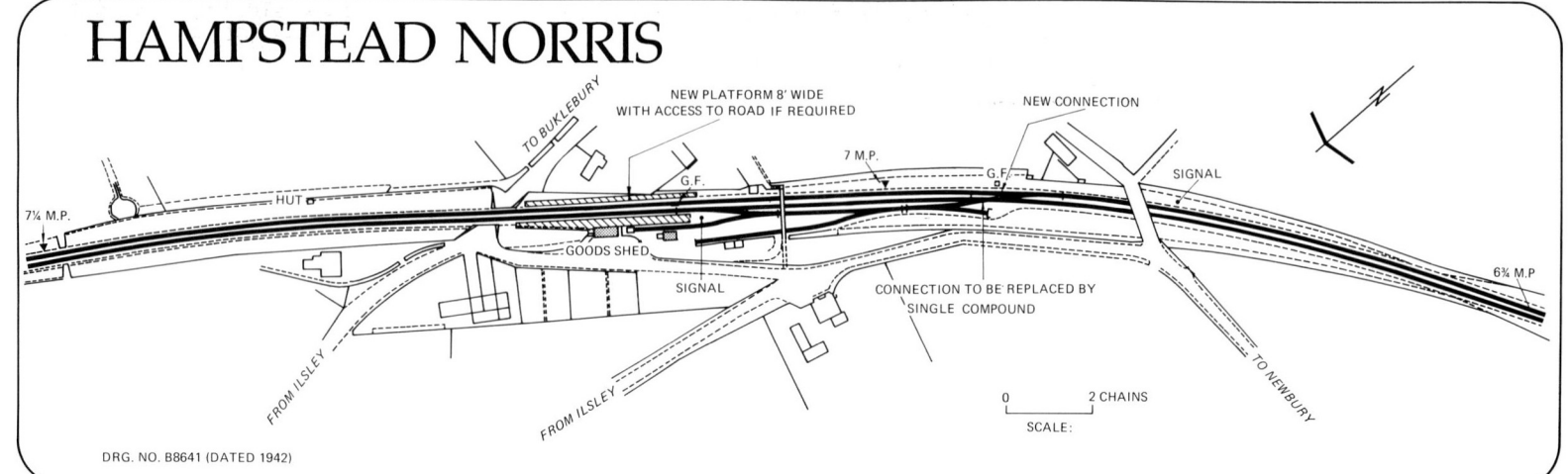

NEW PLATFORM 8' WIDE
WITH ACCESS TO ROAD IF REQUIRED

NEW CONNECTION

TO BUKLEBURY

7 M.P.

G.F.

SIGNAL

7¼ M.P.

HUT

G.F.

GOODS SHED

SIGNAL

CONNECTION TO BE REPLACED BY
SINGLE COMPOUND

FROM ILSLEY

FROM ILSLEY

TO NEWBURY

6¾ M.P.

0   2 CHAINS

SCALE:

DRG. NO. B8641 (DATED 1942)

The 1942 track plan clearly shows the extensive alterations that were to be carried out on the wartime doubling and, as a comparison, *Plate 49* is a view looking north taken in 1919 from the occupation footbridge. This view was probably similar to that when the station was opened, and clearly shows the signal box, point rodding (allowing for the doubling that never took place), the sparse facilities and the small goods shed. A coal wagon can be seen on the far left of the photograph. The top of the signal box was removed and placed on the platform (as seen in *Plate 45*) and used as a parcels office.

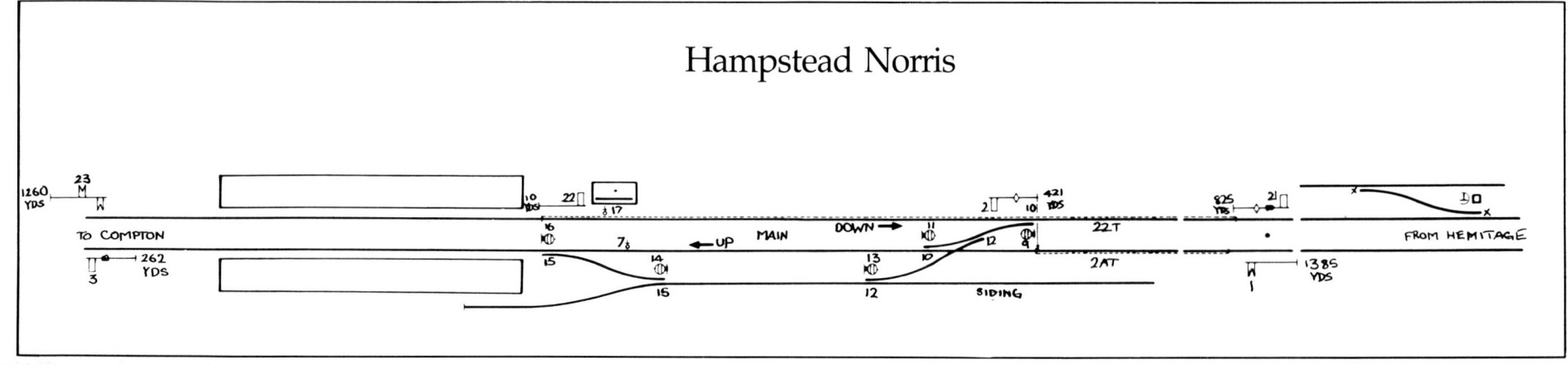

Hampstead Norris

Pinewood Halt

Plate 50: A view looking north in the 1950s.
OPC Collection

PINEWOOD HALT

Plate 51: A fine view of Pinewood Halt showing both 'up' and 'down' GWR pagoda-type waiting shelters. They were of different construction, one having the door much wider but lower than the other, and the original shelter's windows were boarded up during the wartime doubling. This view, photographed during May 1961, looking north, features the brickworks in the background, with the siding bearing right through the gate in the centre of the photograph.

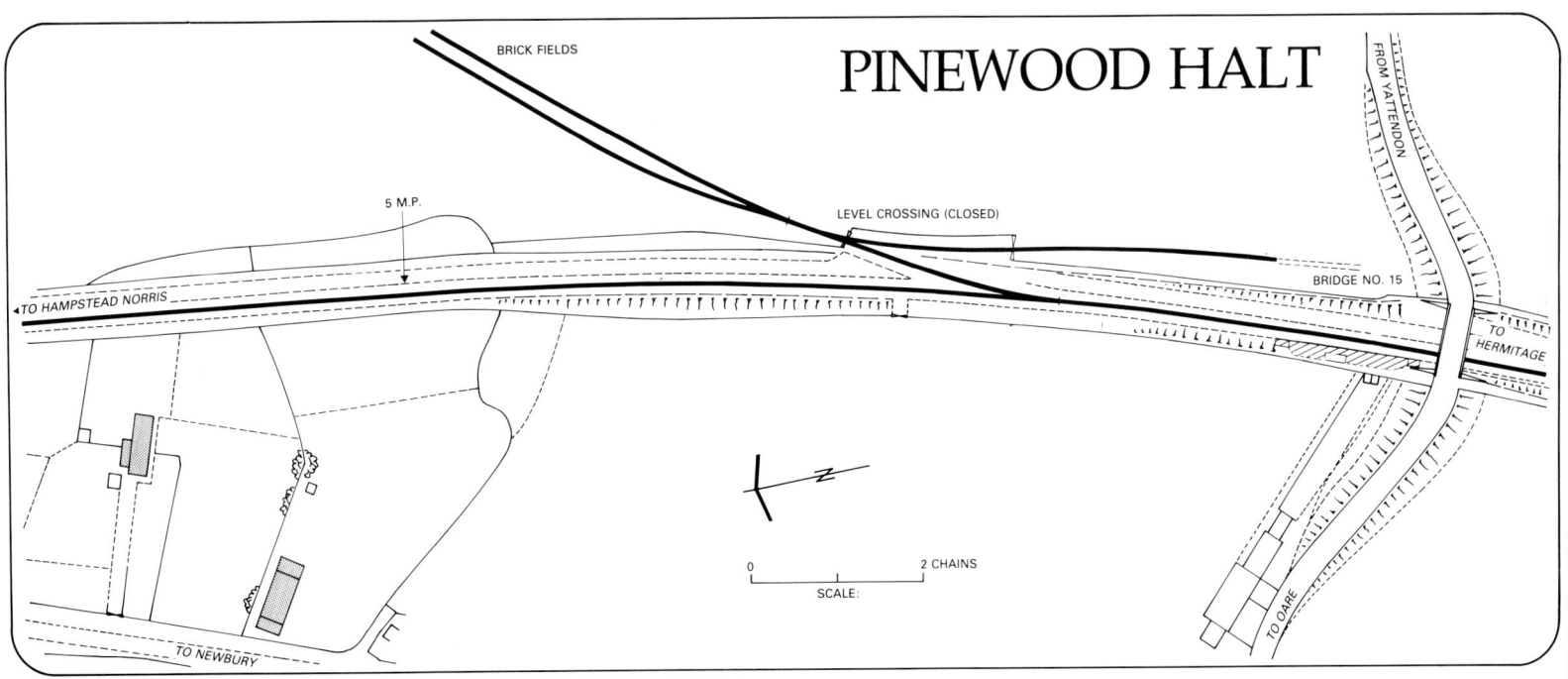

PINEWOOD HALT

BRICK FIELDS

5 M.P.

LEVEL CROSSING (CLOSED)

◄ TO HAMPSTEAD NORRIS

BRIDGE NO. 15

FROM YATTENDON

TO HERMITAGE

TO OARE

TO NEWBURY

0 — 2 CHAINS

SCALE:

Pinewood Halt

Opened: 11th September 1933
Closed to passenger traffic: 10th September 1962
Closed to goods traffic: Freight not handled at this station

This halt was opened to serve and try and attract passengers from the north end of the village of Hermitage. The station 'proper' was about a mile further on. The platform was situated on the 'up' side and consisted of a single platform with a corrugated iron shelter and oil lighting.

The cost is recorded as being £127. Before the halt was established, the siding served a brickfield and was known as Brain's Siding, after the owner. The siding was about one mile north of the station of Hermitage, and joined the main line in the 'down' direction. Inside the brickworks was a small narrow gauge railway. The headshunt to the south was used for some time by a local coal carrier. During the war years, the line was doubled and the extra platform and waiting shelter were installed. The sidings was also used by the 34 RMU unit which was situated nearby.

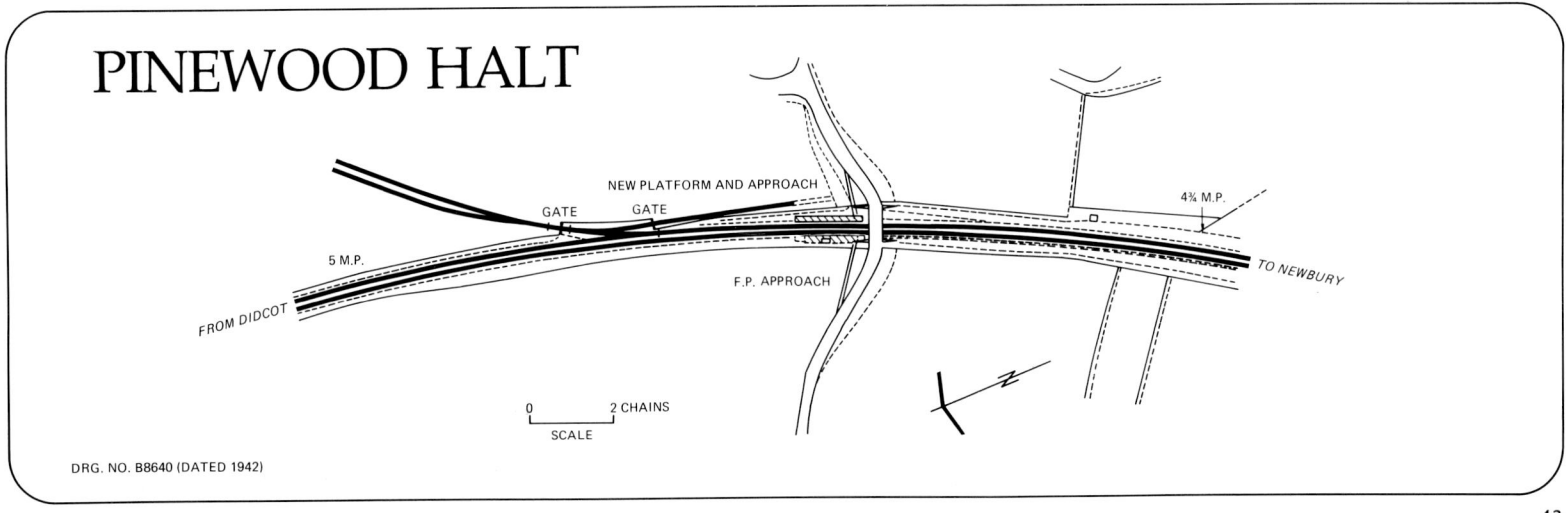

PINEWOOD HALT

NEW PLATFORM AND APPROACH

GATE   GATE

4¾ M.P.

5 M.P.

FROM DIDCOT

F.P. APPROACH

TO NEWBURY

0 — 2 CHAINS

SCALE

DRG. NO. B8640 (DATED 1942)

Plate 52: This view was photographed by the Great Western Railway in 1943, when the new platforms were added and the double line was installed. The siding was reconnected to the new 'down' line at the time of the wartime work. Two wagons can be seen on the south siding just above the pile of rocks on the platform. It is noticeable that there are no lamps on the 'down' platform.

British Rail

Hermitage

Plate 53: A view looking towards Hampstead Norris, showing the fine style of the station buildings, with the signal box just visible at the right-hand side of the picture.

Michael Hale

HERMITAGE

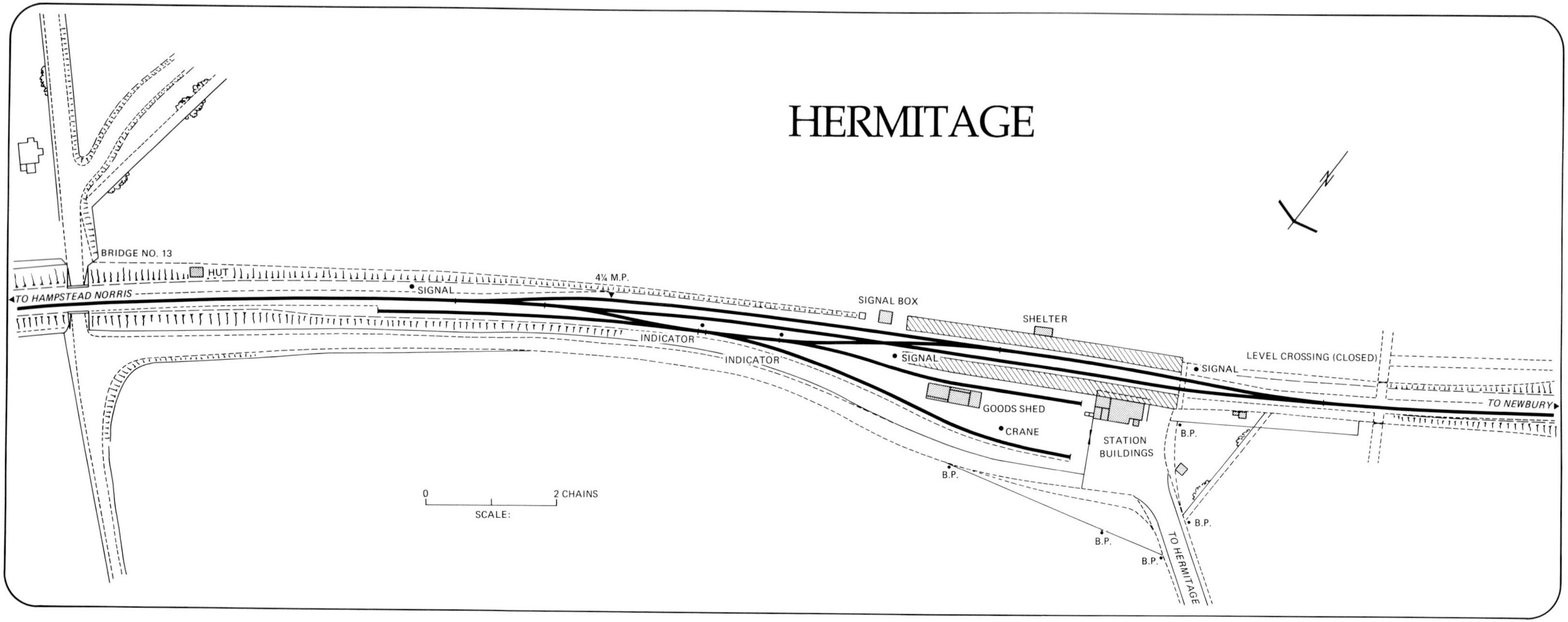

Map labels:
- TO HAMPSTEAD NORRIS
- BRIDGE NO. 13
- HUT
- 4¼ M.P.
- SIGNAL
- INDICATOR
- INDICATOR
- SIGNAL BOX
- SIGNAL
- SHELTER
- GOODS SHED
- CRANE
- STATION BUILDINGS
- B.P.
- B.P.
- B.P.
- B.P.
- B.P.
- TO HERMITAGE
- LEVEL CROSSING (CLOSED)
- SIGNAL
- TO NEWBURY
- N
- 0 ___ 2 CHAINS
- SCALE:

Hermitage

Opened: 13th April 1882
Closed to passenger traffic: 10th September 1962 (closed 4th August 1942 until 8th March 1943 for doubling)
Closed to goods traffic: 10th August 1964

Situated just south of the village, this station served Hermitage and also catered for passengers from the villages of Cold Ash and Frilsham. Being the last station before Newbury, it was busy on market day serving Newbury with the population around and also, on a more regular basis, schoolchildren.

The station itself was equipped with a fairly standard array of station buildings, a smallish goods shed, signal box and a loading dock (added in the early 1900s). One point of note is that the fencing around this station differed inasmuch as it was iron railings and not (as at the other northern section stations) of wooden construction. During the wartime doubling, the siding to the loading bank was extended and new sidings were laid to the cold store, built by the Ministry of Supply. The wartime track plan shows this addition.

Plate 54: A view looking east, towards Hampstead Norris, showing the signal box, permanent way hut alongside, the crossover, and wagons in the goods shed sidings. Note the windlass on the base of the tall station lamps which were added in the 1920s.

Lens of Sutton

HERMITAGE

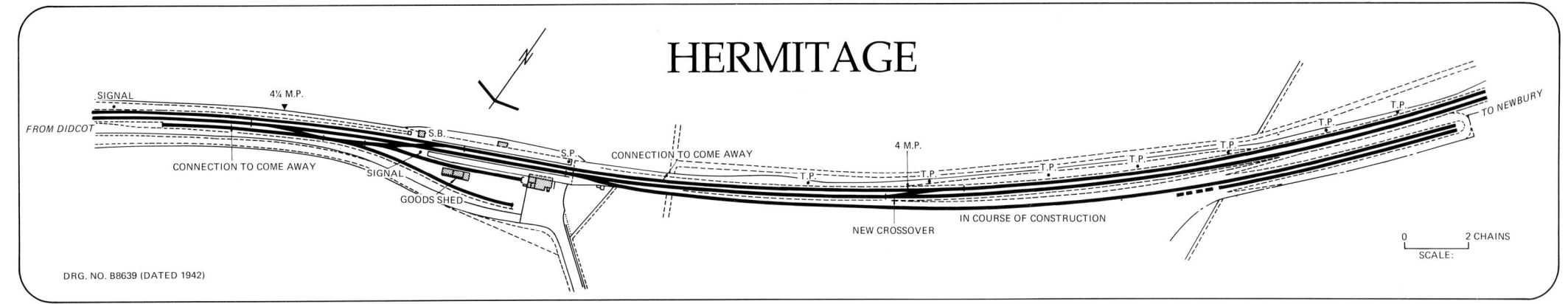

SIGNAL

FROM DIDCOT

4¼ M.P.

S.B.

CONNECTION TO COME AWAY

SIGNAL

GOODS SHED

S.P.

CONNECTION TO COME AWAY

4 M.P.

T.P.

T.P.

T.P.

T.P.

T.P.

T.P.

T.P.

T.P.

TO NEWBURY

NEW CROSSOVER

IN COURSE OF CONSTRUCTION

0   2 CHAINS
SCALE:

DRG. NO. B8639 (DATED 1942)

The above plan shows the official Ministry of Supply diagram for the addition of the meat cold store, and it is clear that there was a plan for two headshunts to be incorporated but, in the eventual building of the site, only one was included. Note also the connections that were removed and the new crossover installed at the 4 mile post.

Plate 55: A view looking towards Didcot, showing details of the station canopy, platform railings and station building. Note the wooden shed at the end of the station buildings which was added in the 1920s for parcels.

British Rail

Hermitage

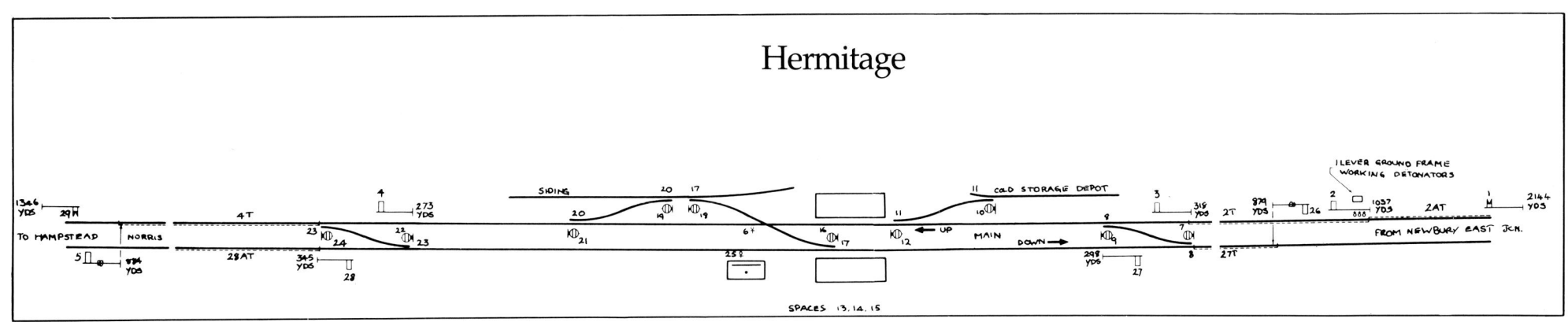

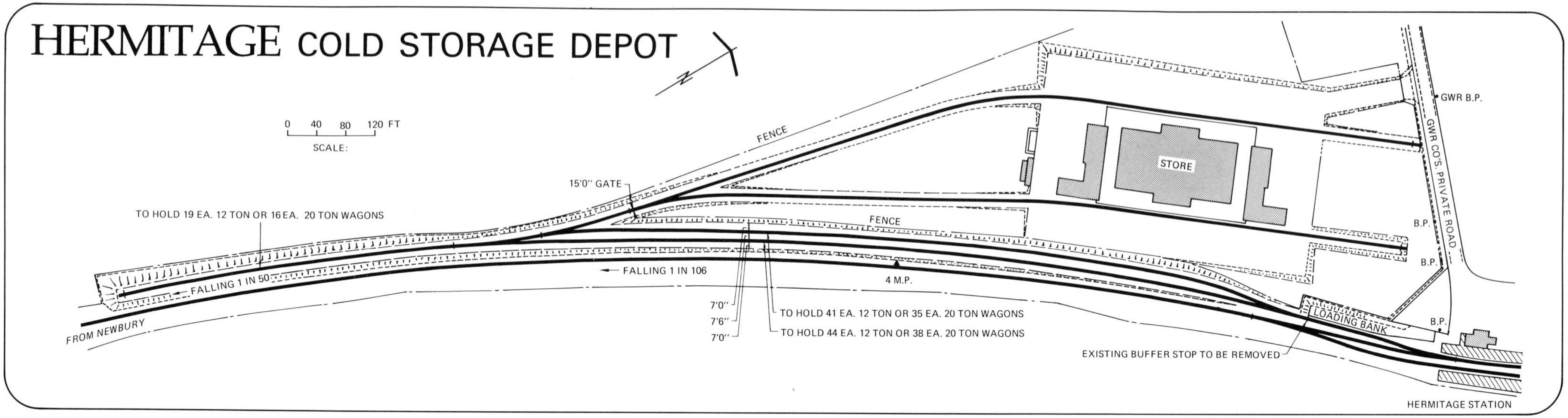

HERMITAGE COLD STORAGE DEPOT

SCALE:
0   40   80   120 FT

FENCE

GWR B.P.

GWR CO'S. PRIVATE ROAD

STORE

B.P.

15'0" GATE

TO HOLD 19 EA. 12 TON OR 16 EA. 20 TON WAGONS

FENCE

B.P.

FALLING 1 IN 50

← FALLING 1 IN 106

4 M.P.

7'0"
7'6"
7'0"

TO HOLD 41 EA. 12 TON OR 35 EA. 20 TON WAGONS
TO HOLD 44 EA. 12 TON OR 38 EA. 20 TON WAGONS

LOADING BANK

B.P.

FROM NEWBURY

EXISTING BUFFER STOP TO BE REMOVED

HERMITAGE STATION

The final plan of this station shows the railway version of the cold storage depot, just one headshunt and all the relevant wagon lengths on each track. The whole site was protected by fencing with a gate across the railway entrance. Note the buffer stop to be removed from the loading dock spur, which was not included on the original survey and was, therefore, an addition in the 1920s. This spur was extended during the wartime extensions of 1942 and was used as the main 'in' road to the cold store. This cold store was also served by road and most of the meat was moved by road transport, but several reports of refrigerated vans on local pick-up goods, serving the meat store, were recorded.

Plate 56: This view, photographed from the 'down' platform waiting shelter, clearly shows the wooden hut constructed for the parcels traffic. Again this is a good photograph and shows details of the heavily-constructed canopies protecting the entrances to the waiting-rooms. The meat cold store and the loading ramp can be clearly seen.

Lens of Sutton

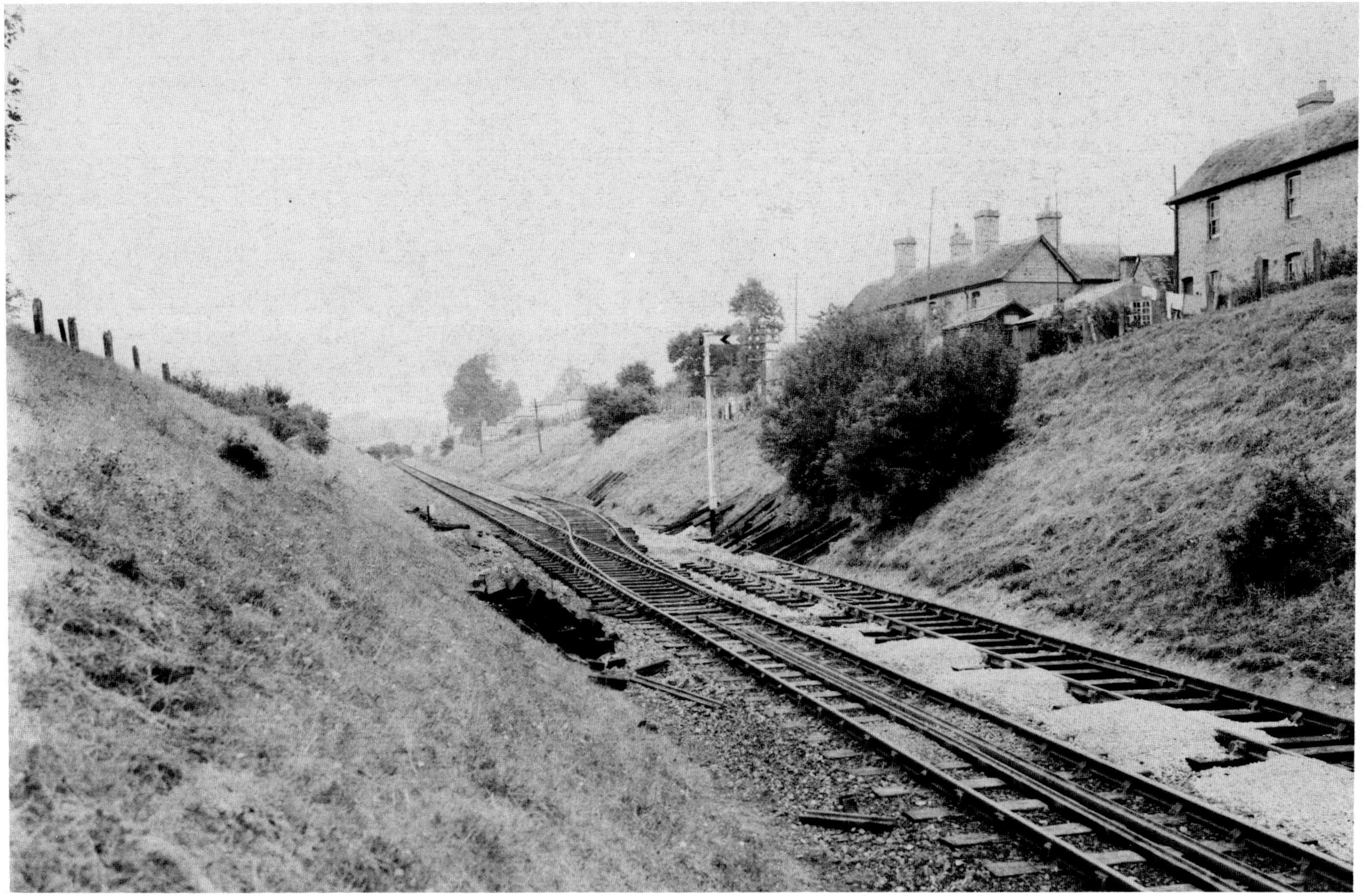

Plate 57: This official Great Western Railway photograph, taken on 28th September 1942, shows the progress of the line doubling. According to records, this was a temporary road and crossover that was installed to help traffic movements and line construction at Shaw Cutting, and it indicates that the photograph was taken near the Kiln Lane road bridge.

British Rail

Fisher's Lane Crossing was a small level crossing provided to allow traffic to and from Fisher's Farm. This crossing had a small keeper's cottage and this (in the early days) was probably manned by a lady who was almost certainly the wife of one of the railway workers. A simple ground frame signal layout was provided, as the 1943 diagram shows.
The 5 lever frame layout is:

Lever	*Released by*	*Locks*	*Releases*
1	2		
2		3	1
3		2.4	
4		3	5
5	4		

Gate Bolt No. 3

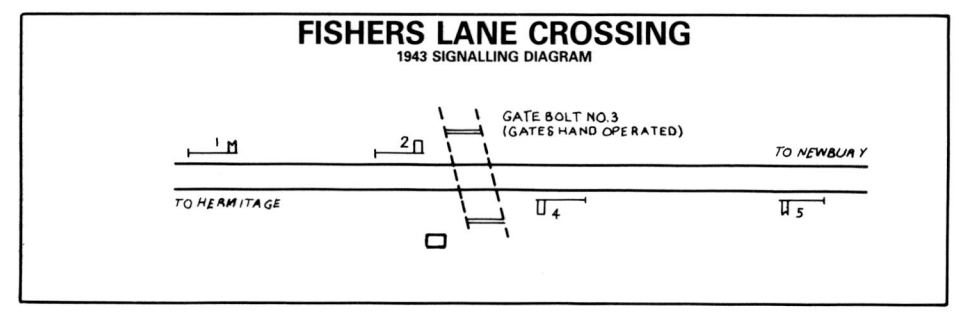

FISHERS LANE CROSSING
1943 SIGNALLING DIAGRAM
GATE BOLT NO.3
(GATES HAND OPERATED)
TO NEWBURY
TO HERMITAGE
1
2
4
5

Plate 58: The curve into Newbury is clearly shown by this 1942 photograph of Hambridge Lane overbridge. The line doubling has recently been carried out and the photograph shows the drainage, cabling and signalling works still in progress.

British Rail

Newbury East Junction

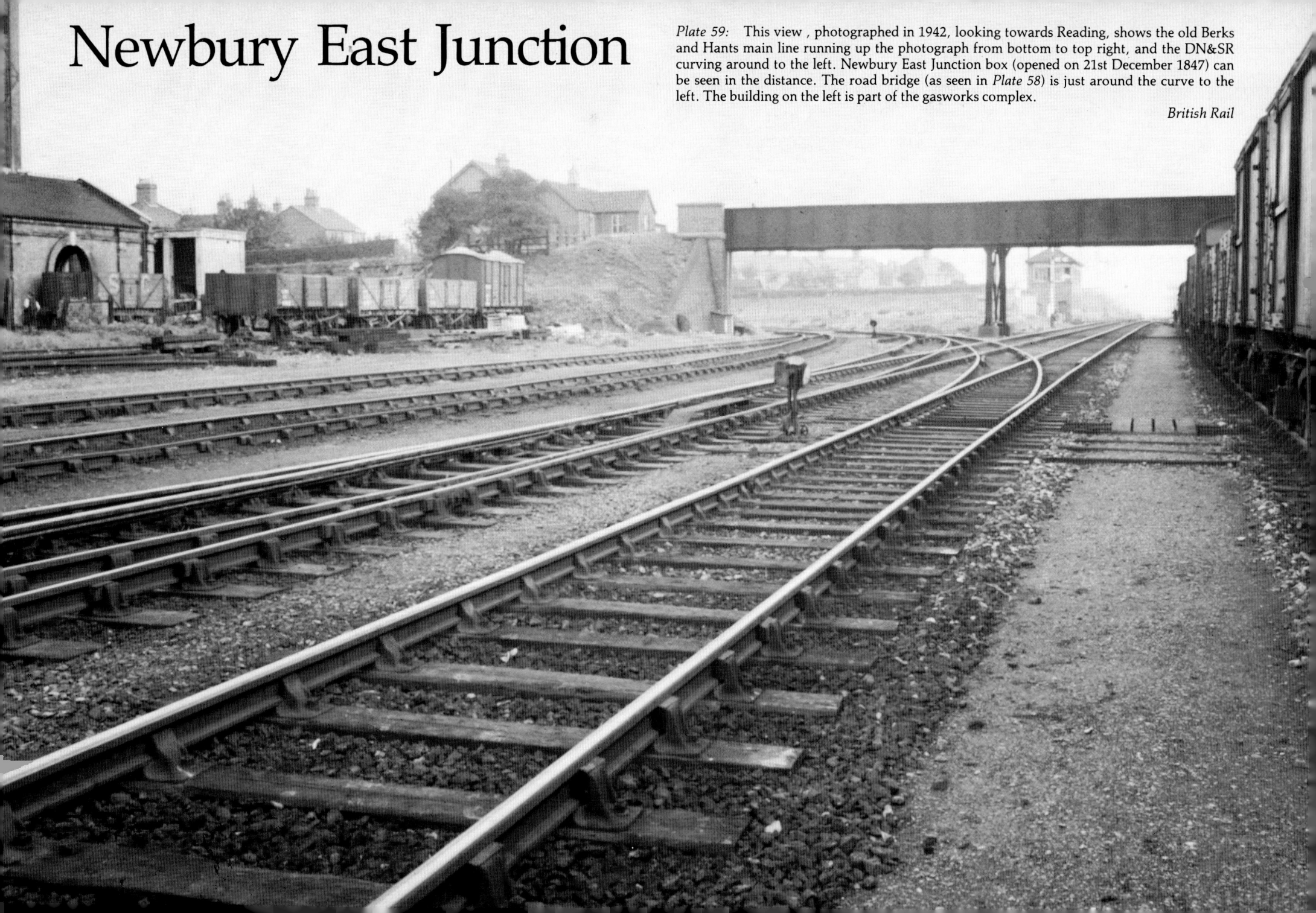

Plate 59: This view , photographed in 1942, looking towards Reading, shows the old Berks and Hants main line running up the photograph from bottom to top right, and the DN&SR curving around to the left. Newbury East Junction box (opened on 21st December 1847) can be seen in the distance. The road bridge (as seen in *Plate 58*) is just around the curve to the left. The building on the left is part of the gasworks complex.

British Rail

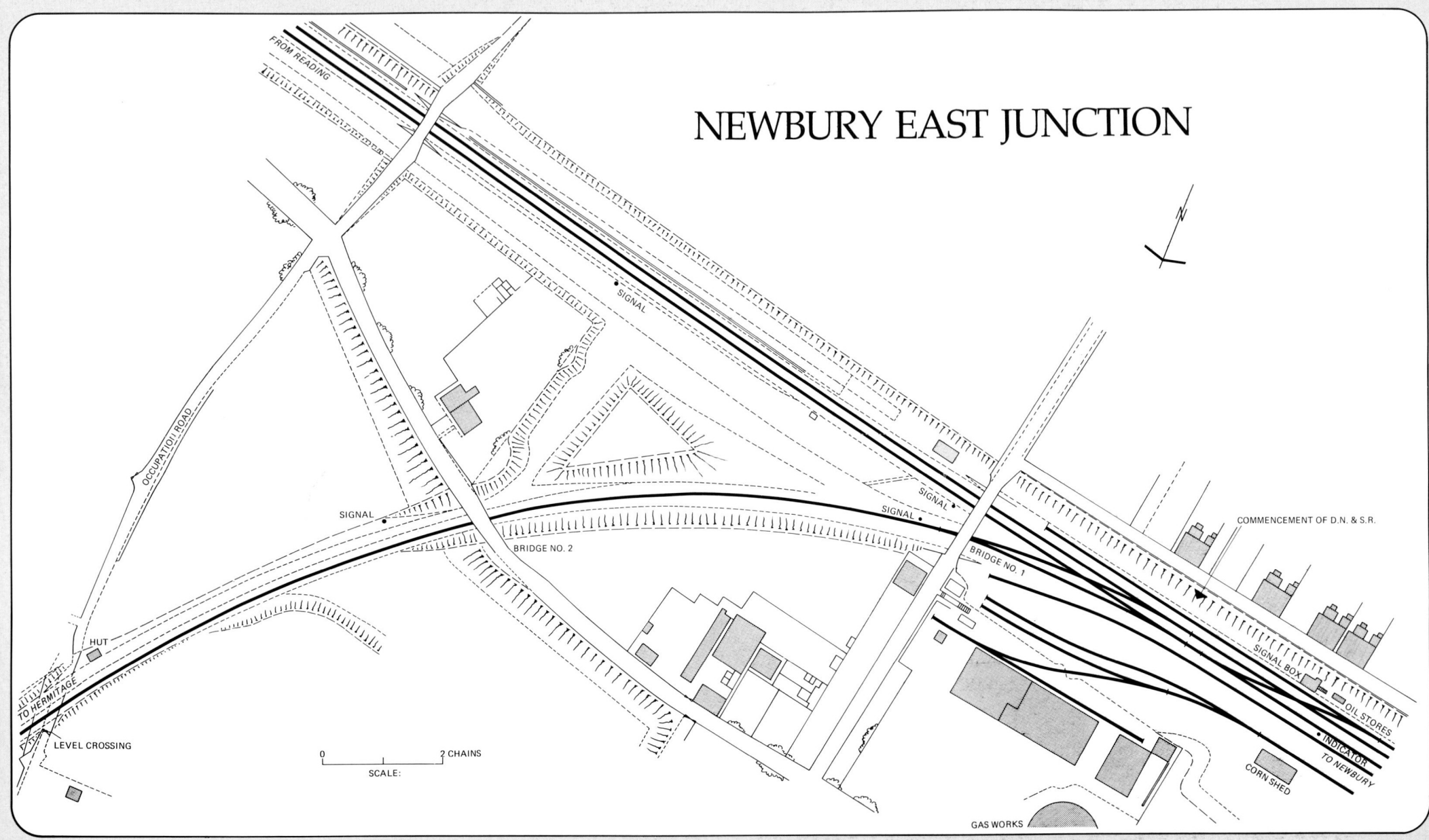

NEWBURY EAST JUNCTION

FROM READING

OCCUPATION ROAD

SIGNAL

SIGNAL

SIGNAL

SIGNAL

SIGNAL

COMMENCEMENT OF D.N. & S.R.

BRIDGE NO. 2

BRIDGE NO. 1

SIGNAL BOX

OIL STORES

HUT

TO HERMITAGE

LEVEL CROSSING

0   1   2 CHAINS

SCALE:

INDICATOR TO NEWBURY

CORN SHED

GAS WORKS

The 1908 survey of Newbury East Junction showing clearly the commencement of the Didcot to Newbury line, around the GWR 52¾ mile post. The permanent way hut, as seen on the left of *Plate 58*, is shown on the extreme left of the above plan.

Newbury

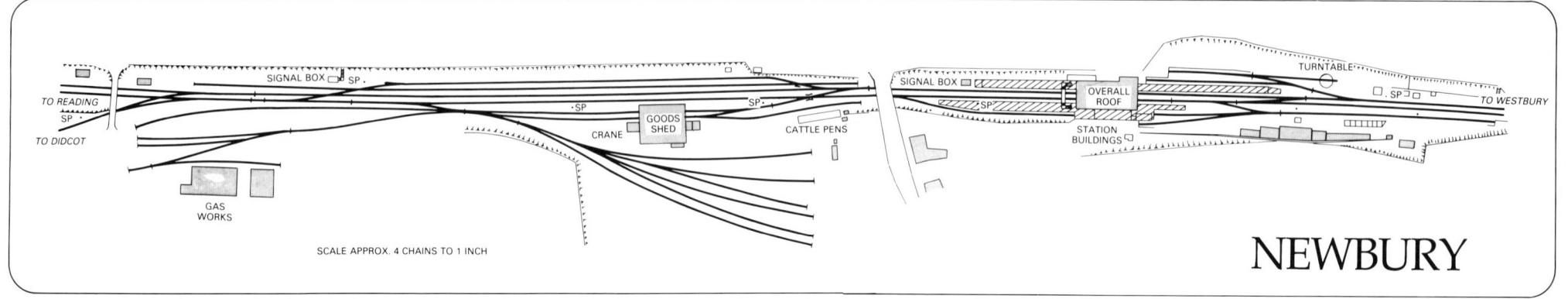

NEWBURY

The original and first track plan (*above*) shows the track lay-out at Newbury, at the turn of the century, when only two main running roads passed through the station. On the left of the station was the Didcot bay and, on the right, the Dorchester and Lambourn Valley bays. The Cheap Street road bridge is clearly shown in the centre of the plan. Note also that the station had an overall roof covering the station complex.

NEWBURY STATION

VALENTINES SERIES

50118

Plate 61: Taken from a 1900s' old postcard, this view, looking west, has been used in previous publications. It is been included here as it is the only known view showing the old overall roof and separate footbridge, spanning just the two main running lines. The DN&SR bay would be on the extreme right.

Lens of Sutton

Plate 60 (previous page): A 1950s view of Newbury Station, looking west from Cheap Street bridge. A local two coach 'stopper' is just leaving for Reading, and the GWR diesel rail-car waits in the bay to leave with the DN&SR stopping service to Didcot.

British Rail

Newbury

Newbury should have been a railway centre, but due to the opposition of local landowners, the GWR drove their main line to the west, via Didcot, instead of taking the natural route along the Kennet Valley. In 1845, the Southampton to Manchester line was planned, taking in Newbury en route, but the contract came to nothing. Meanwhile, the GWR constructed the Berks and Hants branch from Reading to Newbury and Hungerford, which opened on 21st December 1847, and later pushed through to Devizes. The first sod of the Didcot, Newbury and Southampton railway was cut by the Countess of Caernarvon, on 26th August 1879, and was greatly celebrated. The formal opening of the northern section was on 12th April 1882, when it was officially declared open by Lady Loyd-Lindsay. In July 1883, the Bill was passed for the southern section, and this section from Newbury was opened with 'great demonstration' on 1st May 1885. With all this traffic and, of course, the Lambourn line, which was added in 1898, Newbury Station became totally inadequate, and its two main lines under the overall roofing made the junction's facilities used to capacity. With all this in mind, the Great Western Railway decided, in 1907, to place out contracts for quadrupling the track, allowing for two slow stopping lines and two fast lines, and a total rebuild of the station. The contract was placed in 1908 and the following official account of the rebuilding (from the *GWR Magazine*) has been included to sum up the facilities of the 'new' station.

Extract 1909 from GWR Magazine

Newbury Station - Considerable progress has been made with this work; the new buildings are completed and in use, except the refreshment room, which will be opened during June. This has liberated the old buildings for demolition, following which the erection of the veranda covering has been taken in hand. Pending setting back, a wide platform area exists, but, when the rebuilding of Cheap Street overbridge to an increased span is completed, the old platforms will be removed and four lines will exist between platforms, the two centre ones for fast non-stop trains and the platform lines for local services.

Extract 1910 from GWR Magazine

Newbury New Station - The opening of the 'up' platform line at Newbury new station on May 29th brought to a conclusion an important series of engineering works. The necessity for remodelling the station arose largely from the growth of traffic at this historic town, to which the developments of the racecourse and various training establishments in the neighbourhood are contributory; although, at the same time, the conversion of the Berks and Hants Railway into the principal route to the West of England, practically rendered it imperative to free the two main lines of all stopping trains and provide two additional platform lines to admit the satisfactory working of local traffic.

The general features of the scheme, which commenced in May 1908, were the construction of entirely new 'up' and 'down' platforms, station buildings and approach roads, and the reconstruction of three overbridges to the requisite increased span for the additional lines. The buildings on both platforms are of red brick with Bath stone dressings, roofed with dark brindled tiles, and present an effective and pleasing appearance. On the 'up' side, to which a broad approach leads from the town, the platform is 1,065ft. long and 22ft. wide, 330ft. being covered in, a bay 360ft. long being provided at the west end for Lambourn trains, and another bay 440ft. long at the east end for Didcot trains. The main buildings are on this platform and have a length of 206ft. They comprise a booking hall, waiting-rooms, refreshment and tea rooms, postal telegraph office, parcels office, cloakroom and the usual rooms for station staff. The refreshment and tea rooms are panelled in fumed oak and have Roman marble mosaic floors and cathedral glass windows. The 'down' platform, 950ft. long and 20ft. wide (covering being provided over 330ft. of its length), contains, at the west end, a bay 460ft. long for Winchester trains. The usual waiting-room accommodation is also provided. A covered footbridge of a single span of 95ft. connects the platforms, and a loading bank, 310ft. in length, is provided on the 'down' side for horse-boxes, etc. The station is lighted by incandescent gas lamps.

Racecourse Bridge is formed of two plate girders, each 61ft. 5in. in length, with cross-girders at 5ft. intervals (centres), brick jack arches and concrete filling supporting the roadway, which is 13ft. wide.

Greenham Road Bridge comprises two spans, each formed with a pair of plate main girders, one span being carried by a girder 55ft. 4in. long, matched by one 50ft. 8in. long, due to the abutment being on the skew; and the remaining span by girders, each 57ft. long; the inner ends of all the girders being supported on a pair of steel columns braced together. Cross-girders at 5ft. intervals (centres) and jack arches, with concrete filling, support the roadway, which had a width of 18ft. in the clear.

Cheap Street Bridge consists of a single skew span of 87ft. on the square, with four girders, all 96ft. 9in. in length. The curved main girders, between which runs the roadway, 25ft. in width, are 10ft. deep and 27ft. apart (centres); between these girders and the outside girders on each side are the footways, each some 7ft. 6in. wide. Above the footways, curved bracing connects the main and outside girders at three points. The cross-girders under the road are at 10ft. intervals, with rolled steel joists longitudinally at 4ft. intervals. Under the paths, rolled steel joists are placed at 5ft. intervals. The flooring is of buckled plates and the roadway consists of tar asphalt.

Improvements have also been made in the goods yard, a new entrance being made from Cheap Street, with improved gradient compared with the old approach, and a new cart weighbridge, cattle pens and horse landing accommodation have also been provided, these works forming part of the larger scheme for goods yard alteration which is under consideration.

The drawings and contracts for the works were prepared in the office of the engineer, Mr W. W. Grierson and the work was carried out under the supervision of the Divisional Engineer, Mr J. N. Taylor, the contractors being; Station buildings, Mr A. N. Coles, Plymouth, with sub-contractors for the steelwork - Messrs Hill & Smith, Brierley Hill; three road bridges, Messrs Finch & Co., Chepstow. The earthwork, retaining walls, etc., were carried out by the Company's own men.

Plate 61a: A view photographed in the early days of the Didcot bay at Newbury Station, with a set of carriages in the bay on a train to Didcot. Note the enamel signs on the retaining wall.

Real Photographs

A copy of the original 1908 plans, dated and signed by the contractor. The 'notes' are of interest.

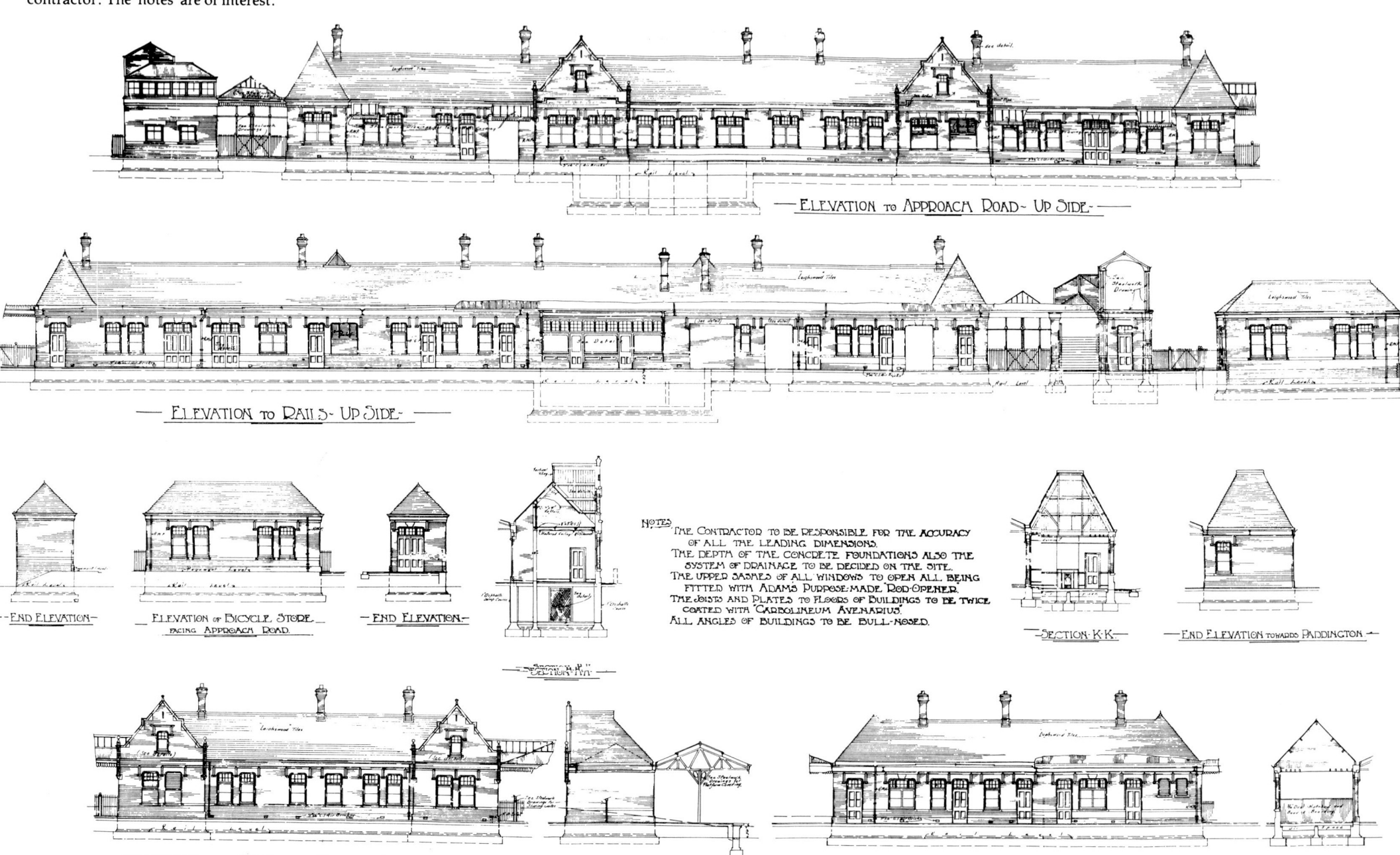

-Elevation to Approach Road - Up Side-

-Elevation to Rails- Up Side-

--End Elevation--

-Elevation of Bicycle Store- facing Approach Road.

-End Elevation-

Notes
The Contractor to be responsible for the accuracy of all the leading dimensions.
The depth of the concrete foundations also the system of drainage to be decided on the site.
The upper sashes of all windows to open all being fitted with Adams purpose-made rod-opener.
The joists and plates to floors of buildings to be twice coated with 'Carbolineum Avenarius'.
All angles of buildings to be bull-nosed.

-Section-K·K-

-End Elevation towards Paddington-

-Section-P·P-

-Elevation to Approach Road - Down Side-

-End Elevation towards Paddington-

-Elevation to Rails - Down Side-

-Section-Y·Y-

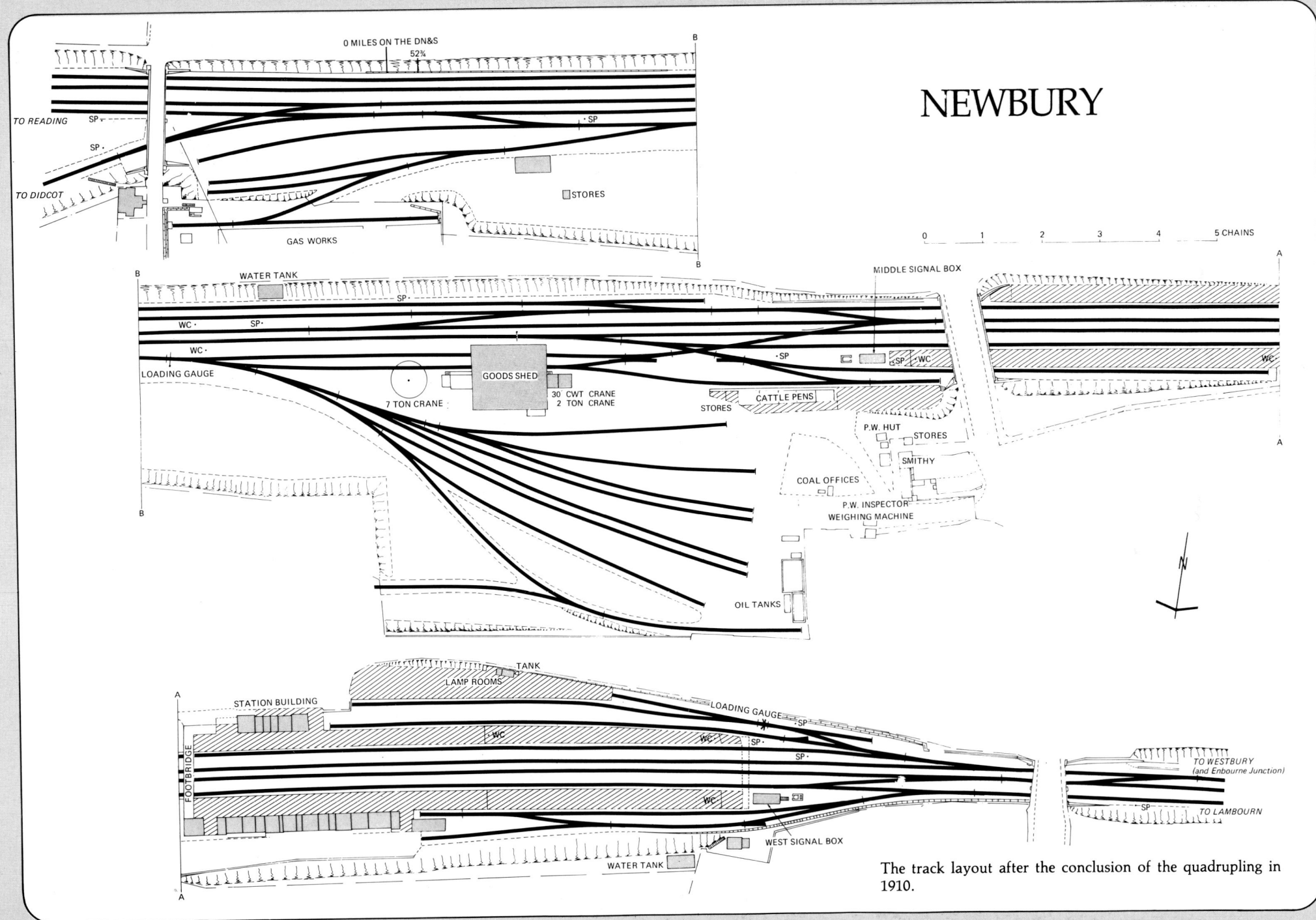

NEWBURY

TO READING

TO DIDCOT

0 MILES ON THE DN&S
52¾

SP
SP
SP

STORES

GAS WORKS

0   1   2   3   4   5 CHAINS

WATER TANK

MIDDLE SIGNAL BOX

SP
WC
WC
SP

LOADING GAUGE

GOODS SHED

7 TON CRANE

30 CWT CRANE
2 TON CRANE

STORES

CATTLE PENS

SP
SP
WC

WC

STORES

P.W. HUT

SMITHY

COAL OFFICES

P.W. INSPECTOR
WEIGHING MACHINE

OIL TANKS

TANK

LAMP ROOMS

STATION BUILDING

LOADING GAUGE

SP

WC

WC

SP

SP

FOOTBRIDGE

WC

TO WESTBURY
(and Enbourne Junction)

TO LAMBOURN

SP

WEST SIGNAL BOX

WATER TANK

The track layout after the conclusion of the quadrupling in
1910.

57

Plates 62 & 63: These views show the 'up' and 'down' side station buildings. In *Plate 62* the construction of the rather unique footbridge can be seen in detail. The steel girders (spanning four tracks and two platforms) rest on the brick-work and support a timber superstructure for the passenger gangway. The bridge was well lit by the glazed windows running the whole length. The buildings themselves, were constructed in English bond bricks using a smooth finish, and giving a polished look to the brickwork. Nearly all the edges were rounded and the gable ends are similar in design to stations on the Princes Risborough to Aynho Line. The small turret designs, coping stones and use of curves in doorways and windows helps to make these buildings rather elegant. Even the chimney design is complicated rather than plain. Note in *Plate 63* how the two windows have been partially bricked up.

Plates 64 & 65: These two views show even more of the rather unique construction of the footbridge. The top photograph (*Plate 64*) is taken from the 'down' side and *Plate 65*, from the approach road to the 'up' side. *Plate 65* dates back to 1967, when car parking was 2s. 6d. for the day.

British Rail

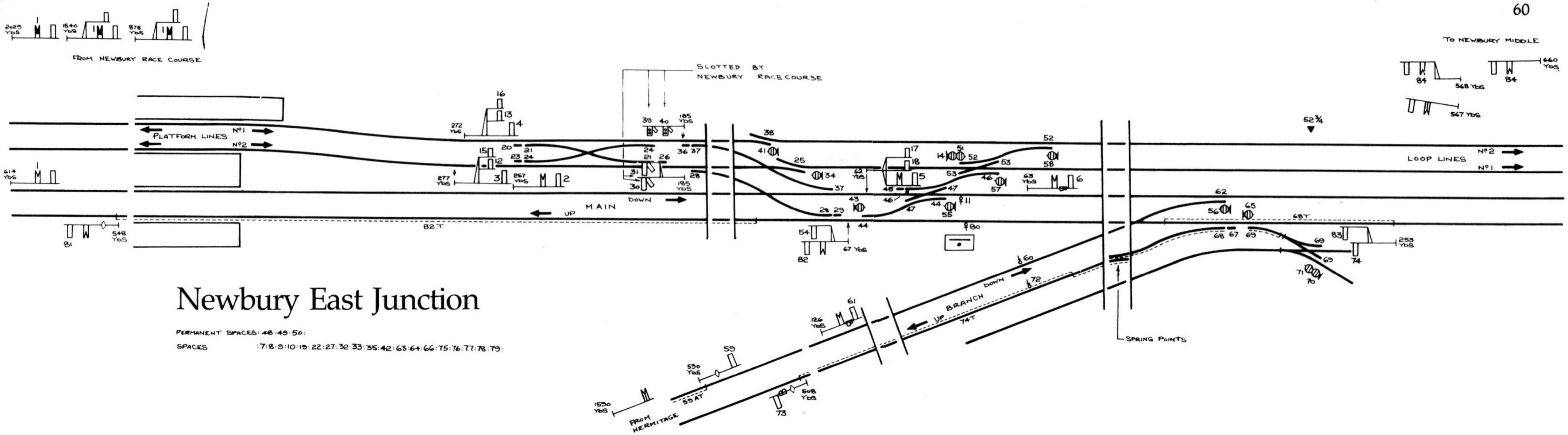

Newbury East Junction

PERMANENT SPACES: 48:49:50:

SPACES :7:8:9:10:15: 22:27: 32:33:35:42:63:64:66:75:76:77:78:79:

Newbury East Junction signalling plan after quadrupling and the doubling of the DN&SR.

Plate 66: This view, taken on 23rd October 1946, although slightly out of sequence, is looking towards Reading, on the 'up' platform, and shows the buffer stops of the Lambourn branch bay. The reason for its inclusion is to give some idea of the platform canopy ends and awnings. The style of lamps is also evident.

British Rail

Newbury (middle)

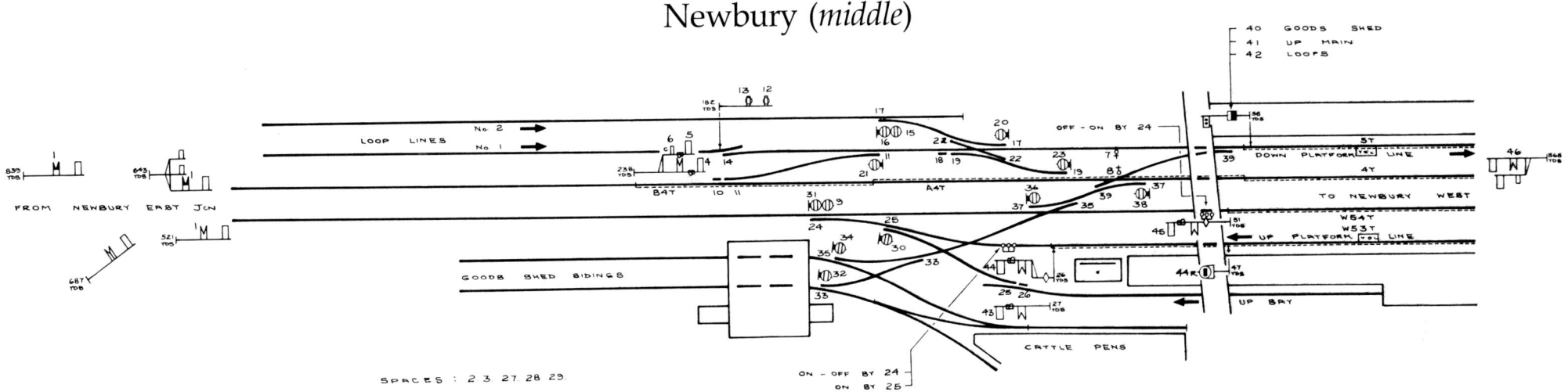

Newbury Middle box signalling diagram. The box was situated right at the end of the 'up' platform and the DN&SR bay, just after Cheap Street Bridge.

Plate 67: A further look at the west end of the station, this time showing the Winchester bay, with a locomotive in attendance, and the GWR style water column.

British Rail

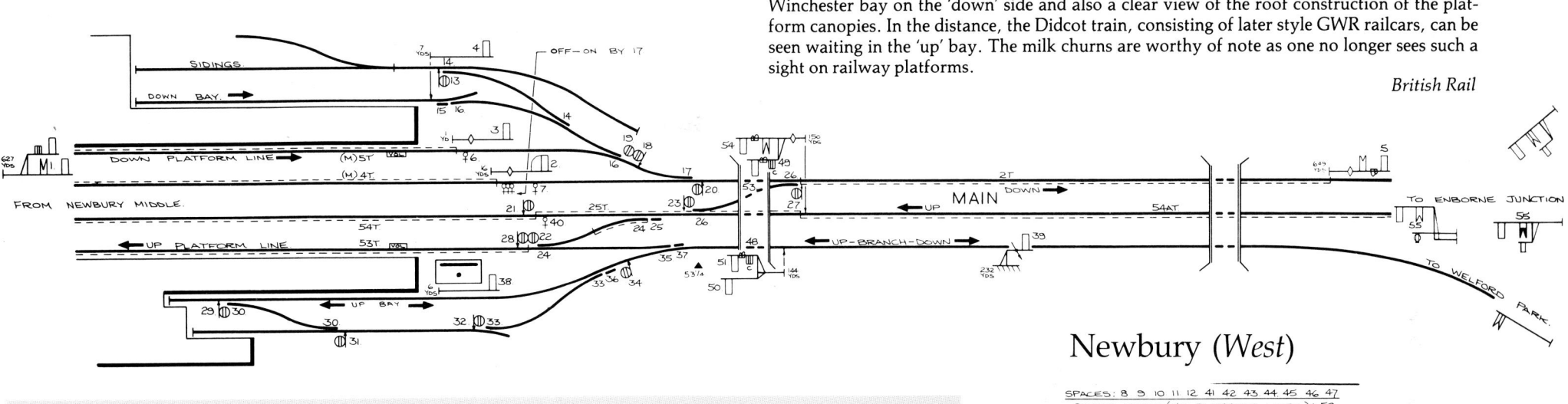

Plate 68 (above): This is the final official view of the west end of the station, and shows the Winchester bay on the 'down' side and also a clear view of the roof construction of the platform canopies. In the distance, the Didcot train, consisting of later style GWR railcars, can be seen waiting in the 'up' bay. The milk churns are worthy of note as one no longer sees such a sight on railway platforms.

British Rail

Newbury (West)

SPACES: 8 9 10 11 12 41 42 43 44 45 46 47
SWITCH LEVER (VIA PLATFORM LINES): 52

The final signalling plan showing the west end of Newbury Station controlled by Newbury West box. The Lambourn branch is independent to the GWR main line and shows it indicated to Welford Park.

Plate 69: No. 3440 *City of Truro* was a locomotive often used on this line in 1957, and she is seen leaving the Winchester bay at Newbury.

Author's Collection

Plate 70: GWR Collett 0-6-0 locomotive No. 2221 was a regular engine on the DN&SR in British Railways' days, and she is seen here awaiting departure to Winchester. A few passengers are seen boarding the train. The grounded coach body on the right was used as a temporary parcels office and lamp room. The single coach train to Lambourn waits on the left, in the bay platform.

Author's Collection

Plate 72: A general view of the west end of Newbury with a Lambourn passenger train standing, wrong road, in the 'up' platform, as the bay is obviously unavailable.

Lens of Sutton

Plate 71: This is not a DN&SR train but an interesting view allowing us to see the West signal box, water-tower and pump room in the background, and also the curve upon which Newbury Station was situated. The train is a local pick-up freight to Lambourn, working the wrong way along the 'up' road.

L. N. Owen

Plate 73: Another view of GWR locomotive No. 3440 *City of Truro* on the local Winchester train. This view shows very clearly the large water-tower, another grounded coach body used as a mess room, and also the engine house at the bottom of the stairs from the water-tower.

Author's Collection

Plate 74: A general view from the 'down' platform, looking west, with the Winchester bay on the left.

Author's Collection

Plate 75: From the road bridge abutment, this photograph has captured the track layout very well indeed. The two bays, horse loading bay and West signal box are being passed, at speed, by GWR 'Castle' class locomotive No. 5014 *Goodrich Castle* with a 'down' milk train, on 27th May 1961.

Michael Hale

Plate 76: Newbury West signal box, as seen on 20th February 1971, with the signalman parking his car alongside the box. All the track of the branch lines had been lifted from this area by this date.

South Devon Railway Museum

Plate 77: A final photograph again showing No. 3440 *City of Truro* leaving Newbury for Winchester and Southampton on 6th June 1957. This is the last bridge before Enborne Junction. The two nearest lines are the GWR main lines and the furthest line, the Lambourn branch.

R. M. Casserley

Plate 78: This photograph completes the scene and shows the Lambourn line rising up and to the left of the picture, leaving the two main GWR lines running on to the west. The bridge in the distance is the same as that in *Plate 77*. It is noticeable that every piece of available land is utilized along the railway embankment for allotments. The railway boundary fence can be clearly seen to the right of the allotments.

British Rail

Plate 79: During World War II, the congestion of the two lines west of Newbury became acute, and so, in 1943, a new 'up' goods loop was laid from just beyond the road bridge to Enborne Junction. This view, looking from the road bridge to Newbury, shows the utility track used for the loop.

British Rail

Plate 80: Looking west to Enborne Junction is this view, also taken from the bridge. This brick built bridge had to be demolished and replaced by a girder style structure to accommodate the three lines.

British Rail

Plate 81: This official view shows the fine brick bridge that was demolished to allow the 'up' loop line to be installed. In the distance the junction signals and signal box of Enborne Junction can be seen. This view was photographed in March 1943, just before the new work was carried out.

British Rail

Plate 82: One final look at the exit point to the 'up' loop, at the Newbury end. The new signal had not yet been installed, but the new bridge and remains of the old brick bridge can be seen in the distance.

British Rail

Enborne
Junction

Plate 83 (above): Although, in this view of Enborne Junction, the Winchester and DN&SR line comes in from the right, in actual fact the line curved to the left after leaving Newbury, as we are looking towards Newbury in this view, taken on the 18th March 1943, before commencement of the loop line.

British Rail

Plate 84: Moving closer to the junction, this view shows details of the original signals before the new 'works'.

British Rail

Plate 85: A view of the same junction, but in June 1943, with maximum work in progress. The new bridge is in situ and the loop is almost complete.

British Rail

Plate 86: This is the final official photograph of the work of installing the 'up' loop, and clearly shows the entry to the loop for the GWR 'up' line, and also the crossover and second entry for the loop for trains from the DN&SR line.

British Rail

ENBORNE JUNCTION

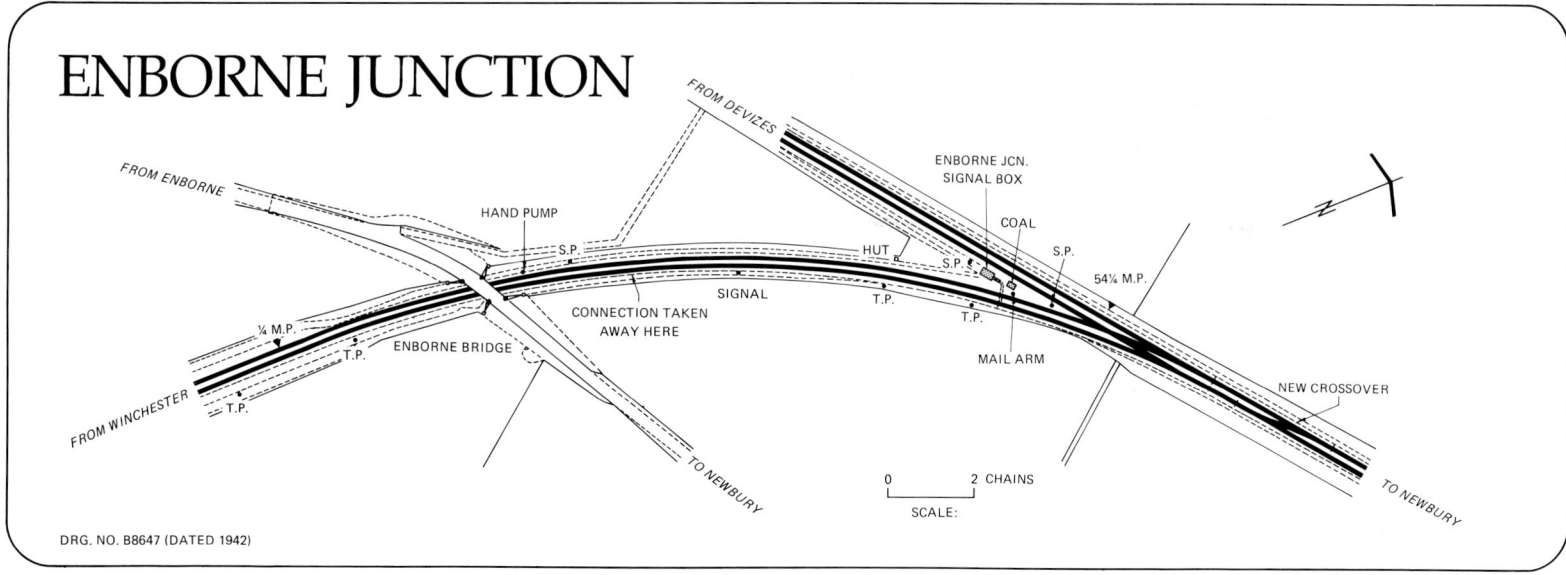

FROM DEVIZES

FROM ENBORNE

HAND PUMP

ENBORNE JCN.
SIGNAL BOX

COAL

S.P.

HUT

S.P.

S.P.

54¼ M.P.

¼ M.P.

SIGNAL

T.P.

T.P.

CONNECTION TAKEN
AWAY HERE

ENBORNE BRIDGE

T.P.

MAIL ARM

NEW CROSSOVER

FROM WINCHESTER

T.P.

TO NEWBURY

TO NEWBURY

0   2 CHAINS

SCALE:

DRG. NO. B8647 (DATED 1942)

This track plan, dated 1942, shows the actual envisaged layout at Enborne with the wartime changes. The crossover was taken away on the DN&SR, and a new one added in the GWR main lines to allow access to the loop. When the loop was finally laid, a further entry was added from the GWR 'up' main line, prior to the junction of the DN&SR.

Plate 87: A general view of the junction, photographed from the road bridge, with the DN&SR coming in from bottom right and the GWR main line running across the picture. A GWR 'Hall' class locomotive, No. 5923 *Colston Hall*, is seen hauling the 4.36 ex-Newbury local stopping service.

Michael Hale

Plate 88: A view, taken in 1960, of the 1910 signal box clearly showing the signals controlling the junction from the DN&SR to the main GWR lines, to Newbury.

R. Kirkland

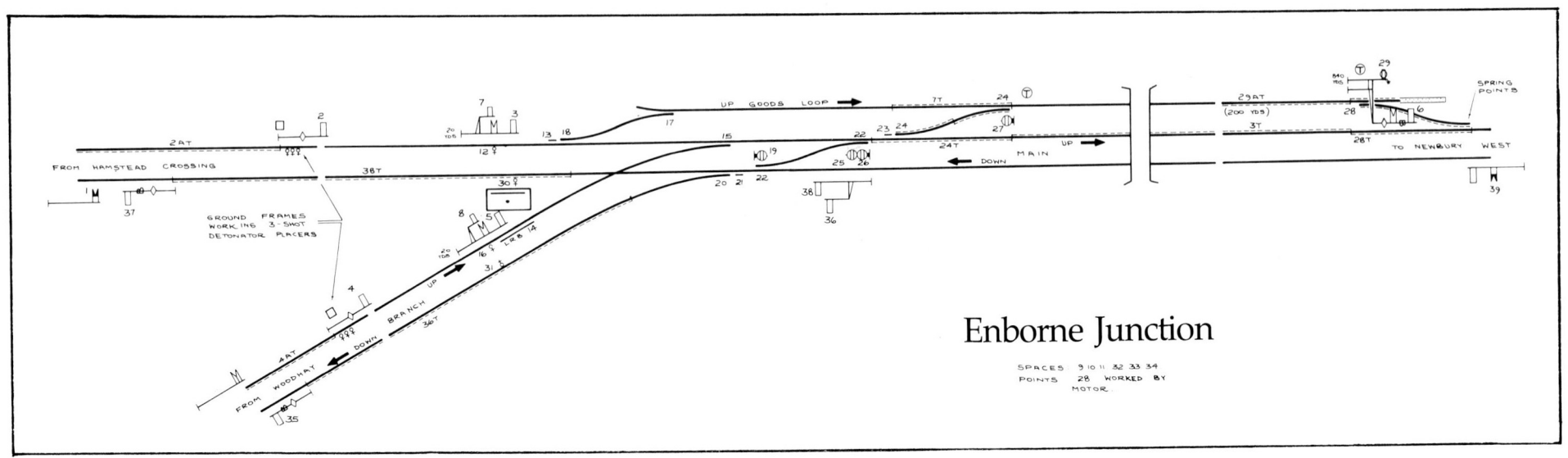

Enborne Junction

SPACES 9 10 11 32 33 34
POINTS 28 WORKED BY
MOTOR.

Plates 89 & 90: A derailment in August 1944 seriously disrupted the wartime effort, when the freight, which had come off the DN&SR line, overran the signals at the end of the 'up' loop. It is reported that thick fog was a hazard at the time.

Author's Collection

Woodhay

Plate 91:   This early 1919 view, looking north from the 'up' platform, clearly shows the different structure of Woodhay to other stations. The milk churns and waiting passengers (with luggage) add to this period piece.

Real Photographs

WOODHAY

The original 1908 plan shows the small goods shed, crane and cattle pens, and the position of the signal box on the 'down' platform. A ground frame controlled the southern yard and was locked to the main box. This was removed when the new signal box was installed.

STATION MASTER'S HOUSE

HUT

CATTLE PEN CRANE GOODS SHED

STATION BUILDINGS

G.F

S.P.

2¼ M.P.

SIGNAL BOX

WASH WATER BRIDGE

B.P.

B.P.

TO WOODHAY

SIGNAL

S.P.

106 LEVEL

TO HIGHCLERE

GRASS ROAD

0   2 CHAINS
SCALE:

RIVER

TO NEWBURY

LEVEL 330

TO NEWBURY

Plate 92:   A 1952 view of the 'down' platform, photographed from a train, showing the sparse waiting shelter and ARP brick-built signal box in the distance. This box was opened on 9th October 1942, and sited approximately 60 yards to the south of the early wooden construction. This box was equipped to be manned for 24 hours per day and, as the line was now doubled from Enborne Junction, Woodhay ceased to be just a crossing point and was therefore the end of the double track section, making this box particularly important.   *H. C. Casserley*

Woodhay

Opened: 4th May 1885
Closed to passenger traffic: 7th March 1960
Closed to goods traffic: 31st December 1962

The line from Enborne Junction was originally single to Woodhay but, during World War II, it was doubled. Woodhay Station, at mile post 2¼, was the first station on the southern section of the DN&SR, and was somewhat different in appearance to the stations on the northern section. The buildings here were even more distinct, as they were constructed of wood, (the only station so constructed on the DN&SR). One reason given for this was the avoidance of extensive ground foundations for the main building, as the station was on a higher embankment and soft ground. The standard stationmaster's house, (*featured in the above plan*), was not far away, as can be seen to the top of the plan. The platform was on a curve, with the main buildings on the 'up' platform, whilst the 'down' platform supported the timber signal box, (supplied by Saxby & Farmer, and having 16 levers), and a small waiting platform shelter. Alongside this shelter was a gentlemen's 'open' lavatory. The main building contained an office, ladies' waiting-room and lavatory, general waiting-room and gentlemen's toilet, booking office and, originally, a lamp room, this later (about 1915) being placed separately in the yard in a hut which had been built by the GWR in 1887. On the platform was also a corrugated iron parcels store and bicycle hut (added in 1915), which had to be constructed on pile supports owing to the angle of the embankment. The yard had the facilities of a brick built goods shed of a standard pattern (see *Plate 94*), and a substantial 3 ton yard crane. Records show that in the early days, Woodhay was one of the busiest stations on this section of the line in both passenger and freight traffic and, that in 1931, a new loading dock was built behind the platform to load mainly the racehorse traffic.

Woodhay

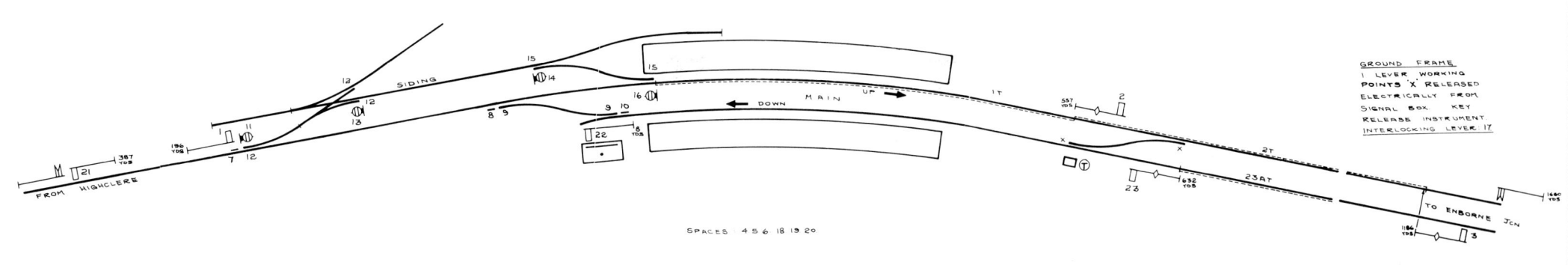

GROUND FRAME
1 LEVER WORKING
POINTS 'X' RELEASED
ELECTRICALLY FROM
SIGNAL BOX KEY
RELEASE INSTRUMENT
INTERLOCKING LEVER: 17

SPACES 4 5 6 18 19 20

The signalling plan (*above*) shows the 'new' box, with the double line from Enborne feeding into the single line in front of the signal box. The ground frame shown on the double section, was near the road bridge connecting Ball Hill to Wash Common, and was electrically released from the Woodhay box.

Plate 93: A view, looking north from the 'down' platform, in the 1950s, and the new horse loading dock, just behind the platform, can be seen. The lamp hut stands at the base of the large telegraph pole and the station platform fencing has been removed, presumably to help loading in the horse dock.

Author's Collection

Plate 94: This view looks south from the 'down' platform, this time in May 1961. It clearly shows the signal box (on the extreme left), at the end on the 'down' platform and, on the 'up' platform the small goods shed and the new style 3 ton yard crane. The lamp hut and wooden station buildings (note some panelling now boarded up) are also visible. The gentlemen's lean-to lavatory and wooden parcels shed can be seen on the right.

Michael Hale

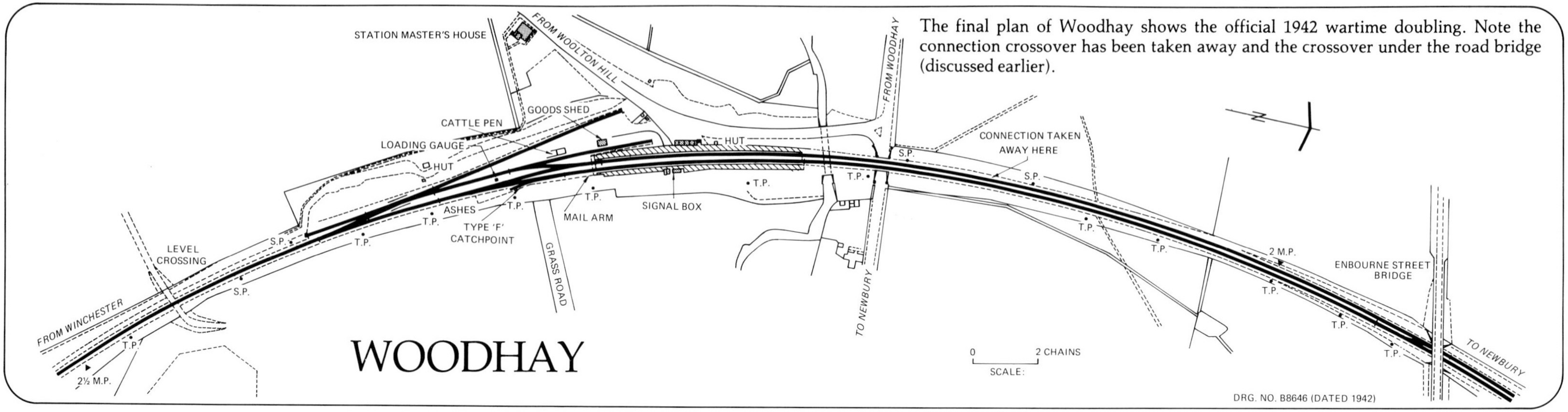

The final plan of Woodhay shows the official 1942 wartime doubling. Note the connection crossover has been taken away and the crossover under the road bridge (discussed earlier).

WOODHAY

STATION MASTER'S HOUSE

FROM WOOLTON HILL

FROM WOODHAY

CATTLE PEN

GOODS SHED

LOADING GAUGE

HUT

HUT

ASHES

TYPE 'F' CATCHPOINT

MAIL ARM

SIGNAL BOX

T.P.

S.P.

LEVEL CROSSING

S.P.

FROM WINCHESTER

2½ M.P.

T.P.

GRASS ROAD

TO NEWBURY

CONNECTION TAKEN AWAY HERE

S.P.

S.P.

T.P.

T.P.

2 M.P.

ENBOURNE STREET BRIDGE

TO NEWBURY

T.P.

0   2 CHAINS
SCALE:

DRG. NO. B8646 (DATED 1942)

Plate 95 (left): This is an interesting view, taken in December 1959, from the back of a moving train, and allows more detail of the horse loading dock to be seen. A horse-box van is in the bay, and the goods shed is on the left.

C. Gammell

Plate 96: The final view of Woodhay is taken from the outside of the main station building looking towards Newbury, and shows how the station was situated on quite a substantial curve. Just past the end of the platforms, the track passed over the Woodhay to Newbury road.

Author's Collection

Highclere

Plate 97:   This early 1900s' photograph, taken from the bridge over the road, has been published previously, but it is an excellent view of this station and shows the short crossing loop. The track layout, station facilities and even the tidy gardens are so clearly defined. The cattle pen appears to be newly-painted. The signal cabin is tucked away under the tree on the platform on the right-hand side.

Lens of Sutton

HIGHCLERE

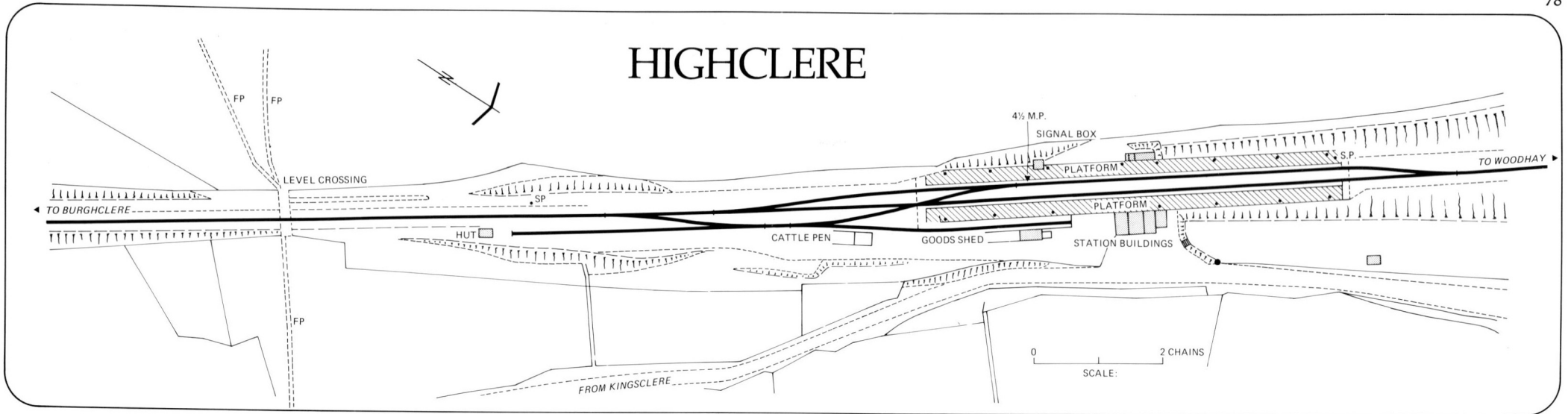

Highclere

Opened: 4th May 1885
Closed to passenger traffic: 7th March 1960
Closed to goods traffic: 31st December 1962

This station was nearer to the village of Burghclere than Burghclere's own station, and so caused some confusion and, consequently, little goods traffic passed through. It was built as a two platform station, and the station building was to the design of buildings on the northern section, even to the degree of the canopy having heavy styled supports. The water supply was taken from a natural spring in front of the station and this was also carried in cans to Woodhay for drinking. The signal cabin on the 'up' platform was again one of the small Saxby & Farmer wooden constructions, with a tiled roof and brick chimney. The 'up' platform also had the usual sparse wooden open passenger platform shelter. The ARP brick signal box was added in 1942 and ceased operation on 6th February 1955, when the crossing loop was taken out, leaving only a single line through the station. At the northern end of the station was a three arch road bridge. The goods yard had a brick-built goods shed, and a 3 ton yard crane (replaced in the 1930s by a more modern 3 ton crane). A cattle pen and loading gauge were also provided.

Plate 98: Another view, taken in 1917, from the same road bridge as that mentioned in *Plate 97,* shows quite a variation, particularly in the track layout. The extension of the passing loop at this end is evident, and also worthy of note is the track, slewing in the distance, bringing the point over to the right rather than the left. The station bushes have all grown but the tree near the signal box has been removed. Single line token apparatus has also been added to the trackside and all the trees have been removed from the rear of the goods yard. The 1908 track plan shows the track layout as shown in *Plate 97,* with the short passing loop and the track at the other end converging left into the main line.

Real Photographs

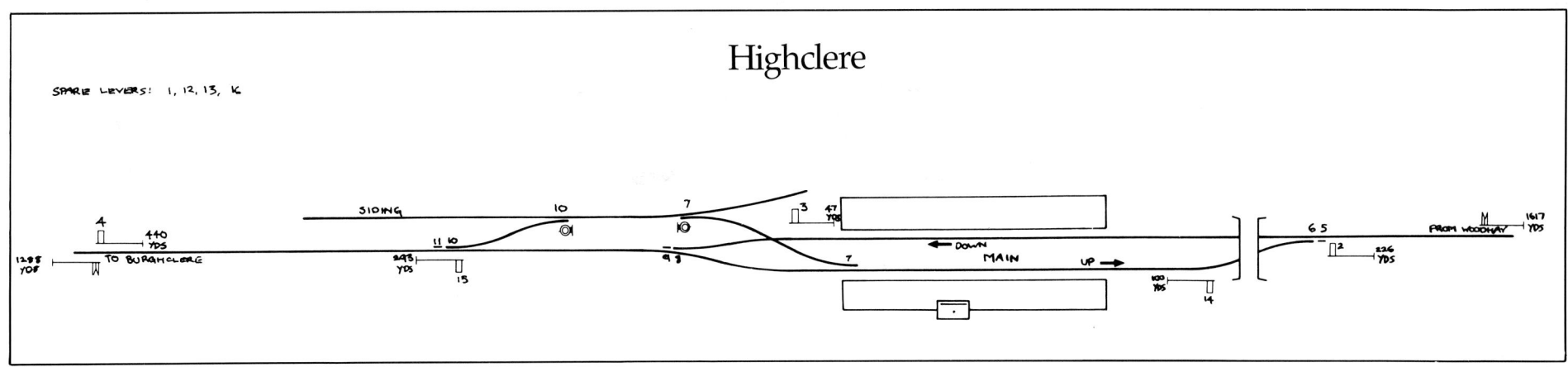

Highclere

SPARE LEVERS: 1, 12, 13, 16

The 1917 signalling diagram shows the extension of the loop and repositioning of the point to obtain better running facilities into the platforms.

Plate 99: A view looking north from the 'up' platform with the three arch brick road bridge in the background. The 'down' platform, with the main station buildings, is clearly shown and the 'heavy' canopy is still intact.

OPC Collection

Plate 100: Looking south from the 'up' platform with the ARP signal box clearly discernible in the distance. The station bushes, as in *Plate 97*, have certainly grown! The area above the embankment behind the station nameboard was once the stationmaster's garden.

OPC Collection

Plate 101: A 1952 view from the window of a train standing in the 'up' platform. The station staff are cutting the grass on the embankment, below the stationmaster's garden.

H. C. Casserley

Plate 103: This time looking from the 'down' platform a clear view of the 'new' signal box is obtained, and also the position of the old box (on the 'up' platform) can be calculated by the gap in the platform front where the rodding passed through.

OPC Collection

Plate 102: A further look from the 'up' platform, but this time in 1960. The station and surroundings seem to·be in very good order and, in this view, we can clearly see the small goods shed, yard crane and signal box (in the distance). The trap between the rails to the water supply spring can also be seen.

C. Gammell

Plate 104: A final view of the derelict station, with its single line and overgrown platforms, taken on 27th May 1961, looking towards Newbury.

Michael Hale

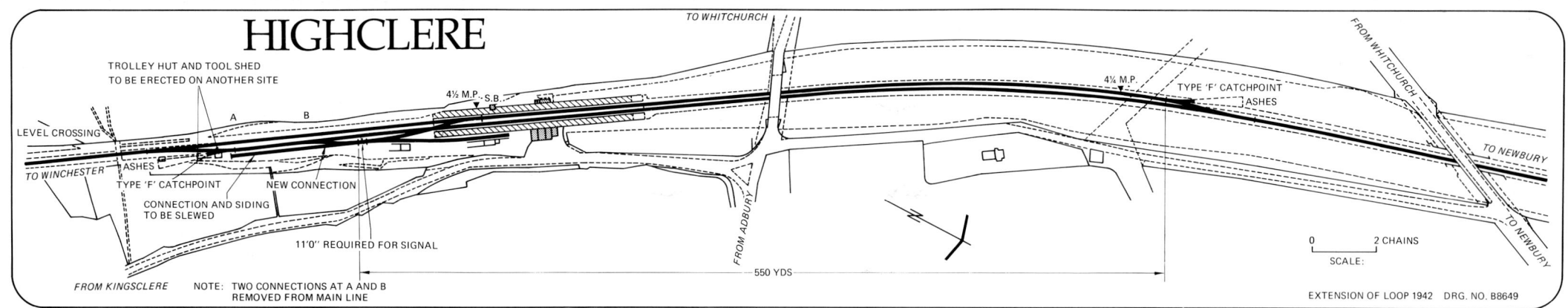

HIGHCLERE

TO WHITCHURCH
FROM WHITCHURCH

TROLLEY HUT AND TOOL SHED
TO BE ERECTED ON ANOTHER SITE

4½ M.P.   S.B.

A   B

4¼ M.P.

TYPE 'F' CATCHPOINT
ASHES

TO NEWBURY

LEVEL CROSSING

TO WINCHESTER   ASHES

TYPE 'F' CATCHPOINT

NEW CONNECTION

CONNECTION AND SIDING
TO BE SLEWED

FROM ADBURY

11'0" REQUIRED FOR SIGNAL

TO NEWBURY

0   2 CHAINS
SCALE:

FROM KINGSCLERE   NOTE: TWO CONNECTIONS AT A AND B
REMOVED FROM MAIN LINE

550 YDS

EXTENSION OF LOOP 1942   DRG. NO. B8649

Plate 105: This official photograph allows detail of the point motors and locking equipment, to be gleaned. This particular point and catch point is at the 4¼ mile post, and can be seen on the wartime 1942 plan above. This was the furthest point of the loop extension on the Newbury side which was added during the wartime doubling. The A34 road bridge, which is discussed in the following few pages, can be seen on the extreme right of the plan.

British Rail

Plate 106 (below): An example of the station nameboard, with cut-out wooden letters screwed to the wooden backboard. The supports were of rail section.

Author's Collection

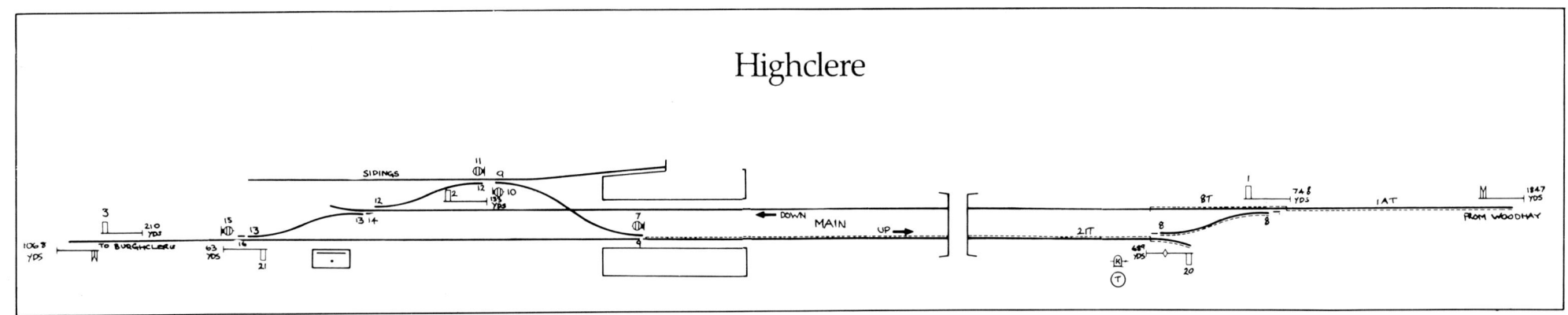

Highclere

81

Plate 108: A GWR motor bus stands on the A34 road bridge, perhaps supplying weight for a bridge-loading test, or a publicity picture for the GWR motor service. It does give a clearer picture of the type of wooden structure supporting the bridge. This view was taken from the small road that led from the A34 to Highclere Station. The 7 ton limit plate can be clearly seen at the entrance to the bridge, but this must have been ignored many times on this busy road.

British Rail

Plate 107: A postcard view of the A34 road bridge over Tothill Cutting, which is, in fact, out of sequence as it came before Highclere Station. This bridge was supported on trestles and this early view shows only the two original main trestles in place. The bridge was bought second-hand and rapidly constructed over the cutting after the original 135ft. long tunnel collapsed before the official line opening.

Lens of Sutton

Plate 110: The final view of the A34 road bridge shows the GWR motor bus standing on the bridge with the camera pointing towards Winchester. There appears to be a complete lack of traffic. The traffic load restriction of 7 tons did, in fact, make the heavier lorries turn left here, and proceed to Highclere Station, turning over the brick three arch road bridge by the station. This too had to be strengthened due to excessive use.

British Rail

Plate 109: This view looks towards Newbury, from the middle of the overbridge at Tothill Cutting. The side structure was of corrugated iron with a wooden rail running along the top. Note the motor bus is running on trade plates. In 1942, the bridge had to be strengthened to take the wartime traffic (military) and so an additional large trestle was added, and the original drawing can be seen on *Page 83*. This drawing allows all the detail of the wooden structure to be seen, and would make an interesting model.

British Rail

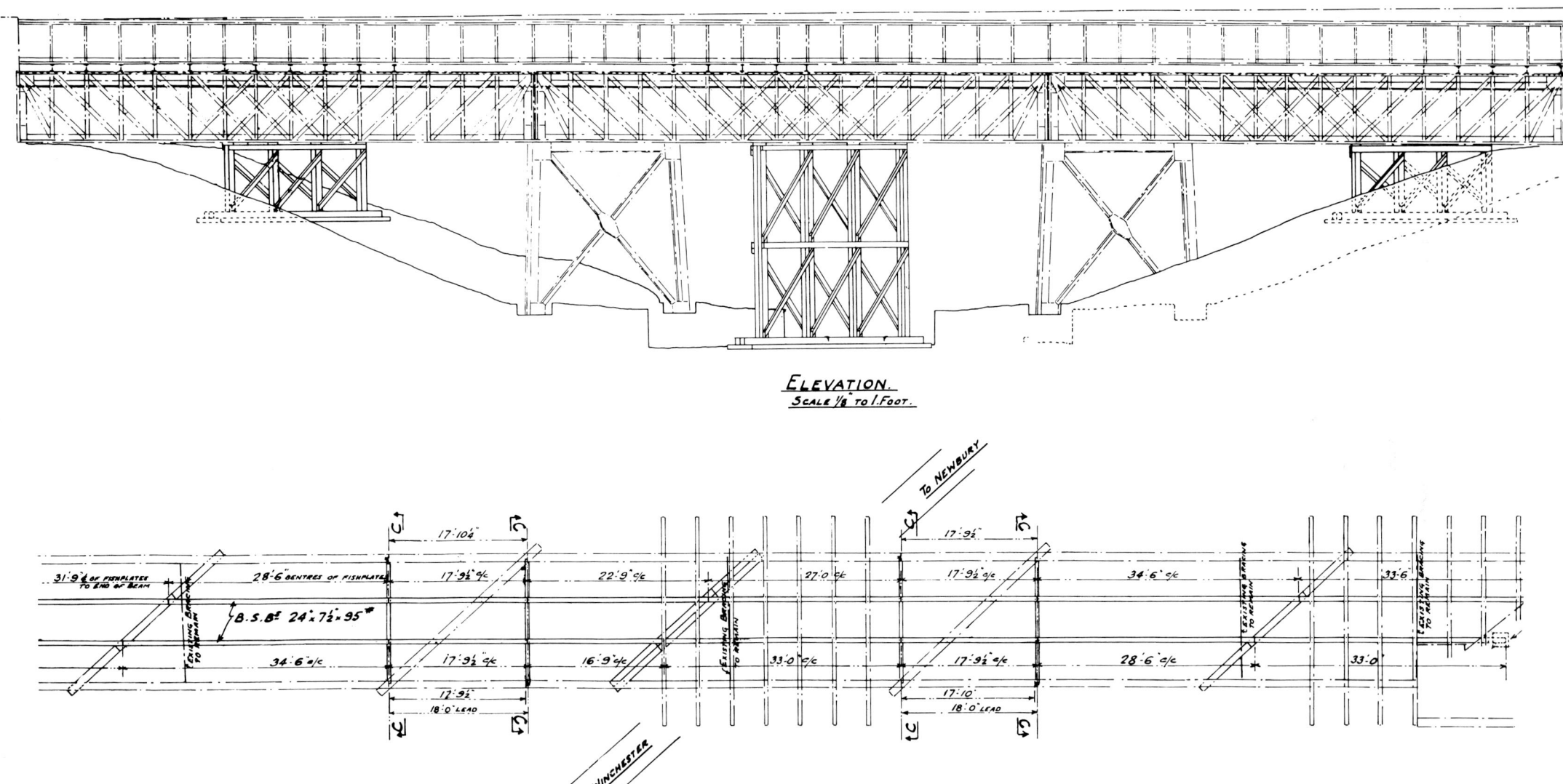

ELEVATION.
SCALE ⅛ TO 1 FOOT.

Burghclere

Plate 111: This view looks north through the station and road bridge, towards Highclere. The goods shed can just be seen on the left and, on the track in front of the goods shed, (just behind the station nameboard), the water tank wagon can be seen. The water wagons bore the name of the appropriate station and were filled up at Winchester. After arrival at Burghclere, the wagon would be emptied into a tank behind the platform. The water was then pumped by hand, (the pump being in the lamp room), to the white tank on the side of the main building. Again, this scene was photographed from the back of a train in 1960.

C. Gammell

BURGHCLERE

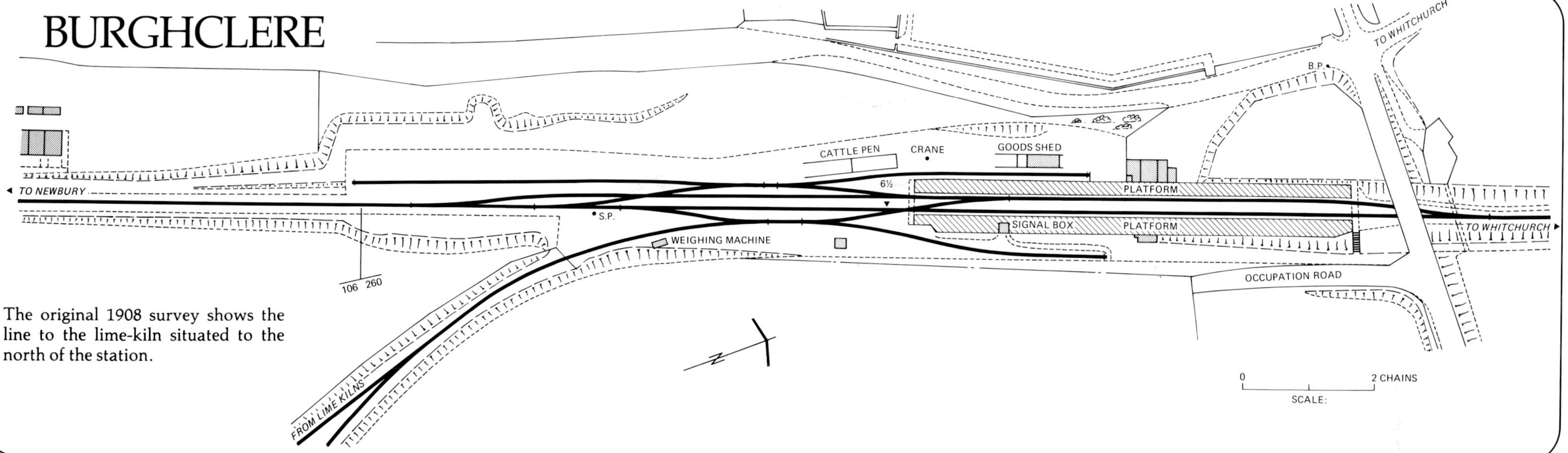

The original 1908 survey shows the line to the lime-kiln situated to the north of the station.

TO NEWBURY

FROM LIME KILNS

CATTLE PEN · CRANE · GOODS SHED · PLATFORM · 6½ · SIGNAL BOX · PLATFORM · WEIGHING MACHINE · S.P. · OCCUPATION ROAD · 106 260 · TO WHITCHURCH · B.P. · TO WHITCHURCH

0 — 2 CHAINS
SCALE:

Plate 112: A view from the road bridge, in 1960, showing the passenger crossing at the end of the platform, as no footbridge was provided. Note the steps on the left, which were provided for passengers to gain access to the 'down' platform from the road. In this view, the original 'up' trailing connection to the siding to the lime-kilns had been removed.
R. Kirkland

85

Burghclere

Opened: 4th May 1885
Closed to passengers: 7th March 1960
Closed to Goods Traffic: 6th May 1963

Situated at the 6½ mile post, Burghclere Station served the surrounding villages of Ecchinswell, Kingsclere and Sydmonton. The station was originally called Sydmonton but after discussion, the GWR insisted that it should be renamed Burghclere. The station buildings, with a parcel shed built alongside, were again of a standard pattern, with two storey design main buildings (the usual platform canopy here being supported by cast-iron brackets instead of pillars), and were situated on the 'up' platform. The 'down' platform possessed a small wooden passenger shelter and a gentlemen's 'open' lavatory. At the Highclere end of the station was a red brick road bridge, with the loop point intersection beneath. This bridge led to the large and pleasant forecourt of the station. Both the 'up' and 'down' lines had siding facilities, with a goods shed and a 3 ton hand crane, which broke down in the 1930s and was never replaced. The cattle pens were also on the 'up' side. The 'down' side had the siding headshunt and the private siding (installed in 1888) to the lime-kilns, which was protected by a gate. Also on this side was a weighing machine, which was situated on the company's side of the gate to the lime-kilns. The original signal box was situated on the 'down' platform until the wartime doubling, when a new brick ARP box was built. This was at the end of the loop and became operational in November 1942. Passengers had to cross the line by means of a 'line' crossing at the north end of the station, as no footbridge facility was provided. During World War II, the loop at the Highclere end of the station was extended, but cut back slightly at the south end. Due to the length of the loop, the point had to be powered by a hand generator (see *Plate 116*). The loop was also protected by a catch point and a runaway ash pile. The 'down' sidings, lime-kiln private sidings and diamond crossing were removed in 1946. During 1902, there was a scheme to build a light railway to Kingsclere, to help eliminate the 4 mile walk which residents of that village had to catch their trains, but this did not materialize due to lack of local fund raising. The Tilley lamps were installed on the station in 1949 and the whole station was used in the famous film 'Ghost Train', starring Arthur Askey.

Plate 113 (top left): A general view of the station, looking south, with the 'new' signal box in the background. The wooden waiting shelter for passengers, with the gentlemen's lavatory on the side, is clearly visible.

Michael Hale

Plate 114 (above): Ex-SR Class T9 4-4-0, No. 30292, pulls out of the station with a train to Newbury, in June 1953. This month was the first time that southern engines worked the line. Mrs Bessie Sheerman, the stationmistress, can be seen on the platform.

Lens of Sutton

Plate 115 (left): This view, taken in 1960, looks north towards the road bridge. Note the water wagon behind the station nameboard. Above this can be seen the approach road to the station, through an archway of trees. The station was still in good order, with the flower beds ringed by painted white stones, and all the trees on the platform are neatly trimmed.

R. Kirkland

BURGHCLERE

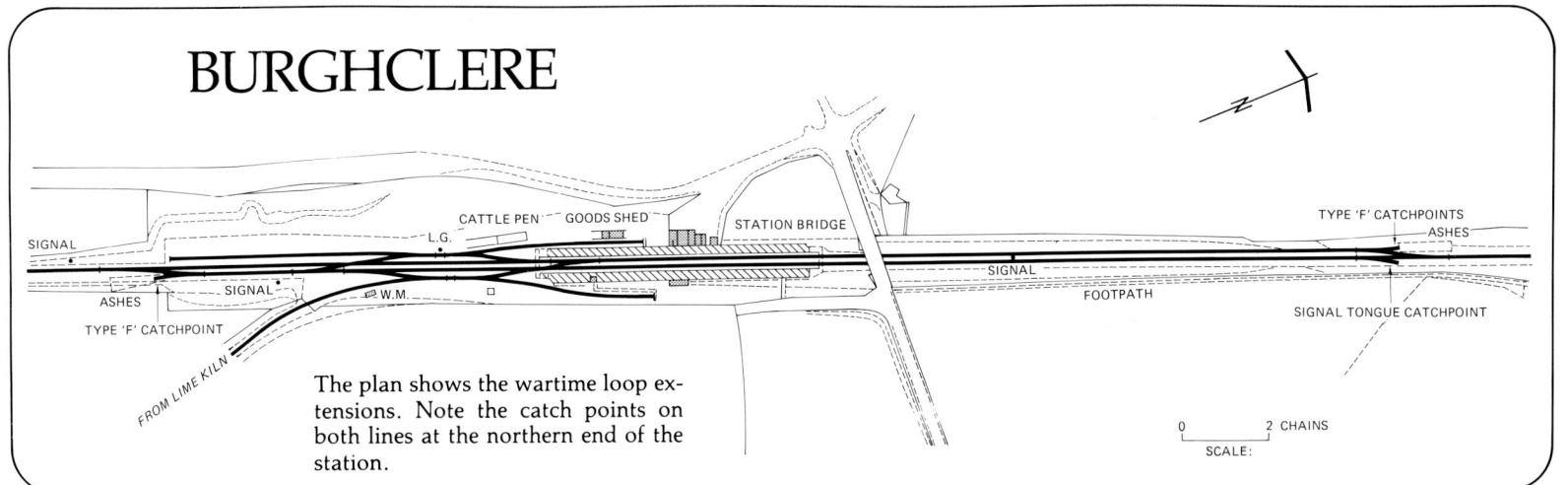

The plan shows the wartime loop extensions. Note the catch points on both lines at the northern end of the station.

Plate 117 (below): A view of the 'down' platform, taken from a train, on 4th May 1952.

H. C. Casserley

Plate 118 (below right): This is a final view of the station, in May 1961, with the wooden waiting shelter and gentlemen's lavatory now having disappeared, as has the goods yard shed and crane. Passenger traffic had ceased and only freight trains now passed this way.

Michael Hale

Plate 116 (top right): The hand generator that powered the new crossover which was 'remote' from the new box. Working these points was achieved by pulling the point lever half way (two notches on the lever), then by winding the electrical hand generator until the points had changed. The lever was then pulled over to the second notch.

Burghclere
(1943)

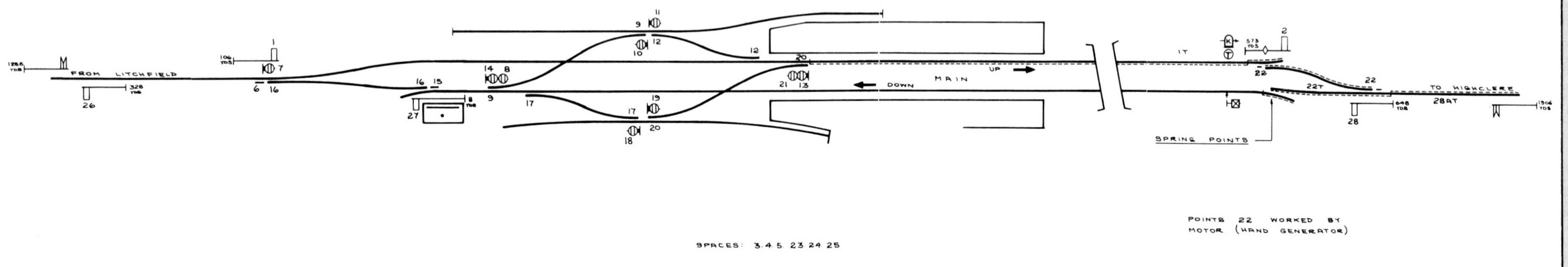

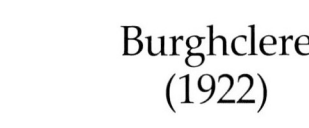

SPACES: 3.4.5. 23 24 25

SPRING POINTS

POINTS 22 WORKED BY
MOTOR (HAND GENERATOR)

FROM LITCHFIELD

MAIN

DOWN

UP

TO HIGHCLERE

Burghclere
(1922)

Two signalling diagrams to show the alterations between 1922 (with the box on the station) and 1943, after the new signal box and wartime alterations had taken place.

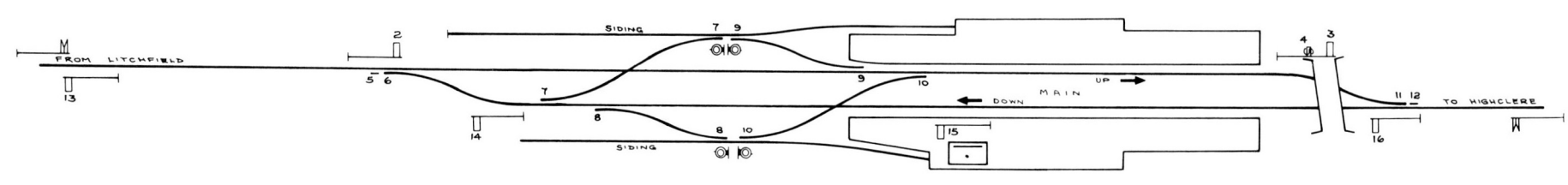

SPARE LEVERS 1·17

FROM LITCHFIELD

SIDING

S'DING

MAIN

DOWN

UP

TO HIGHCLERE

Plate 119: A view facing south, photographed on 6th June 1943, from the northern end of the wartime loop alterations. The station is just beyond the brick road bridge. This point system was operated by electrical point motors, as explained in *Plate 116*. The black box on the left, held track circuiting batteries, while the white hut near the signal was the 'token' box. Note the catch point in the left-hand line and the runaway ash pile on the right.

British Rail

Plate 121 (below): The south end of the loop crossing, seen on 6th June 1943, with the new signal box operational (opened 13th November 1942). The lime-kiln sidings on the extreme left are loaded with wagons. The two small lines are to take the platelayers' motorized trolleys. The goods yard was on the extreme right. Single line token apparatus and the catch point warning board are also visible, just in front of the coal bunker, and the signalman's toilet of pre-cast construction. The white sighting signal panel was actually painted on the signal box brickwork and the long lens hood was fitted to the lamp, illuminating the token setting-down post, to prevent the light being seen from the air during World War II.

British Rail

Plate 120 (above): The same points as those shown in *Plate 119*, but looking north, with the catch point and ash runaway, plus the 'limit of shunt' and signals all operational in 1943.

British Rail

Litchfield

Plate 122:   A view of the station, in 1919, looking north towards Burghclere. The original signal box and wooden waiting shelter are seen on the 'up' platform.

Real Photographs

LITCHFIELD

SCALE: 0 — 2 CHAINS

(track diagram showing:) SIGNAL BOX · 9 M.P. · HUT · S.P. · PLATFORM · TO BURGHCLERE · TO WHITCHURCH · S.P. · STATION BUILDINGS · GATE · GOODS SHED · PLATFORM · CATTLE PEN · CRANE · WELL · TO NEWBURY · 106 330 · 330 106

Litchfield

Opened: 4th May 1885
Closed to passengers: 7th March 1960
Closed to goods traffic: 13th August 1962

This picturesque station (often confused with Lichfield in Staffordshire), was situated in a small chalk cutting, but on high ground overlooking the village it served, at the 9 mile line post. The station nameboard did, in fact, have 'HANTS' displayed underneath the name of LITCHFIELD. Again, this station had the standard type of design, of a two storey main building situated on the 'down' side platform with a small wooden (open) passenger shelter on the 'up' platform. The original signal box was also on the 'up' platform, controlling the small station passing loop and a siding (with headshunt) serving the goods shed and cattle pens. The goods shed was also of a standard pattern and had the use of a 3 ton yard crane, but, according to records, this yard and its facilities were not put to very much use, as both freight and passenger traffic was very sparse (about 20 passengers per week). It is interesting to note that, in 1936, the 697ft. loop was taken out of commission and also the signal box was removed, the remaining goods yard being controlled by a small ground frame and the station only having a single line. The wartime doubling re-established the crossing loop with a much extended length of around 2,000 yds., the 'up' platform and a new brick-built signal box (commissioned in 1943) controlling the new complex. After the war, and with the decline of the traffic on the line, this section was again singled and the signal box was demolished in 1955. As with the previous station, the passengers had to cross the line by means of a sleeper crossing at the Burghclere end of the station. Another interesting construction to point out was the sleeper hut built in the area near the cattle pens, which served as a permanent way hut and a loading gauge across the exit of the yard.

Plate 123 (below): In 1959 the line had been singled and, in this view looking north, the 'new' signal box (now out of service) can be seen. The entry to the goods yard (now controlled by a ground frame) with the loading gauge is also visible.

C. Gammell

Plate 124 (bottom right): A small view of the station looking south in the 1960s. The nameboard still has the word 'HANTS' beneath the name.

Author's Collection

LITCHFIELD

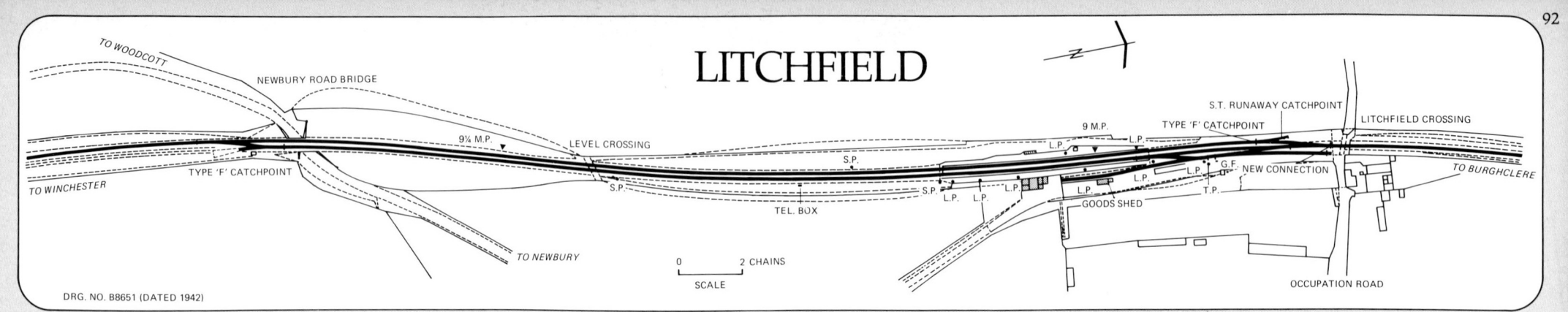

DRG. NO. B8651 (DATED 1942)

Litchfield
(1920)

The top plan shows the long loop installed in the wartime improvements, and the two signalling plans offer the comparison to the 1908 and World War II layouts. The points were again electrically-operated by a hand generator in the signal box.

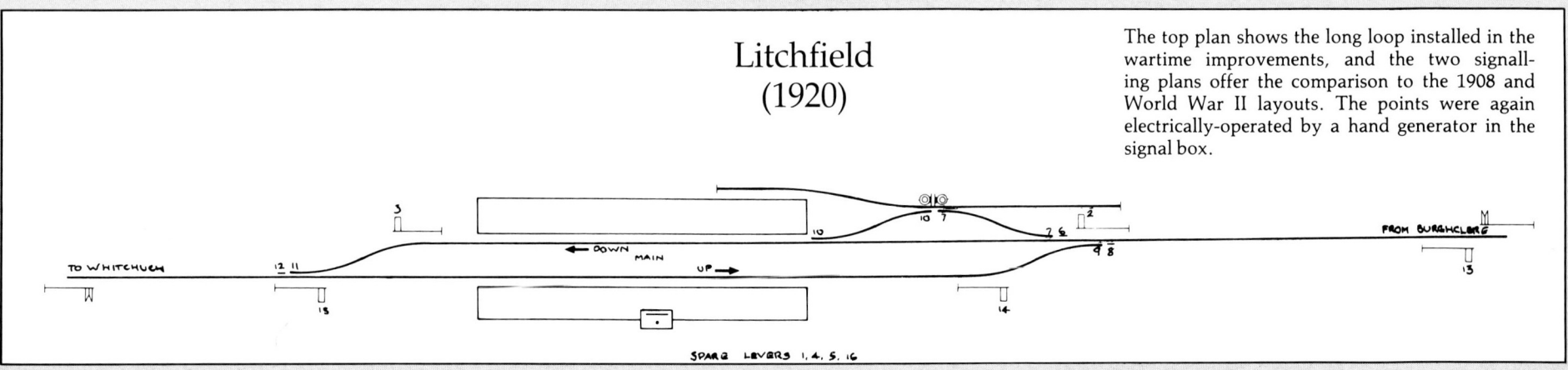

Litchfield
(1942)

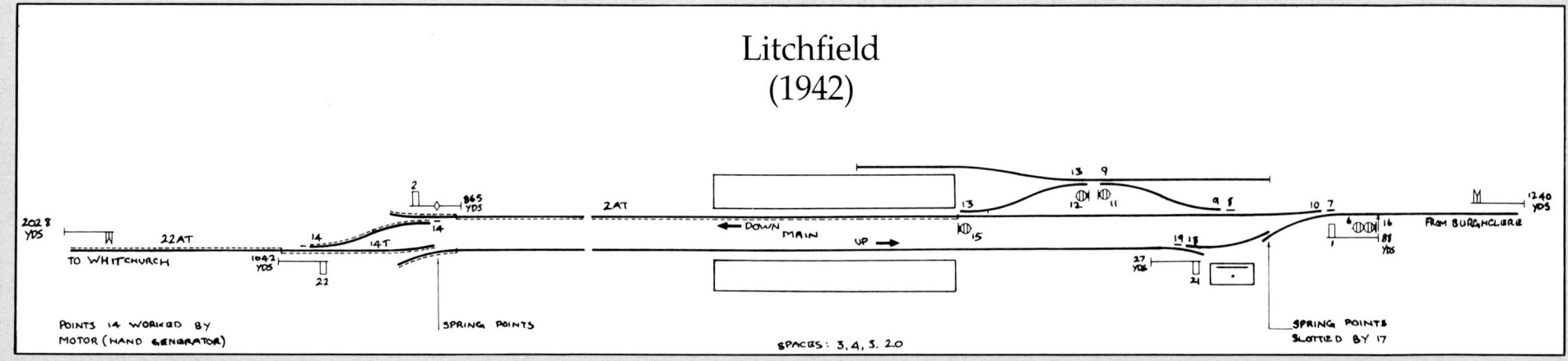

Whitchurch

Plate 125: A view looking north, showing the standard DN&SR double storey station building, canopy and also the 'up' side wooden waiting shelter for passengers.

Lens of Sutton

WHITCHURCH

The track plan of 1908 shows the more comprehensive layout at this station. Note the position of the subway, signal box and ground frame.

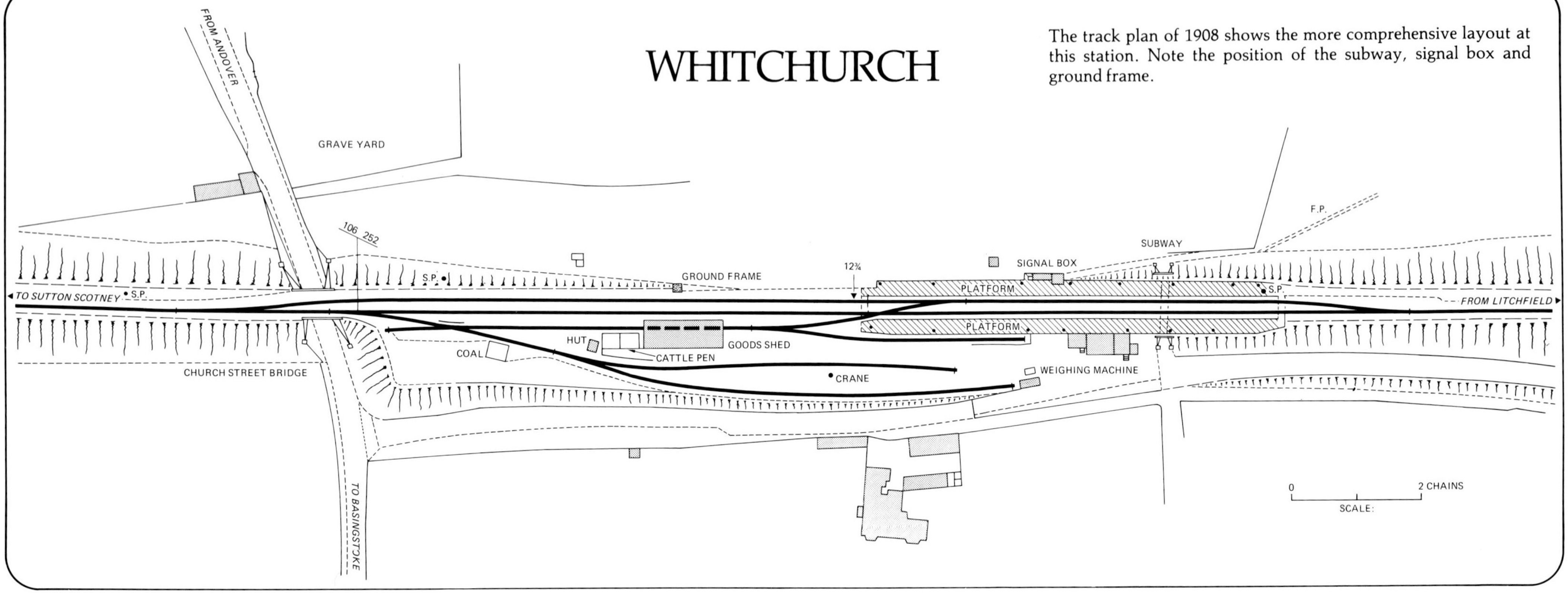

FROM ANDOVER

GRAVE YARD

106 252

TO SUTTON SCOTNEY   S.P.

S.P.

GROUND FRAME

12¾

SIGNAL BOX

SUBWAY

F.P.

PLATFORM

PLATFORM

S.P.

FROM LITCHFIELD

CHURCH STREET BRIDGE

HUT

COAL

CATTLE PEN

GOODS SHED

CRANE

WEIGHING MACHINE

TO BASINGSTOKE

0   2 CHAINS

SCALE:

Whitchurch

Opened: 4th May 1885
Closed to passenger traffic: 7th March 1960
Closed to goods traffic: 6th May 1963

The station of Whitchurch was the second railway station to be built in this town, as the LSWR had opened its station earlier. As the two stations were quite some way apart, the use as a changing place for passengers between railways did not materialize. As no actual rail link ever took place, the nearest the two lines came to each other was where the DN& SR passed under LSWR metals through a short tunnel (seen in *Plate 133*). The station (mile post 12¾) was one of the largest stations on this section of the line and although named Whitchurch 'HANTS' in 1924, was renamed Whitchurch 'TOWN' around 1950. The facilities included a goods shed, cattle pens, a 3 ton yard crane, a small headshunt and three sidings and, in fact, compared favourably with the layout at Compton Station. Also near the entrance to the goods yard was a weighbridge and office. The station, in the early days, had a water crane at the end of the platform. The goods yard dealt with a considerable variety of traffic, including coal, cattle, sheep, watercress and other vegetable products. The signal box was

again situated on the 'up' platform, next to the small open standard wooden waiting shelter for passengers, which had its roof cut-back to help the signalman's view. Here the station buildings were again typically two storey (main building with platform canopy), but with extensions to the waiting-room. The building also contained an office, ladies' waiting-room, gentlemen's lavatory, lamp room and booking hall with the stationmaster's office. This station also boasted a subway for passengers to cross from one platform to the other. A ground frame of 8 levers was provided to control the goods yard double-slip, and was released from the main signal box by an interlocking lever. A new large 11,500 gallon water tank was installed during the war and was situated behind the platform shelter on the 'up' platform. This was necessary to feed the two water cranes installed at the end of the extended wartime loops of 1,850ft. This was completed in 1943 together with a new brick-built signal box, the inside of which can be seen in *Plate 130*. Other buildings in the station complex were a brick-built hut for the permanent way men, and situated behind the ground frame, was a timber construction used for the gangers' trolleys and equipment. There was a corrugated iron hut at the end of the 'down' platform, which was used as a lamp hut.

Plate 126: A postcard view, in the early 1900s, of the main station buildings.

Author's Collection

Plate 127: Looking towards Sutton Scotney, in a southerly direction, this photograph, taken on 1st May 1960, clearly shows the word 'TOWN' under the station nameboard, the goods shed and the wartime signal box (which was approximately on the site of the old ground frame).

R. Kirkland

Plate 128: A view looking north towards Litchfield with the small tunnel under the LSWR line in the far distance. The new (1943) water-tower of 11,250 gallons, on the 'up' platform, was built to supply the new locomotive water cranes which were installed at the end of the new long loop. The passenger waiting shelter and the old signal box had long since gone when this picture was taken in 1961.

Michael Hale

Plate 129: Whitchurch 'TOWN' nameboard on the 'down' platform with a good view of the town itself, showing how the station was built on high ground overlooking the town.

Author's Collection

Whitchurch (1922)

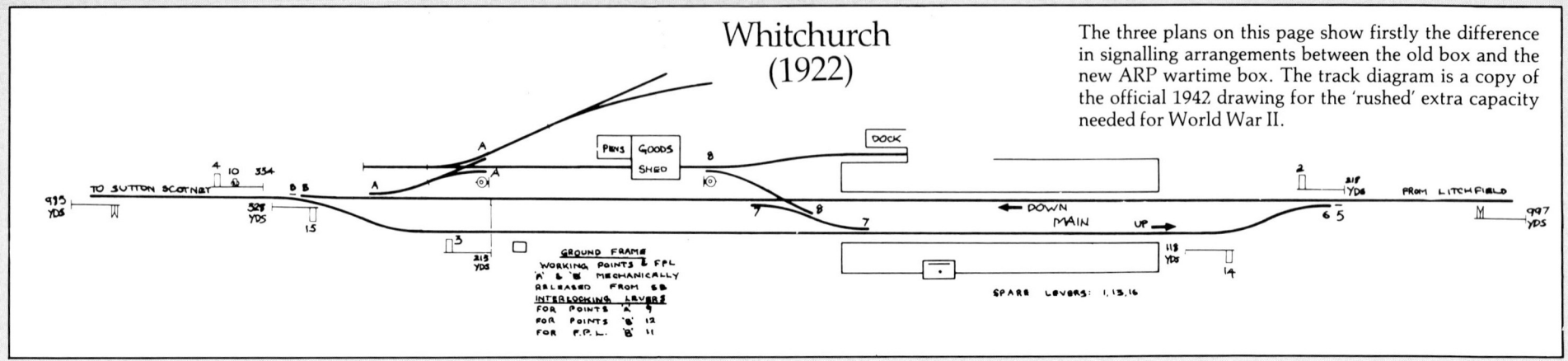

The three plans on this page show firstly the difference in signalling arrangements between the old box and the new ARP wartime box. The track diagram is a copy of the official 1942 drawing for the 'rushed' extra capacity needed for World War II.

WHITCHURCH

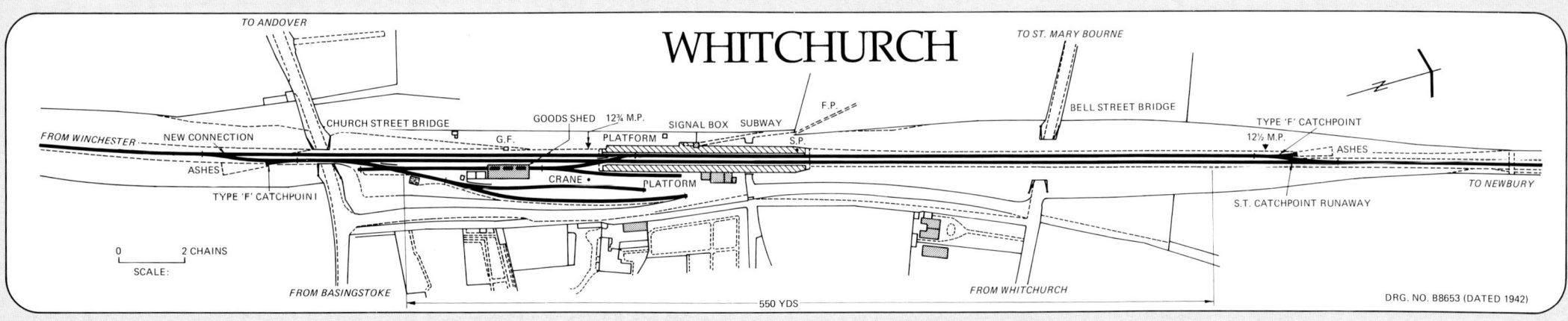

DRG. NO. B8653 (DATED 1942)

Whitchurch (1942)

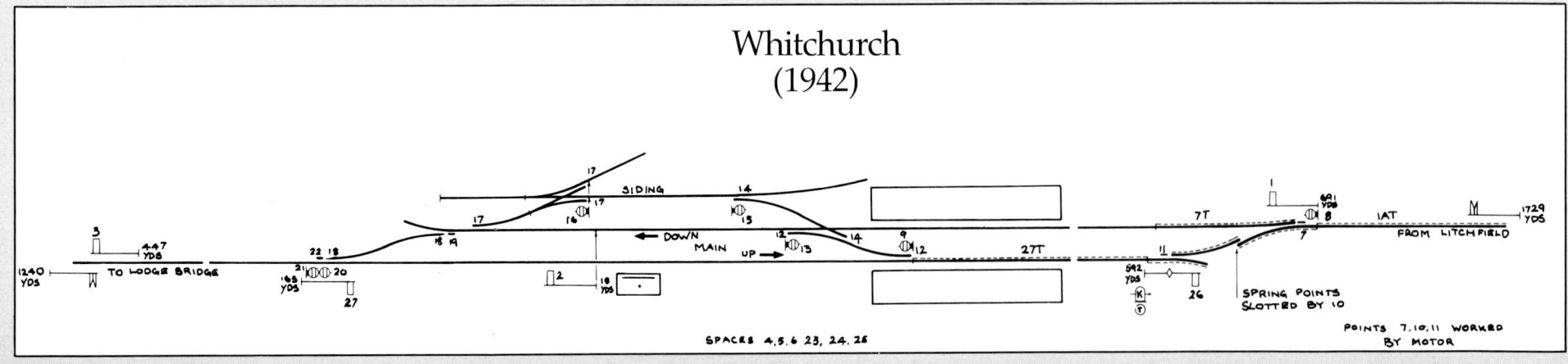

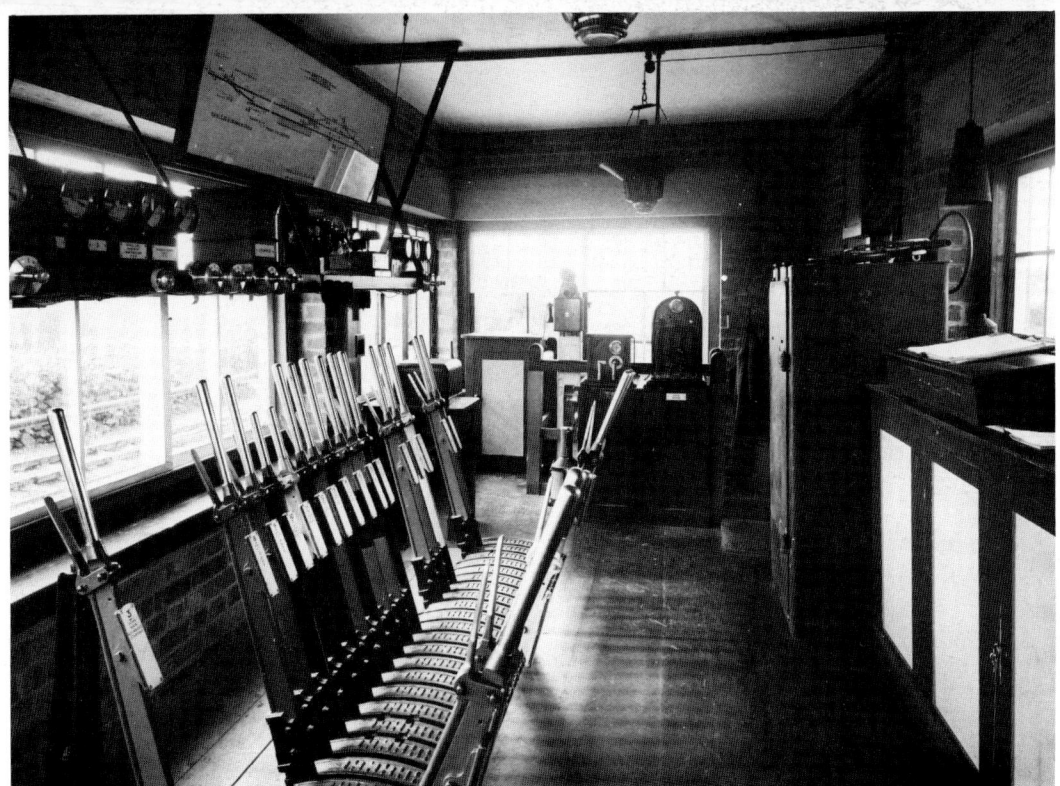

Plate 130 (top left): The interior of the new ARP brick signal box built during 1942/3 and opened in 1943. This view, looking towards the south, shows the token apparatus marked 'Lodge Bridge', which was the next box on the line. The levers 7, 10 and 11, are the ones for the points at the end of the loops, and the two stage positions on the guide rails can be seen at the base of the lever. The operation of these points is explained in *Plate 116*. The metal cabinet was installed for the signalmen to take cover in case of air raids, and the bowls were fitted to the lamps to reduce light to a minimum during wartime.

British Rail

Plate 131 (above): Whitchurch Town, on 12th December 1959, showing a close up of the station buildings. The notice to the subway also stands out, pointing out to passengers the way to the station courtyard. They then proceeded past the station buildings to a small damp brick arch subway underneath the line, which then came up alongside the field and along a narrow path to the 'up' platform.

C. Gammell

Plate 132 (left): The 'up' platform with wartime water-tower and the wooden shelter for passengers still in place. The bushes show signs of topiary but other stations on the line surpassed the efforts of Whitchurch.

Author's Collection

Plate 133: This photograph has been included to show the short tunnel that allowed the DN&SR to pass under the SR main line. The relaying of the DN&SR track is recorded in the railway records as 1926, and it would appear that the SR are also relaying track, as the wagons on the horizon are all of permanent way stock.

British Rail

Plate 134: The tunnel is more clearly visible in this photograph, looking north. Taken to record the extended loop (1,850ft.) alterations, this official view shows the new water-crane (fed by the water tank on the 'up' platform), the new token box and the runaway ash pile after the catch points.

British Rail

Plate 135: A further look at the northern end of the loop, but this time looking south back at the station. The water-tower on the 'up' platform can be picked out, as can the new signal box after the station platform, the white edges of which stand out clearly.

British Rail

LODGE BRIDGE

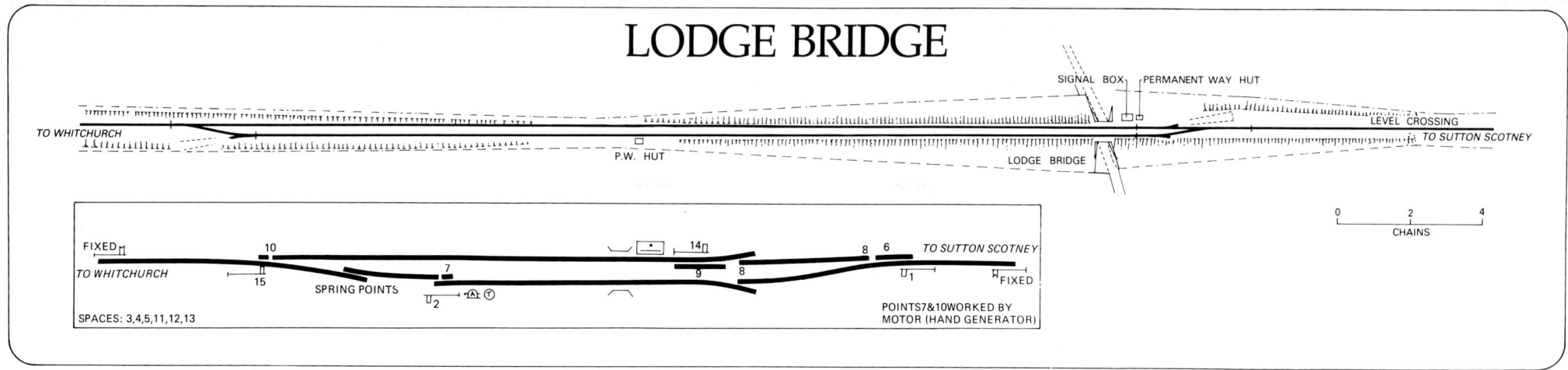

Between Whitchurch and the next station down the line, Sutton Scotney, a distance of approximately 6 miles, the wartime measures provided a new passing loop. This called for a new signal box and permanent way hut, built near Lodge Bridge, and was named after the bridge. The standard ash runaway catch points were provided and, again, the point motors were worked by electrical hand generators. This loop was taken out of service in March 1950. Working this box during the winter would have been a particularly lonely and cold occupation.

Barton Stacey Halt

It is appropriate here to include a plan, traced from the original survey of 1908, to show the exact position of Barton Stacey Halt. This was obviously added to this old survey just before wartime work in 1940, when it was built. It was a wooden platform to serve the Barton Stacey Army Camp and, from late February 1940, a regular workers' train, usually consisting of five coaches, was run from Southampton. The train was quite often worked by an Adams 4-4-0 locomotive and the coaches were stored during the day at Winchester Chesil. As it was technically a wartime private halt, no details of opening or closing dates are officially available, but it is presumed it ceased operation at the end of the war.

BARTON STACEY HALT

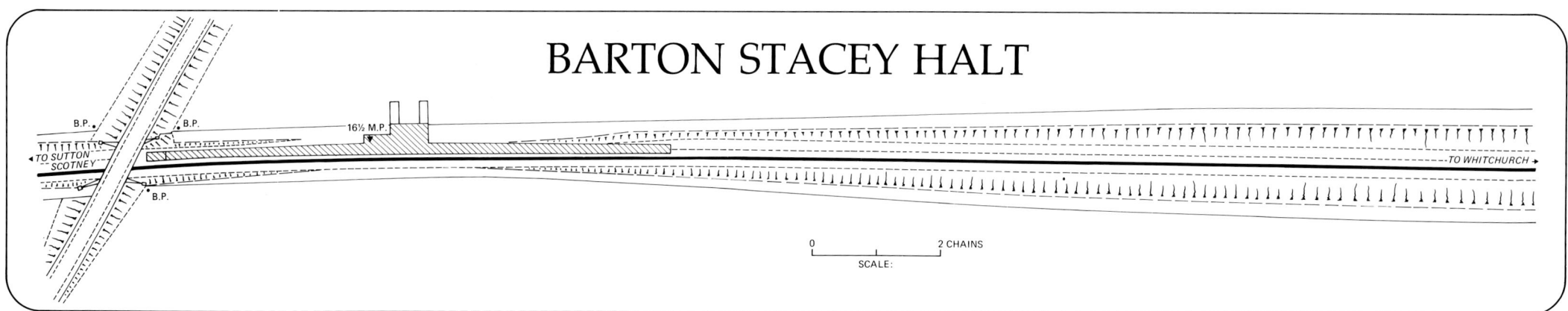

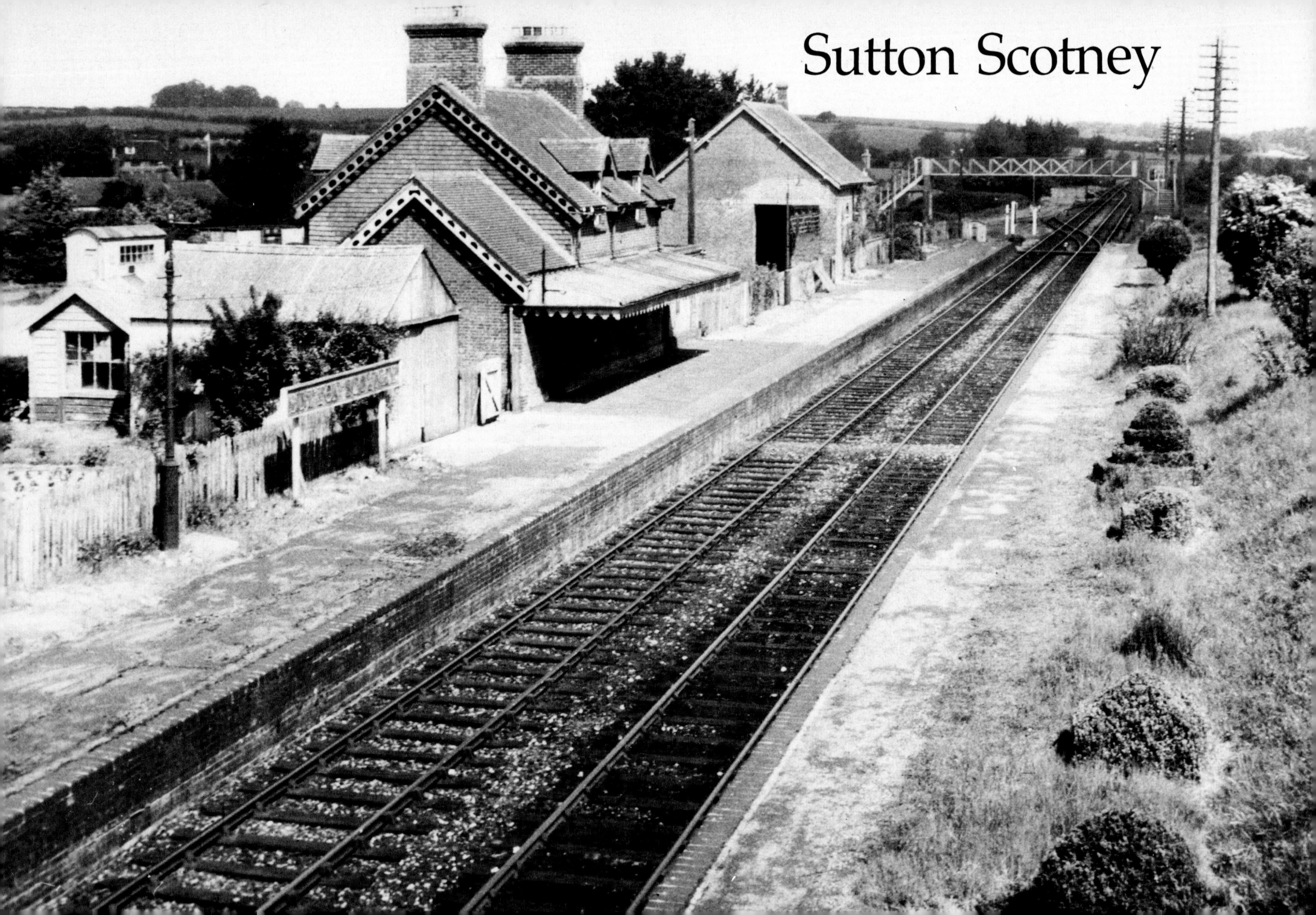

Sutton Scotney

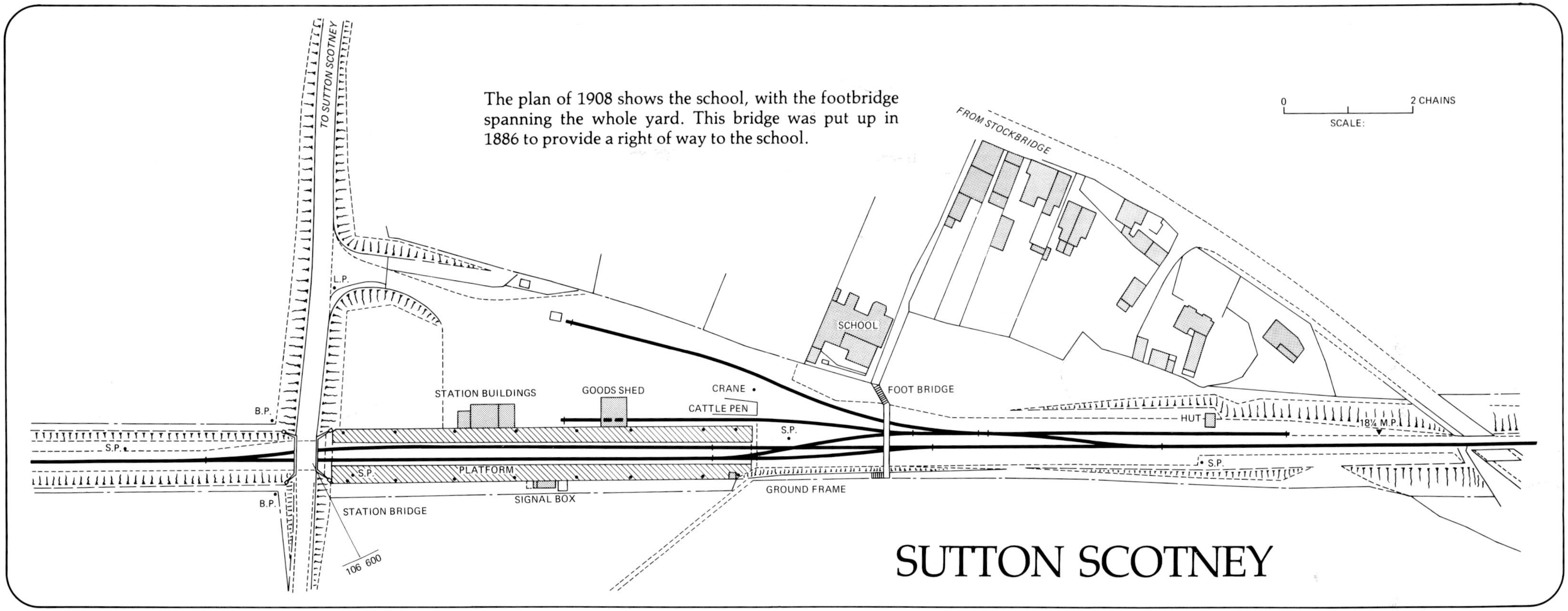

The plan of 1908 shows the school, with the footbridge spanning the whole yard. This bridge was put up in 1886 to provide a right of way to the school.

TO SUTTON SCOTNEY

FROM STOCKBRIDGE

0   2 CHAINS
SCALE:

L.P.

SCHOOL

B.P.

STATION BUILDINGS

GOODS SHED

CRANE

CATTLE PEN

FOOT BRIDGE

S.P.

HUT

18¼ M.P.

S.P.

PLATFORM

GROUND FRAME

S.P.

S.P.

B.P.

STATION BRIDGE

SIGNAL BOX

106 600

SUTTON SCOTNEY

Plate 136 (previous page): A panoramic view of Sutton Scotney, photographed in May 1961, looking towards Whitchurch, showing the goods shed, the unusual footbridge and wartime signal box. The corrugated asbestos building in the foreground was used as an additional office, with the old ground frame signal box moved behind and used as a garden shed. The weighbridge office (a corrugated iron hut) can be seen over the top of the old ground frame hut. The Pooley weighbridge was No. 02277, of 10 ton capacity and had a 12ft. x 7ft. base, being installed in 1907.

Michael Hale

Plate 137 (left): A fine old postcard showing the station buildings, goods shed and station yard. Note the coal office in the station yard.

Lens of Sutton

Plate 138 (right): The station nameboard on the 'up' side of the line.

C. Gammell

Sutton Scotney

Opened: 4th May 1885
Closed to passenger traffic: 7th March 1960
Closed to goods traffic: 3rd February 1964

The station of Sutton Scotney was originally intended to be the last station before Winchester, at approximately the 18¼ mile post. Again it was a typical station, with a two storey brick building and a large platform canopy. The building contained the booking office, ladies' waiting-room and goods office and was situated on the 'up' platform. The 'down' platform originally had a standard small wooden shelter for passengers, with the signal box standing alongside on the platform. A small 4 lever ground frame stood at the north end of the 'down' platform, and controlled the entry to the goods yard. This yard had a large goods shed, a cattle pen and a 3 ton yard crane. An unusual footbridge was used to maintain a right of access across the whole site. The usual wartime loop extensions were carried out, the loop being 600 yards long. The 'new' signal box was sited at the north end of the station complex, just past the footbridge, and a weighbridge was also added in 1907. In the 1920s, the crossover was removed and the goods yard was only accessible from the 'up' main line. The ground frame signal box was also moved to the platform to be used as an additional office, only later to be moved again to its final resting place behind the asbestos hut, and used as a garden shed.

Plate 139 (above):   A general view, taken in May 1960, looking north, with the 'new' signal box, footbridge, goods shed, single line token apparatus and asbestos shed all visible.

R. Kirkland

Plates 140 & 141 (below left &below right):   Two views, taken from a train window, on 4th May 1952, shows the 'down' platform in both directions. In *Plate 140*, the cut bushes stand out, as does the white square of paint on the bridge, showing where the starter signal once stood before the loop was extended. *Plate 141* shows a view looking in the other direction towards the footbridge and signal box.

H. C. Casserley

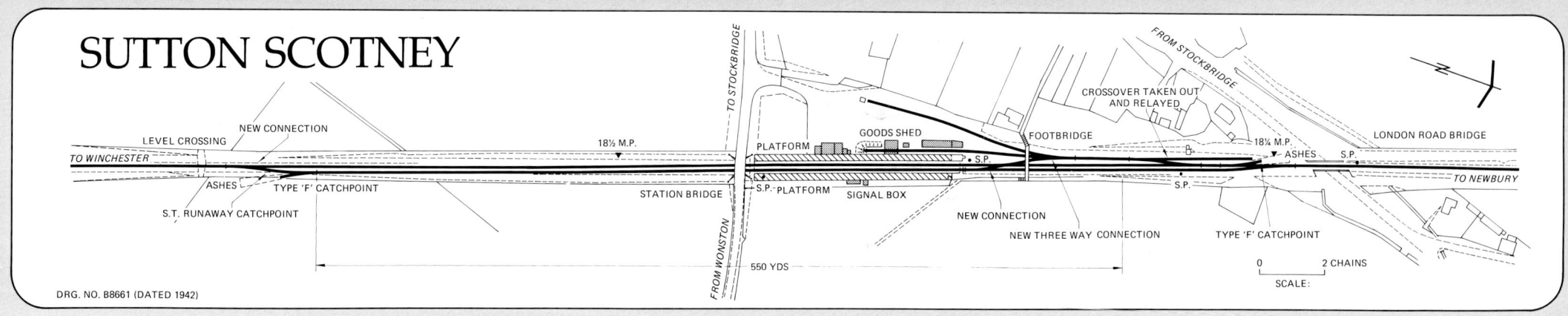

SUTTON SCOTNEY

TO STOCKBRIDGE

FROM STOCKBRIDGE

NEW CONNECTION

LEVEL CROSSING

TO WINCHESTER

18½ M.P.

PLATFORM

GOODS SHED

FOOTBRIDGE

CROSSOVER TAKEN OUT AND RELAYED

18¼ M.P.

LONDON ROAD BRIDGE

ASHES

S.P.

ASHES

S.P.

S.P.

TO NEWBURY

S.T. RUNAWAY CATCHPOINT

TYPE 'F' CATCHPOINT

STATION BRIDGE

S.P. PLATFORM

SIGNAL BOX

NEW CONNECTION

NEW THREE WAY CONNECTION

TYPE 'F' CATCHPOINT

FROM WONSTON

550 YDS

0   2 CHAINS

SCALE:

DRG. NO. B8661 (DATED 1942)

The 1942 wartime official plan of the extension of the loops and new crossover to be installed. The signalling plan of 1922 shows the original crossover removed, allowing access to the goods yard only via the 'up' running line. Note also the 1943 diagram has a point, via a diamond crossing, allowing access to the yard from the 'down' main line.

Sutton Scotney
(1922)

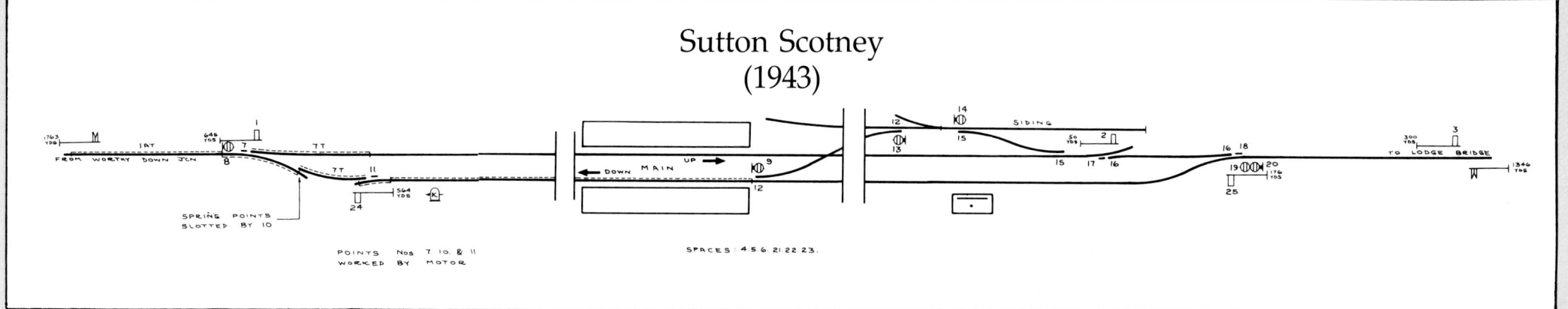

Sutton Scotney
(1943)

Worthy Down

Plate 142:   A general view of Worthy Down, looking towards Sutton Scotney, in December 1959, showing the wartime station construction with the middle island platform. The camp was situated on the left when this photograph was taken, and all the sidings had been removed.

C. Cammell

Worthy Down

Opened: 1st April 1918
Closed to passenger traffic: 7th March 1960
Closed to goods traffic: Freight not handled at this station

This outpost station, at the 21¼ mile post, was opened to serve the Royal Flying Corps Station on Worthy Down, two miles north of King's Worthy. Firstly, two sidings were constructed on the west side of the line, with a RFC yard asphalted for the airbase use, in October 1917, and a platform was built on the other side of the main line. This platform was used by workmen, whilst they were constructing the airbase, and was eventually made permanent in April 1918, when it opened for public service and became a recognized station halt. The platform was 450ft. in length with two nameboards. The booking office was initially a 'grounded' horse-box body, but was later replaced by the GWR (in the 1920s) with a corrugated hut. A small wooden parcels office was also provided. In the early days, the sidings were controlled by two ground frames, north and south, with levers operating the double slips feeding the sidings. This platform was closed in 1942, when a new island platform was built and reopened in 1943 with, also, a new ARP brick signal box, brick platelayers' hut and a small station booking office. An unusual waiting shelter and store were constructed on the platform, and the official drawings are reproduced on *pages 109 & 111*. As the station was constructed on a down gradient of 1 in 106, a catch point was installed to protect the next station of King's Worthy, but this was over 2 miles away, and several hair-raising incidents did take place concerning runaway wagons, etc. During the war, special forces' trains were put on at night to bring service personnel back to the camp, these trains terminating at Worthy Down and returning empty to Winchester. During 1953, all the sidings were removed and the track reverted to just a passing loop. Again, no drinking water was on site, so supplies were usually obtained from the camp or nearest station.

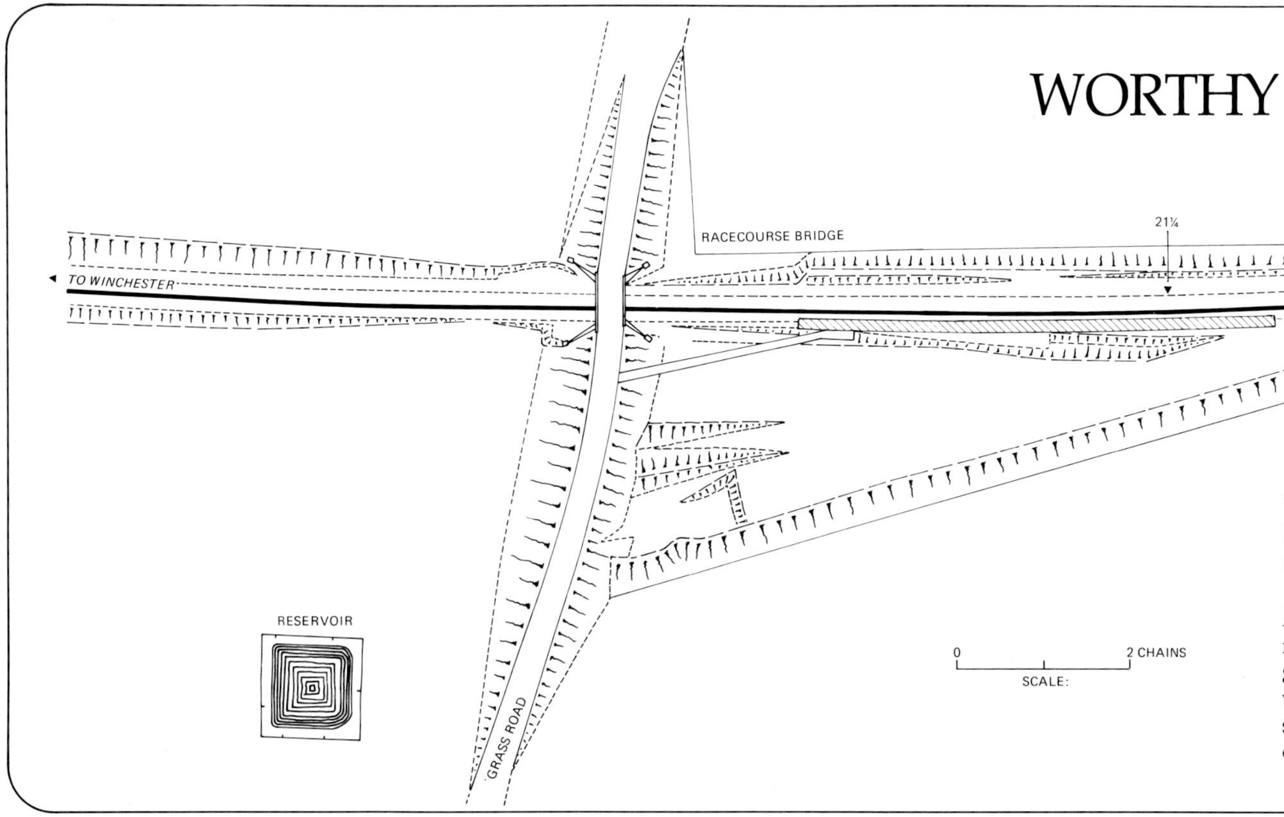

WORTHY DOWN

TO WINCHESTER
RACECOURSE BRIDGE
21¼
TO SUTTON SCOTNEY
RESERVOIR
GRASS ROAD
0   2 CHAINS
SCALE:

The 1908 survey showing just the single line. The platform had obviously been drawn in afterwards on the official survey to show the site of the first station platform.

Plate 143 (top left): An earlier view, in 1953, just before the sidings were removed. The wartime signal box and platelayers' hut are seen in the foreground. Behind the signal box was a further brick single storey hut, which was used as the station building and booking office. The sidings can be seen above the four coach train, and the army camp appears in the top left of the picture.

Author's Collection

Plate 144: This wintry view, photographed by the GWR in 1943, shows the new island platform built, but not the waiting shelter. The signal box is still inoperative, but the platelayers' hut seems to have a good 'steam up'. The army camp on the left, with an unusual crane between rail and road, is clearly visible.

British Rail

Plate 145: Photographed in May 1960, this view shows that the sidings have disappeared. Details of the signal box and station buildings can also be seen.

R. Kirkland

Plates 146 & 147 (below): Two more views, taken from the road bridge, in May 1961, giving an overall view of the station area and station shelter.

Michael Hale

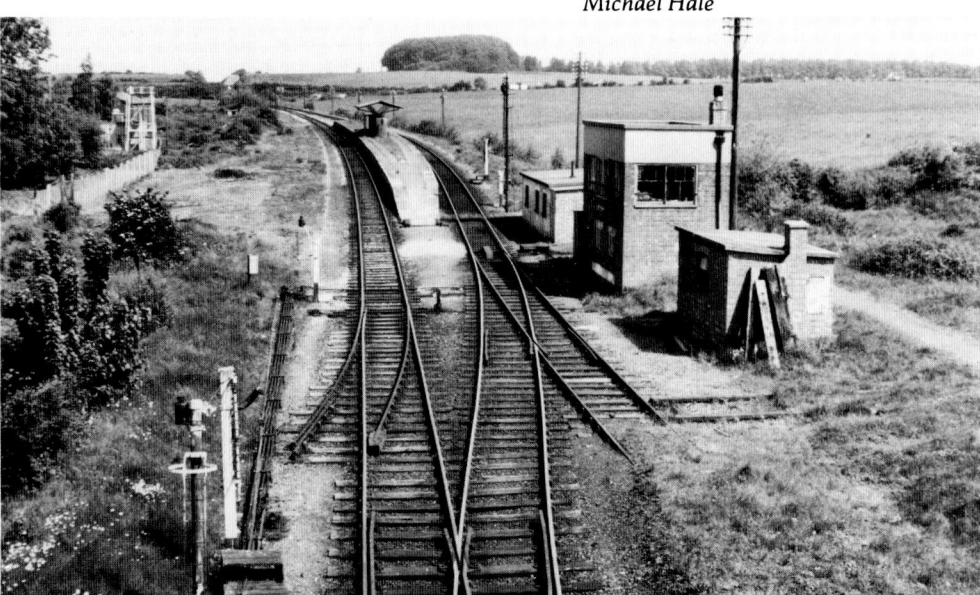

WORTHY DOWN

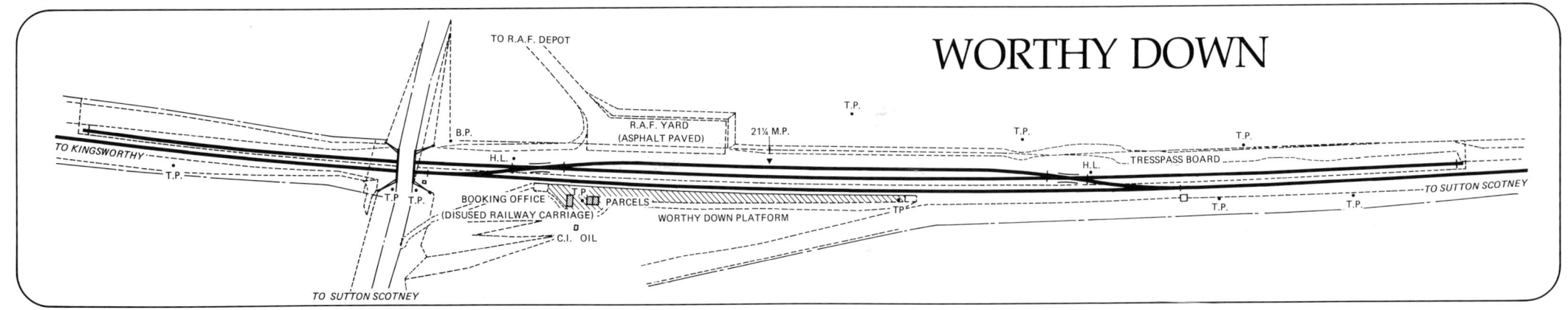

The plan (*above*) shows the 1918 layout when the station was opened for public service. Note the official plan states 'disused railway carriage' for the booking office. The black corrugated lamp hut is marked 'oil'.

Worthy Down

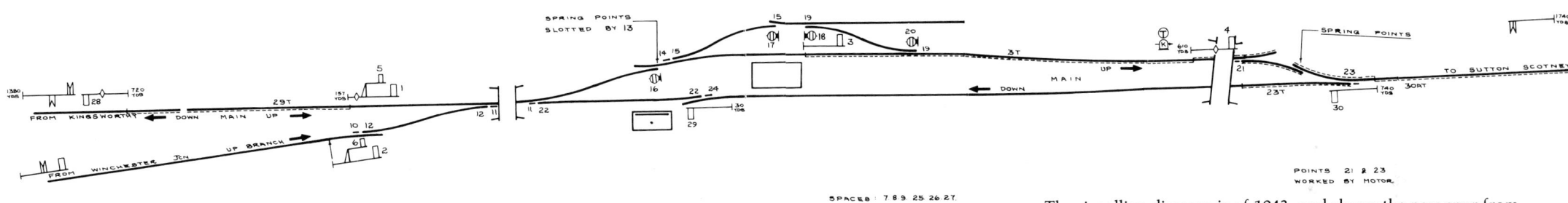

The signalling diagram is of 1943, and shows the new spur from Winchester Junction and the Southern Railway section.

Worthy Down

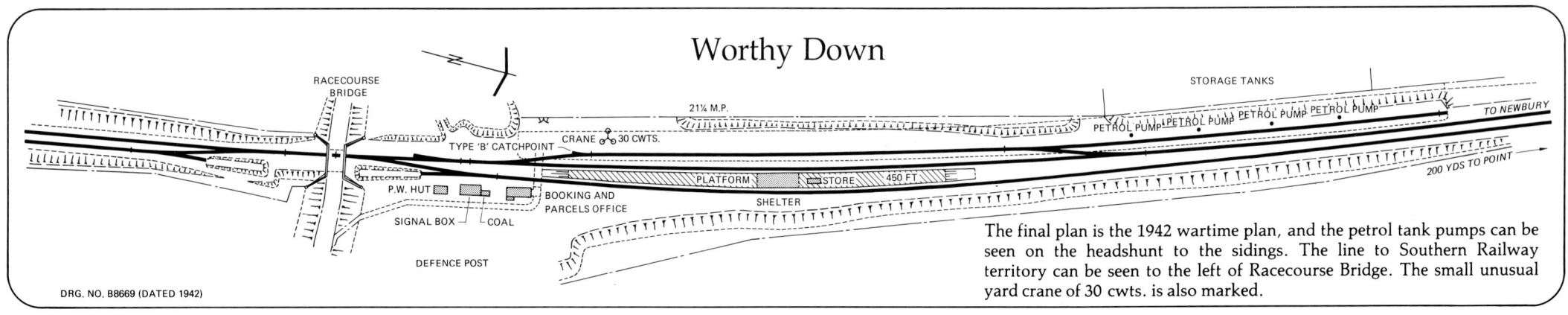

DRG. NO. B8669 (DATED 1942)

The final plan is the 1942 wartime plan, and the petrol tank pumps can be seen on the headshunt to the sidings. The line to Southern Railway territory can be seen to the left of Racecourse Bridge. The small unusual yard crane of 30 cwts. is also marked.

Plate 148: During the extensive alterations in World War II, the old platform has, in this view, just been removed and one can see where the double-slip has also been dismantled. The original booking office shed, in corrugated iron, is still in situ on the right, and the new wartime signal box is well under construction. The unusual yard crane used by the RAF is also visible.

British Rail

Plate 149: A further stage of construction with the island platform in being, the track realigned and the platelayers' hut, signal box and booking office all in various stages of completion. The siding and revised point work is also in place.

British Rail

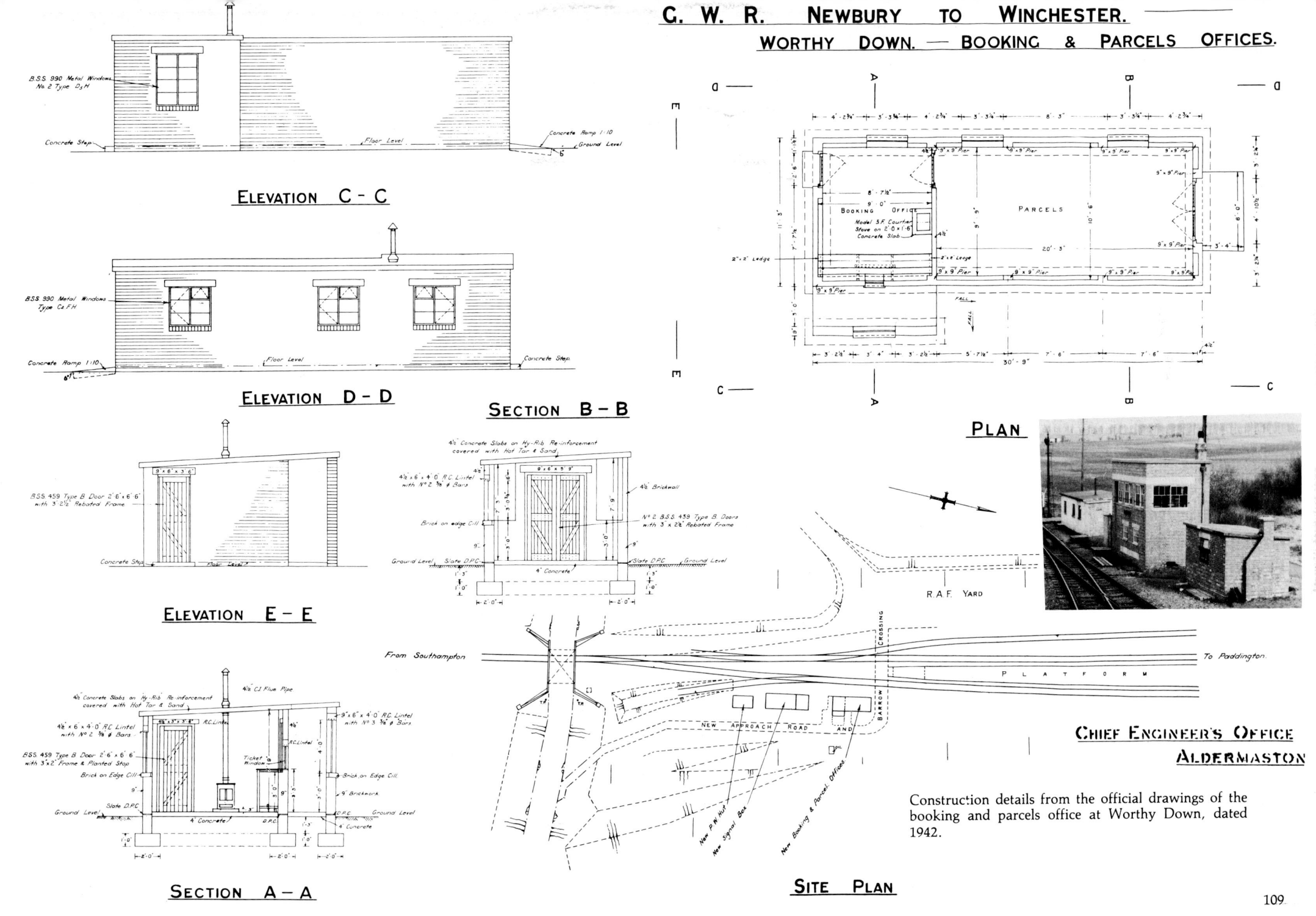

ELEVATION C - C

BSS 990 Metal Windows No 2 Type D5H

Concrete Step
Floor Level
Concrete Ramp 1:10
Ground Level

ELEVATION D - D

BSS 990 Metal Windows Type C2 F.H.

Concrete Ramp 1:10
Floor Level
Concrete Step

ELEVATION E - E

9"x 6"x 3' 6"
BSS 459 Type B Door 2'6 x 6'6 with 3'2½" Rebated Frame.
Concrete Step
Floor Level

SECTION B - B

4½ Concrete Slabs on Hy-Rib Re-inforcement covered with Hot Tar & Sand.
4½ x 6 x 4'0 R.C. Lintel with No 2 ⅜ Ø Bars
9"x 6"x 5' 9"
4½ Brickwall
Brick on edge Cill
No 2 BSS 459 Type B Doors with 3'x 2½' Rebated Frame
Ground Level   Slate D.P.C.
Slate D.P.C.   Ground Level
4" Concrete
2'-0"   2'-0"

SECTION A - A

4½ Concrete Slabs on Hy-Rib Re-inforcement covered with Hot Tar & Sand.
4½ CI Flue Pipe
4½ x 6 x 4'0 R.C. Lintel with No 2 ⅜ Ø Bars
9"x 6"x 4'0" R.C. Lintel with No 3 ⅜ Ø Bars
9"x 8"x 3' 6"
R.C. Lintel
BSS 459 Type B Door 2'6 x 2' Frame & Planted Stop
R.C.Lintel
Ticket Window
Brick on Edge Cill.
Brick on Edge Cill.
9" Brickwork.
Slate D.P.C.
Ground Level   D.P.C.
D.P.C.   Ground Level
4" Concrete   4" Concrete
2'-0"   2'-0"   2'-0"

PLAN

4' 2¾"   3' 3¾"   4' 2¾"   3' 3¾"   8' 3"   3' 3¾"   4' 2¾"

9"x 9" Pier   9"x 9" Pier
9"x 9" Pier
BOOKING OFFICE   PARCELS
Model 3.F. Courtier Stove on 2'0 x 1'6 Concrete Slab
8' 7½"
9' 0"
2"x 2" Ledge
2"x 2" Ledge
9"x 9" Pier   9"x 9" Pier   9"x 9" Pier
FALL
20' 3"
10'- 6"
11' 3"
7'- 7½"
3' 2¾"   3' 4"
6'- 0"
4'- 10½"
FALL
3' 2½"   3' 4"   3' 2½"   5' 7½"   7' 6"   7' 6"
30'- 9"

SITE PLAN

From Southampton
To Paddington.
R.A.F. Yard
PLATFORM
BARROW CROSSING
New P.W Hut
New Signal Box
New Booking & Parcel Offices
NEW APPROACH ROAD AND

CHIEF ENGINEER'S OFFICE
ALDERMASTON

Construction details from the official drawings of the booking and parcels office at Worthy Down, dated 1942.

Plate 150: This view of an unidentified Southern Railway Q class locomotive, hauling a long coal train, shows the stark structure of the waiting shelter on the island platform, and also gives a view of the road bridge from where most of the photographs of this station were taken.

L. Elsey

Plate 151: On 4th May 1952, GWR Collett 0-6-0 locomotive, No. 3211, waits with a three coach train for the crossing 'up' train to clear the points. Note the store shed on the platform and the single line token instrument.

H. C. Casserley

Plate 152: Obviously a 'special', as passenger traffic on this line was not as prolific as the photograph suggests.

L. Elsey

Plate 153: No. 3440 *City of Truro*, with the usual three coach train leaves on a 'down' service in 1957.

Author's Collection

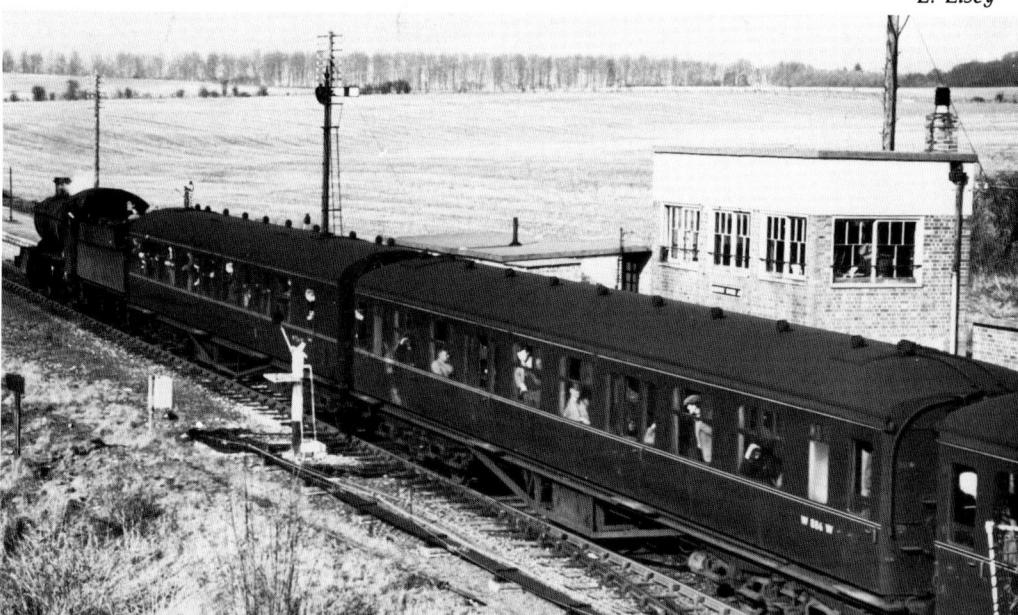

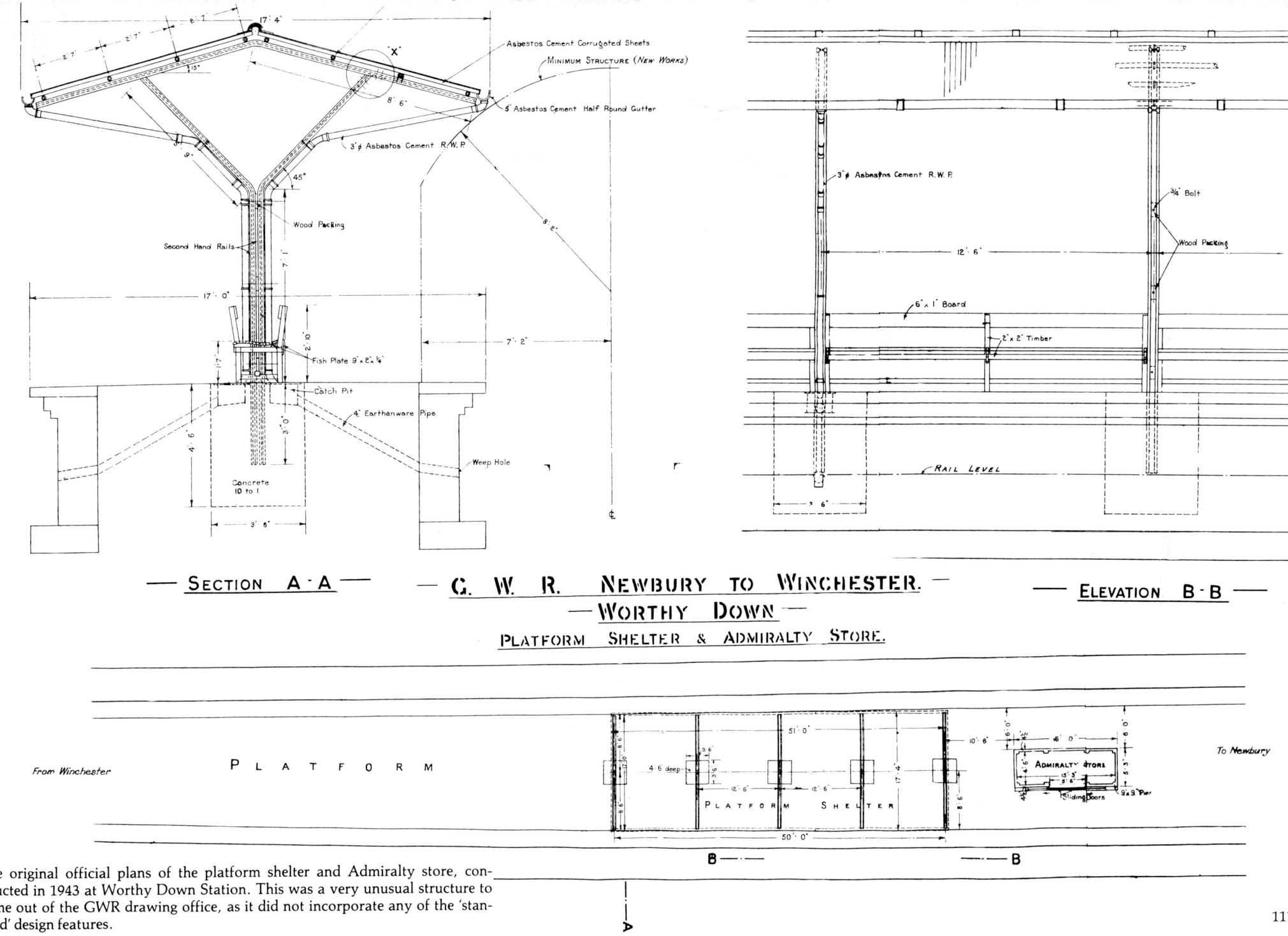

— SECTION A·A — G. W. R. NEWBURY TO WINCHESTER. —

— WORTHY DOWN —

PLATFORM SHELTER & ADMIRALTY STORE.

— ELEVATION B·B —

The original official plans of the platform shelter and Admiralty store, constructed in 1943 at Worthy Down Station. This was a very unusual structure to come out of the GWR drawing office, as it did not incorporate any of the 'standard' design features.

Winchester Junction

Plate 154: A fine view of the junction with the Southern Railway, incorporated in 1943 with the wartime improvements. The line from the left is, in fact, the connecting line from Worthy Down, and the gradient dropping away from the junction is visible. The two main lines continue to Waterloo and the line on the right sweeps round to Alton, making this signal box an important and busy junction. The bridge seen in the foreground is, in fact, the overbridge where the DN&SR line passed under this junction and the Southern Railway, as can be seen on the 1942 plan.

WINCHESTER JUNCTION

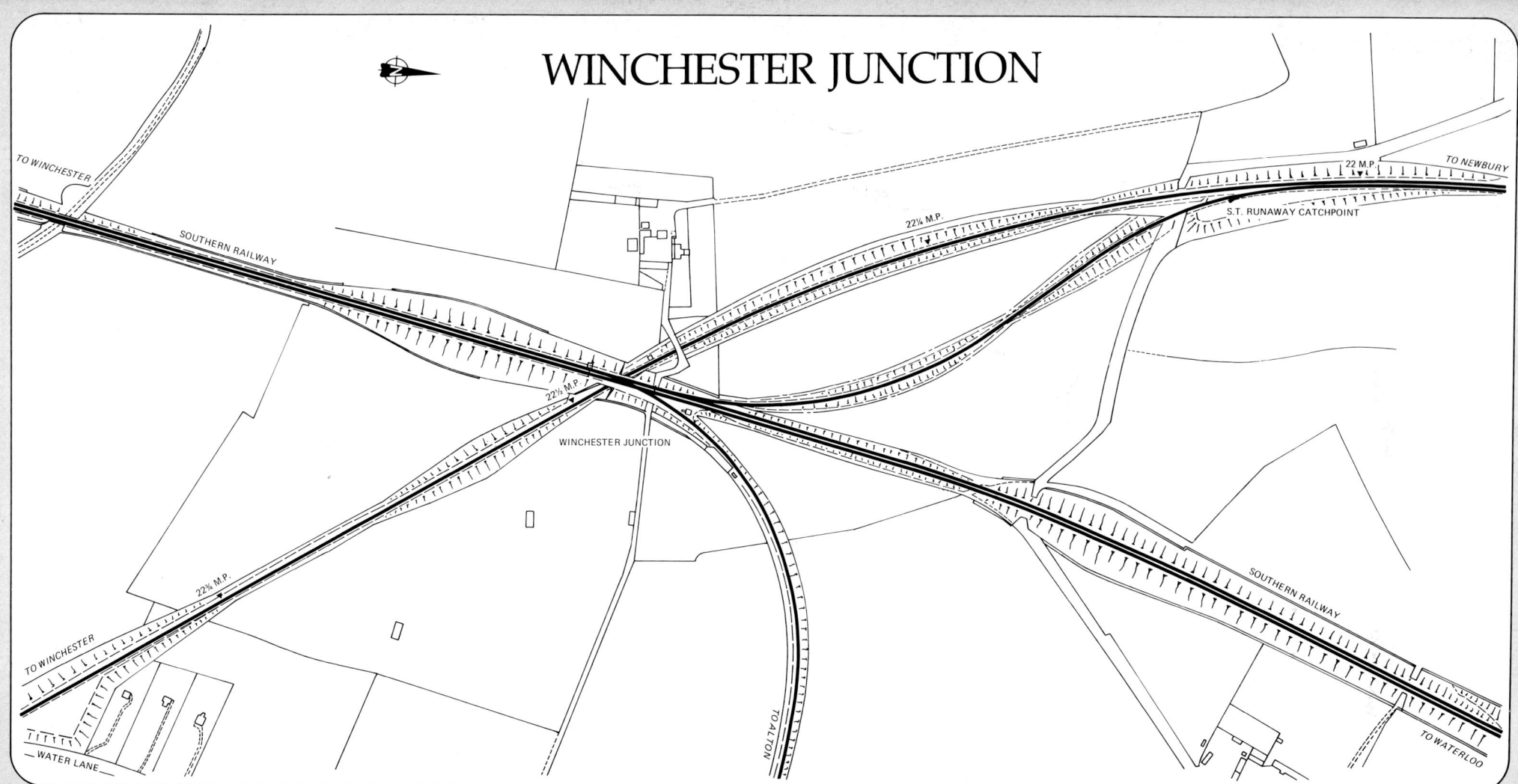

TO WINCHESTER

TO NEWBURY

22 M.P.

SOUTHERN RAILWAY

22¼ M.P.

S.T. RUNAWAY CATCHPOINT

22½ M.P.

WINCHESTER JUNCTION

22¾ M.P.

TO WINCHESTER

SOUTHERN RAILWAY

TO ALTON

WATER LANE

TO WATERLOO

Plate 155: Another view of the junction with the spur to the DN&SR line completely out of action, as can be seen by the frog of the point having been lifted and the continuous line inserted. The Alton branch train driver had just passed the token to the signalman, who is returning to his box.

Author's Collection

Plate 157: This view shows the line about to be put in, with the initial connecting line to the SR having just been laid.

British Rail

Plate 156: A view of the amount of earth removal that took place to allow the connection between the DN&SR and the SR main line.

British Rail

Plate 158: Looking from Worthy Down, on 6th October 1942, the DN&SR is seen running into a cutting and beneath the underbridge to the SR main line. The new connecting spur can be seen under construction in the centre of the photograph. Close examination of the photograph reveals the telegraph poles of the SR main line along the horizon on the left. The junction from the DN&SR to the new spur connecting line appears in the official photographic registers as being named Woodham Junction.

British Rail

King's Worthy

Plate 159: King's Worthy in the 1920s, from an old postcard, looking northwards from the 'up' platform towards Sutton Scotney. When this photograph was taken, the whole station area was virtually only ten years old, hence the 'clean' look to the scene. On the 'down' platform can be seen the signal box at the far end and, just beyond, the goods yard.

Author's Collection

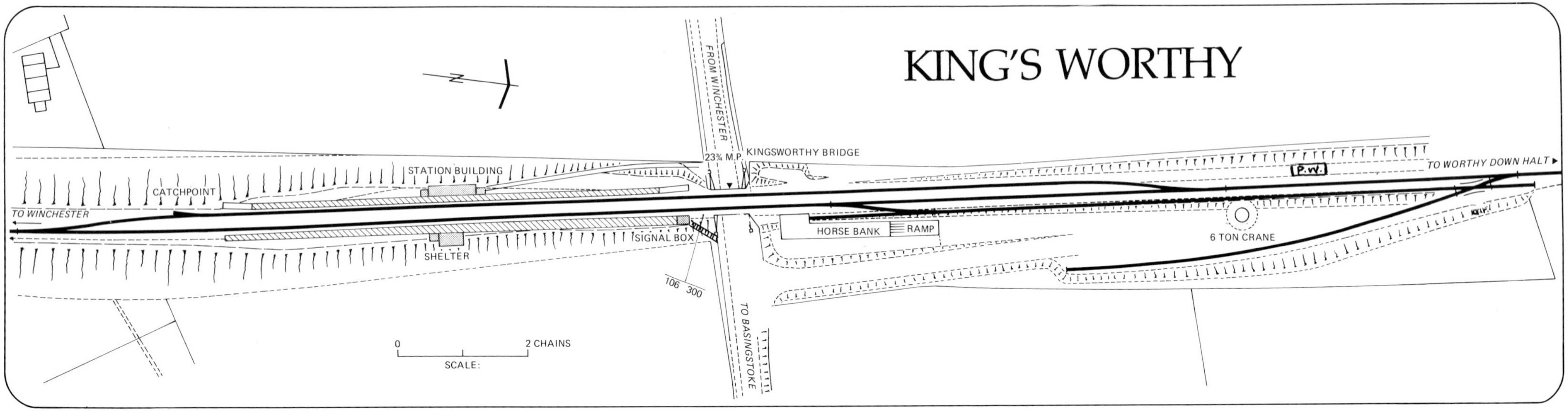

KING'S WORTHY

[Map/track diagram labels:]

FROM WINCHESTER

23¾ M.P. KINGSWORTHY BRIDGE

STATION BUILDING

CATCHPOINT

TO WINCHESTER

SHELTER

SIGNAL BOX

106 300

TO BASINGSTOKE

P.W.

TO WORTHY DOWN HALT ▶

HORSE BANK RAMP

6 TON CRANE

0   2 CHAINS

SCALE:

Plate 160: A view looking at the 'down' platform from an 'up' train in May 1952.

H. C. Casserley

King's Worthy

Opened to passenger traffic: 1st February 1909
Opened to goods traffic: 29th April 1909
Closed to passenger traffic: 7th March 1960
Closed to goods traffic 10th October 1962

King's Worthy was authorized as a new station in May 1908. It was opened for passengers in February 1909 and had seven 'down' and five 'up' trains daily. The station was situated at the 23¼ mile post serving the villages of Easton, Abbotts Worthy, King's Worthy, Martyr Worthy and Headbourne Worthy, and its buildings were GWR-constructed and quite different from the other DN&SR buildings. This gave the DN&SR a further crossing place, with a loop of approximately 800ft. at this station.

The buildings and signal box were constructed in wood and, as seen in *Plate 159*, appeared attractive, and the individual GWR notice-boards stand out well on each platform. The signal box was situated at the end of the 'down' platform, just above the main Winchester to Basingstoke road which ran underneath the railway at this point. Both platforms had access from the road, the 'down' by a set of steps and the 'up' by a cinder path. The goods yard had its own approach road, and a 6 ton yard crane, but it was not until Christmas 1909 that a goods shed was erected by the GWR. It was a corrugated iron shed with sliding doors. A horse/cattle loading dock was also built and extended in 1931. As no full size weighbridge was provided, a weighing machine was provided in the goods shed. The main station building contained a general station office, ladies' room and booking office, and waiting-room.

The wartime measures extended the loop, and the old signal box was moved from the 'down' platform end to the northern end of the new loop (reportedly by a local labourer, on a platelayer's trolley). This box was capable of holding all the new wartime equipment and also replaced the small ground frame that existed there. This small box was moved to the platform alongside the station buildings and was used for a lamp room, and can be seen in *Plate 161*. Two further small buildings were built near the signal box to house permanent way equipment and gangers' trolleys.

In 1955 the crossing loop was removed and the signal box closed in January 1955, the 'up' line remaining as the single line between Worthy Down and Winchester. The goods yard remained and was controlled by a ground frame.

King's Worthy

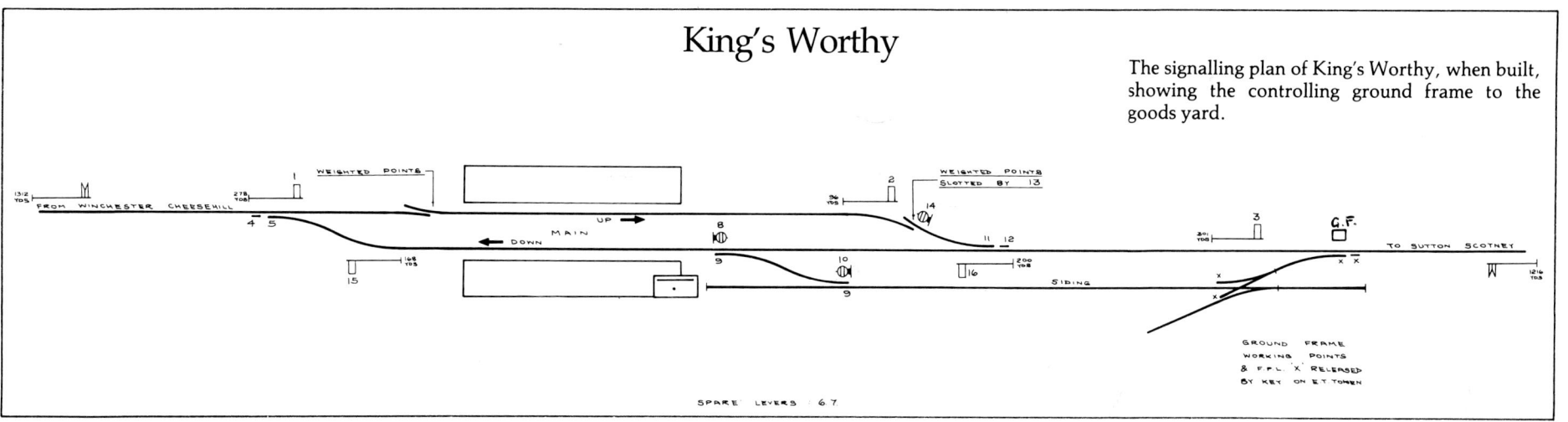

The signalling plan of King's Worthy, when built, showing the controlling ground frame to the goods yard.

Plate 161: Photographed from a train, speeding away from King's Worthy in December 1959, this picture has captured the derelict state of this station. Note the station staff's bicycle outside, and how the 'down' platform has been totally demolished and, in consequence, become overgrown.

C. Gammell

Plate 162 (below): After passenger closure, King's Worthy is at rest, in May 1961. Seen here from the 'down' platform position, it is already becoming overgrown as only freight trains now pass infrequently up and down this line. *Michael Hale*

KING'S WORTHY

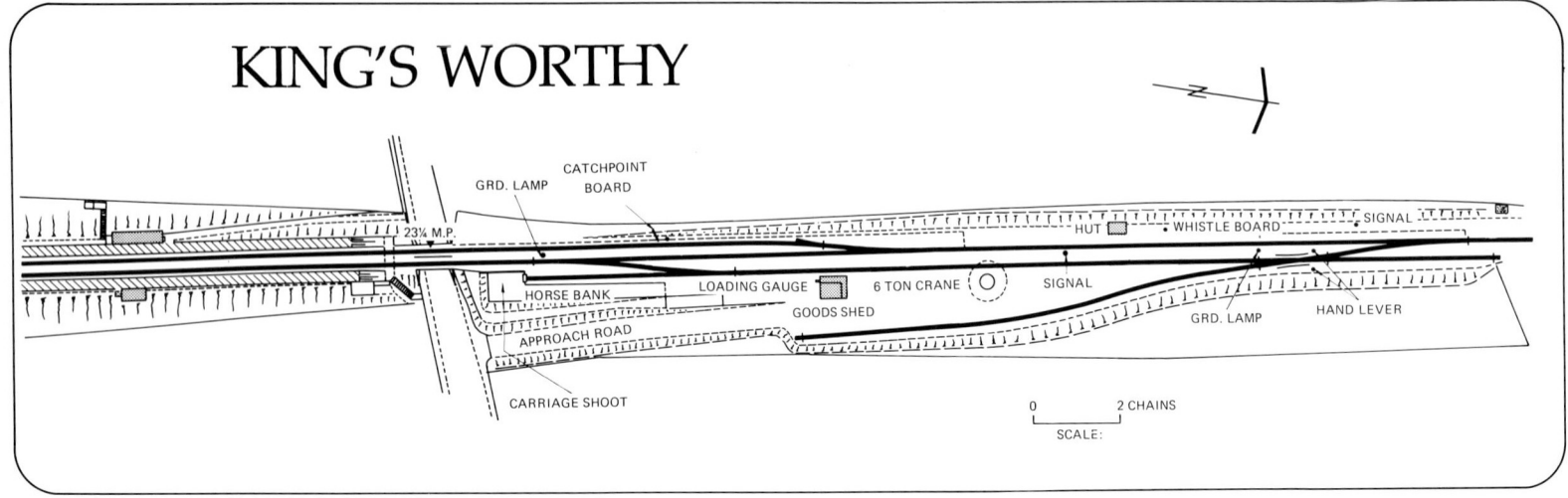

CATCHPOINT
BOARD

GRD. LAMP

SIGNAL

HUT · WHISTLE BOARD

23¼ M.P.

HORSE BANK

LOADING GAUGE

6 TON CRANE

SIGNAL

GRD. LAMP

HAND LEVER

APPROACH ROAD

GOODS SHED

CARRIAGE SHOOT

0   2 CHAINS

SCALE:

The top plan shows the 1931 alterations
and the middle plan, the 1942 wartime
additions. The bottom signalling plan is
dated 1943.

King's Worthy

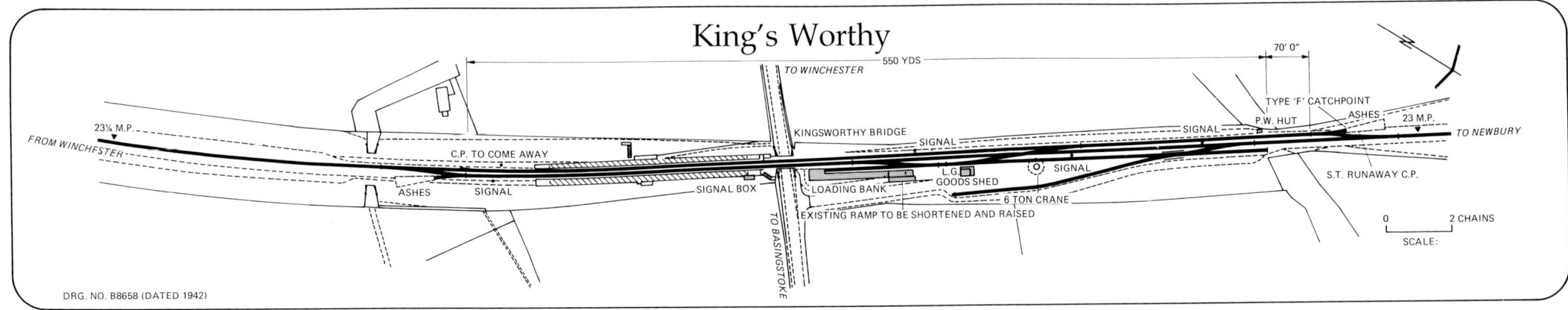

TO WINCHESTER

70' 0"

550 YDS

TYPE 'F' CATCHPOINT

23¼ M.P.

KINGSWORTHY BRIDGE

SIGNAL

SIGNAL

P.W. HUT

ASHES

23 M.P.

FROM WINCHESTER

C.P. TO COME AWAY

SIGNAL

TO NEWBURY

ASHES

SIGNAL

SIGNAL BOX

LOADING BANK

L.G

GOODS SHED

SIGNAL

S.T. RUNAWAY C.P.

TO BASINGSTOKE

EXISTING RAMP TO BE SHORTENED AND RAISED

6 TON CRANE

0   2 CHAINS

SCALE:

DRG. NO. B8658 (DATED 1942)

King's Worthy

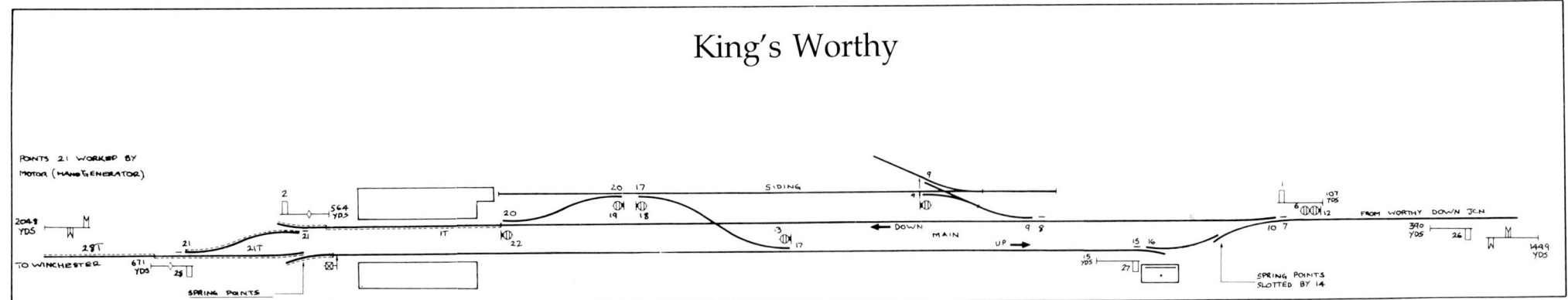

POINTS 21 WORKED BY
MOTOR (HAND GENERATOR)

2

20 17

SIDING

9

107
YDS

564
YDS

20

19 18

9

FROM WORTHY DOWN JCN

2048
YDS

21

21T

1T

3

DOWN MAIN UP

9 8

10 7

6 12

370
YDS

26

28T

22

17

15 16

1499
YDS

TO WINCHESTER

671
YDS

25

15
YDS

27

SPRING POINTS
SLOTTED BY 14

SPRING POINTS

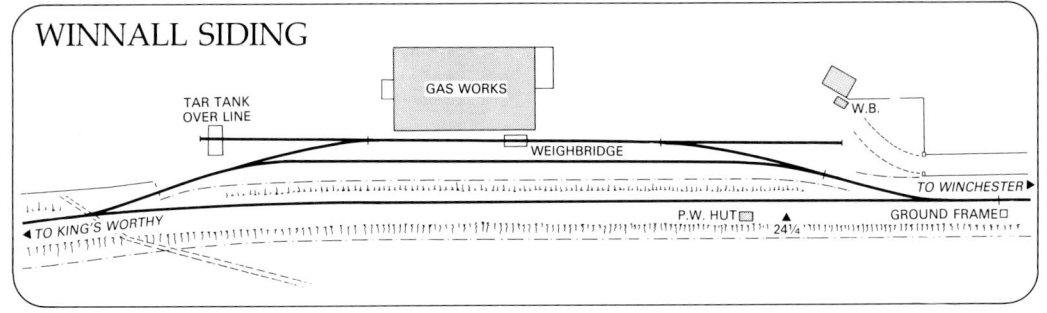

WINNALL SIDING

TAR TANK
OVER LINE

GAS WORKS

W.B.

WEIGHBRIDGE

TO WINCHESTER ▶

◀ TO KING'S WORTHY

P.W. HUT ▢   GROUND FRAME ▢

▲ 24¼

Winnall Siding

These sidings, situated near the 24¼ mile post, served the gasworks for Winchester, and were constructed in 1905 when the gasworks were opened. Having a capacity of 38 wagons (plus a weighbridge), the yard was controlled by two ground frames, Winnall North and Winnall South. The sidings were 'private' and generally not maintained by the GWR. The gasworks closed in 1957 and the siding was taken over by a construction firm but was not utilized by this company. The sidings were situated just past the bridge, as can be seen in *Plate 164*.

Plate 163: The north end of the wartime Winchester loop, photographed on 18th November 1942, by Winnall Farm. The Winchester Tunnel can just be seen under the Winnall Farm bridge, with St. John's Road houses, Winchester, above the tunnel. A new permanent way hut is being built on the left and the electric point motors, controlling the loop, have just been installed. Note the whistle board to the right of the wagon.

British Rail

Plate 164: A further view, photographed by the GWR on 13th January 1943, about two months after that in *Plate 163*, but this time looking north towards Newbury. The work is finished and the permanent way hut is on the right. Winnall gasworks was just beyond the bridge seen in the distance. Between this bridge and the camera was a further siding, called Camp Sidings, going off to the right. It was near the 24½ mile post and served Alvington Park War Department Sidings. It was commissioned in October 1918 but was closed and removed in 1920.

British Rail

Winchester (Chesil)

Plate 165: A GWR 4-4-0 'Duke' class locomotive, No. 3266 *Amyas*, emerges from the tunnel and arrives at Winchester Chesil, on 20th May 1935, with a two coach train from Newbury.

H. C. Casserley

WINCHESTER (CHESIL)

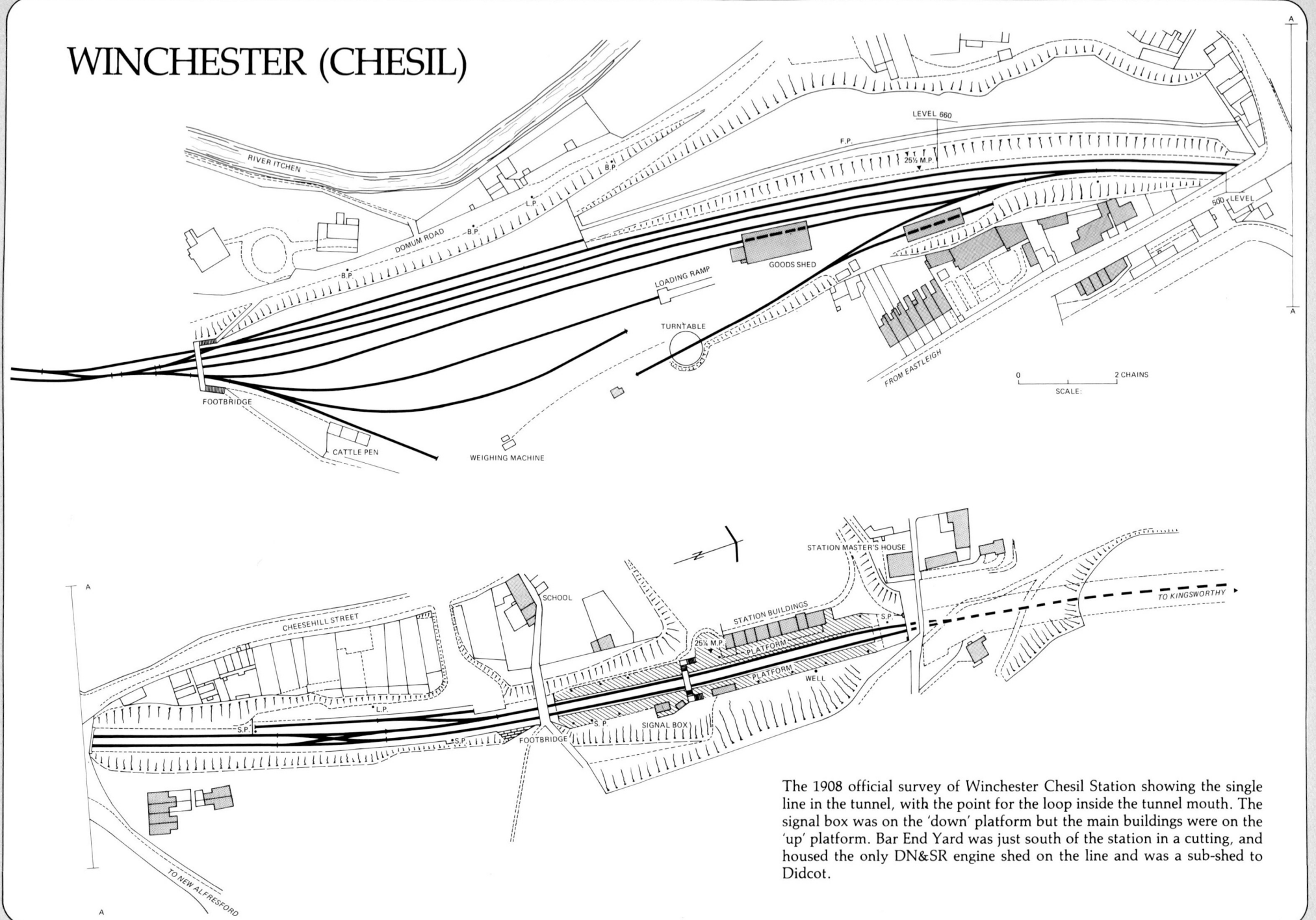

RIVER ITCHEN

LEVEL 660

F.P.

25½ M.P.

500 LEVEL

DOMUM ROAD

B.P.

L.P.

B.P.

B.P.

LOADING RAMP

GOODS SHED

TURNTABLE

FROM EASTLEIGH

0   2 CHAINS

SCALE:

FOOTBRIDGE

CATTLE PEN

WEIGHING MACHINE

STATION MASTER'S HOUSE

SCHOOL

STATION BUILDINGS

TO KINGSWORTHY

CHEESEHILL STREET

25¼ M.P.

PLATFORM

S.P.

PLATFORM

WELL

L.P.

S.P.

S.P.

FOOTBRIDGE

SIGNAL BOX

A

A

TO NEW ALRESFORD

The 1908 official survey of Winchester Chesil Station showing the single line in the tunnel, with the point for the loop inside the tunnel mouth. The signal box was on the 'down' platform but the main buildings were on the 'up' platform. Bar End Yard was just south of the station in a cutting, and housed the only DN&SR engine shed on the line and was a sub-shed to Didcot.

Plates 166 & 167: These two identical views of this idyllic station setting represent a gap in time of 42 years. *Plate 166* was taken in 1919 and shows the signal box on the 'down' platform but, in *Plate 167*, taken in 1961, this had disappeared and had been moved further away revealing the gentlemen's toilet. Three points of interest are: (a) in the 1961 view the pillar bases of the gas lamps remain on both platforms; (b) the platform nameboard had been removed; (c) the stationmaster's house can be seen high up on the left overlooking the station complex.

Real Photographs and Michael Hale

Winchester (Chesil)

Opened: 4th May 1885
Closed to passenger traffic: 7th March 1960
Closed to goods traffic: 4th April 1966
(reopened Saturdays only from 18th June 1960 until 10th September 1960, and from 17th June 1961 until 9th September 1961)

This station was the last on the line at the 25¼ mile post and built to the standard GWR design (except for the familiar style of signal box supplied by Saxby & Farmer). The line entered the 441 yard curved tunnel from King's Worthy. This tunnel was noted for its dampness and in the 1920s and 1930s had to be relined due to the decaying brickwork. The northern loop crossover was just inside the tunnel mouth and was in an awkward position for the engine crews. The main station buildings were on the 'up' platform and housed a ladies' waiting-room and toilets for 'three' classes, general waiting-room, booking hall and office, a store, porters room, lamp room, gentlemen's toilet and oil store. Before 1914, there was also a small bookstall. The 'down' platform was cut into an 80ft. chalk embankment and had a timber-constructed waiting-room, consisting of a general waiting-room and ladies' waiting-room. There was an outside gentlemen's toilet on the other side of the covered footbridge which joined the two platforms. The station, although named 'Cheesehill' originally, was renamed 'Chesil' in 1950. The station was originally the DN&SR terminus and remained so for about six years.

When the final plans had been agreed for the DN&SR extension to Shawford, the track layout was altered and was opened up to Shawford on 1st October 1891. Due to a large land slip on to the now 'down' platform, the new waiting-room was not provided until 1892. Station facilities were restricted due to the location of the buildings so only a small loading dock was provided and the goods yard, etc. was placed further down the line at Bar End.

A new signalling and point system was installed in 1922/3 where the GWR tried out a joint venture with Siemens Bros. Signalling Company. They built a new brick box of standard GWR design, south of the station. The scissors crossover was replaced by two separate crossovers and all coupled (including point locks) to the electrically-operated box. A full account of this novel installation was included in the *Great Western Magazine* and this has been reproduced in full on *pages 126 and 127*. The whole system was taken out of service in 1933 after many faults due to moisture and dampness, and was replaced by the conventional mechanical system.

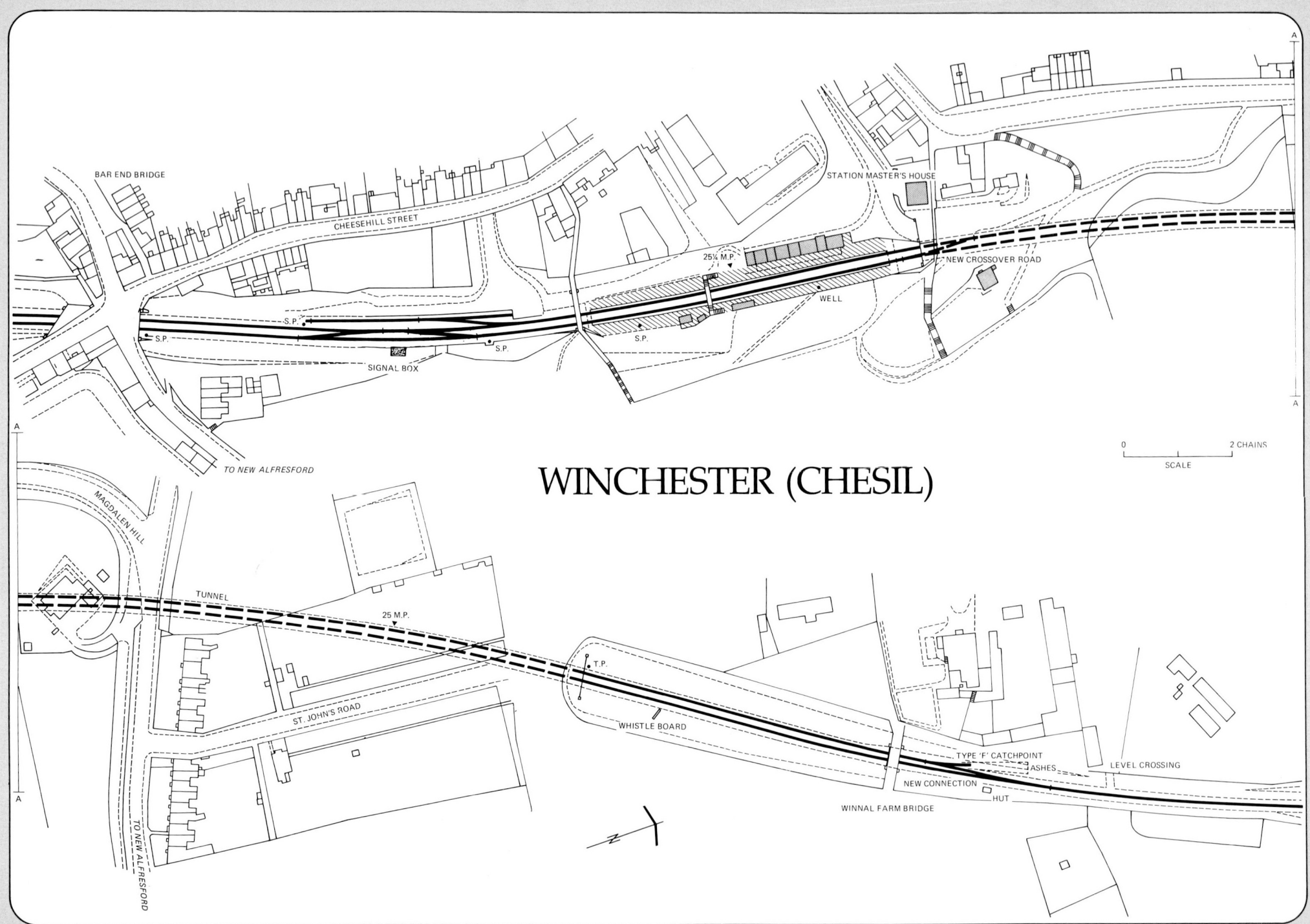

BAR END BRIDGE

CHEESEHILL STREET

STATION MASTER'S HOUSE

25¼ M.P.

NEW CROSSOVER ROAD

WELL

S.P.

S.P.

S.P.

S.P.

SIGNAL BOX

A

A

A

A

TO NEW ALFRESFORD

0   2 CHAINS

SCALE

WINCHESTER (CHESIL)

MAGDALEN HILL

TUNNEL

25 M.P.

T.P.

WHISTLE BOARD

TYPE 'F' CATCHPOINT

ASHES

LEVEL CROSSING

ST. JOHN'S ROAD

NEW CONNECTION

HUT

WINNAL FARM BRIDGE

A

A

TO NEW ALFRESFORD

N

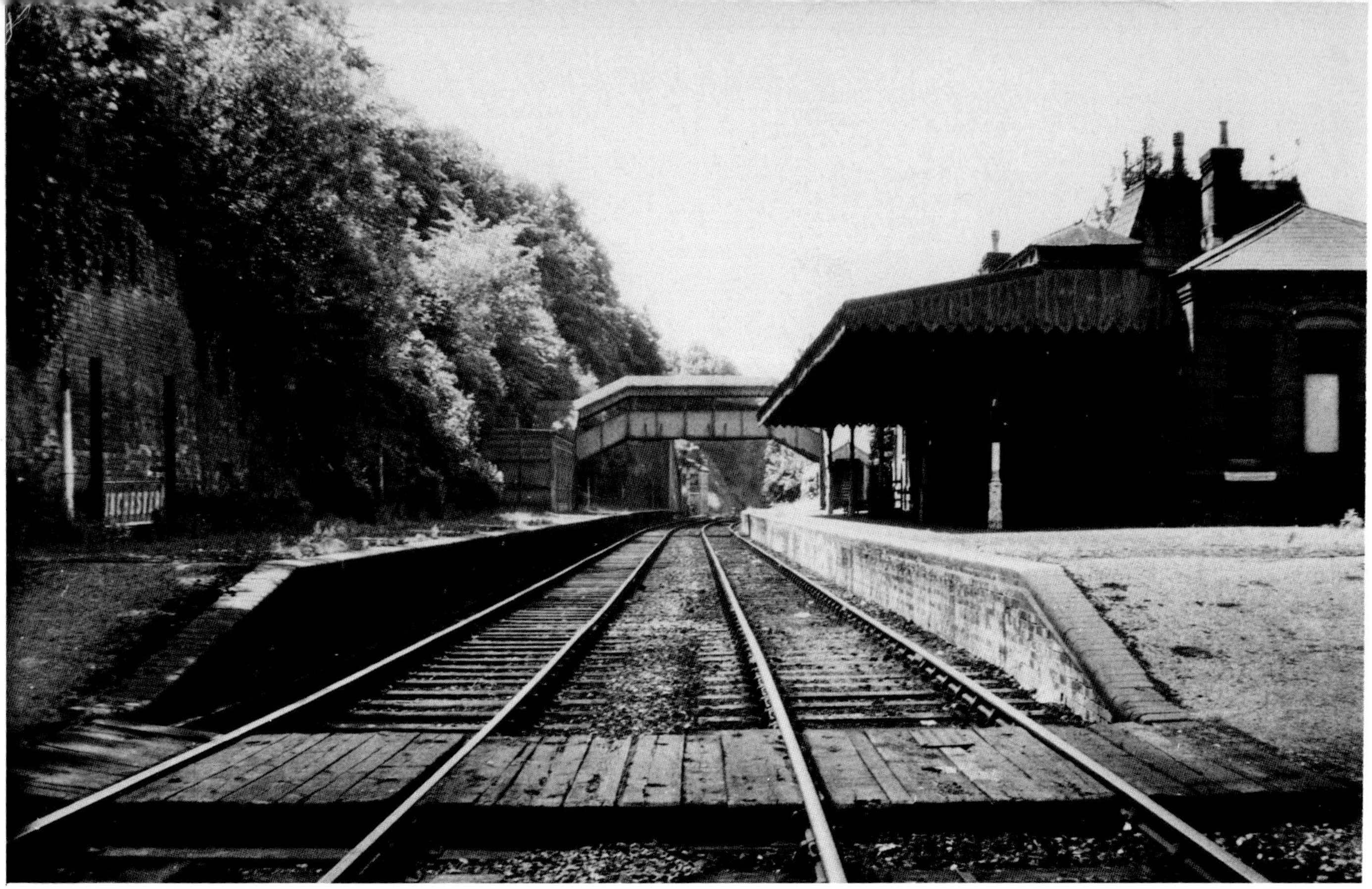

The 1942 wartime diagram *(above page)* showing the removal of the scissors crossings in 1922, the station signal box, and the replacement crossovers and new brick signal box. The box housed the experimental electric power frame. The box was again altered in the 1943 wartime measures and enlarged by 50 per cent to accommodate more levers. The outside staircase was, at this time, replaced by an internal staircase. It was noted that, in the 1950s, when this section became Southern Region, this box was painted in cream and green. The bridge between this new signal box and the 'down' platform was a high girder footbridge which carried a footpath from St. Giles Hill to Chesil Street. The tunnel was originally constructed for two lines, and so the wartime loop extension did not present too many problems, and a new crossover was placed just inside the tunnel. The bridge (almost a tunnel) at the southern end of the station was called Bar End Bridge.

Plate 168: A view, taken in May 1961, looking from the tunnel mouth towards the south and Bar End Yard. The footbridge serving the station is in front of the high girder bridge which can be seen through the top of the footbridge. The new signal box lies just beyond the brick abutment of the girder bridge on the left. The station awning facia border is not of GWR style but is that of the DN&SR, but the building has the standard GWR look about it. Note the towers and ornate ironwork on the roof.

Michael Hale

The 1922 signalling plan shows the new crossover plan after removal of the original scissors crossing.

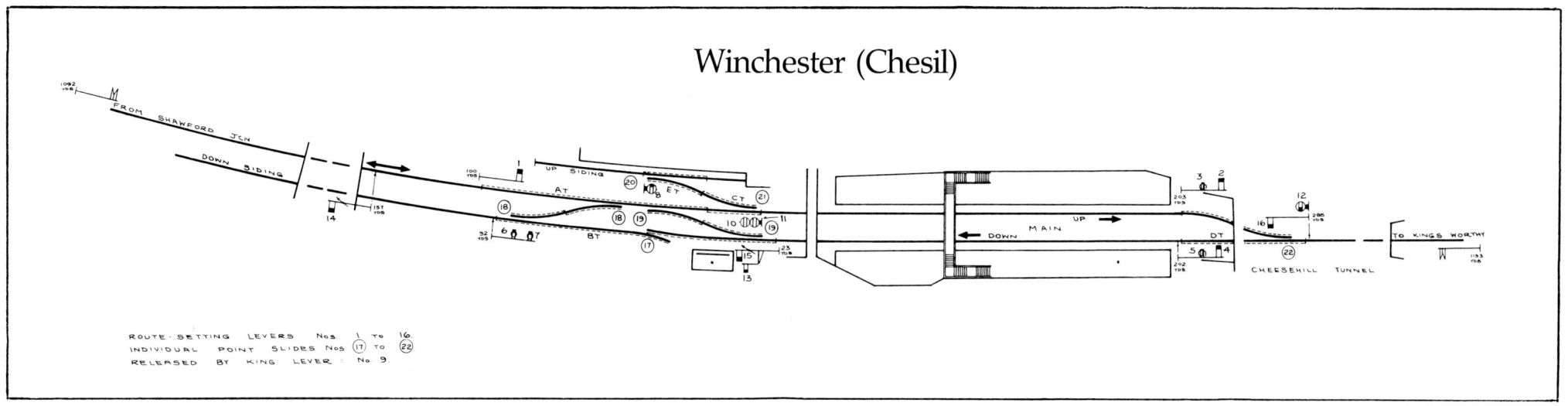

Winchester (Chesil)
FROM SHAWFORD JCN
DOWN SIDING
UP SIDING
MAIN
UP
DOWN
TO KINGS WORTHY
CHEESEHILL TUNNEL
ROUTE-SETTING LEVERS Nos 1 TO 16.
INDIVIDUAL POINT SLIDES Nos (17) TO (22)
RELEASED BY KING LEVER : No 9.

Winchester (Chesil)

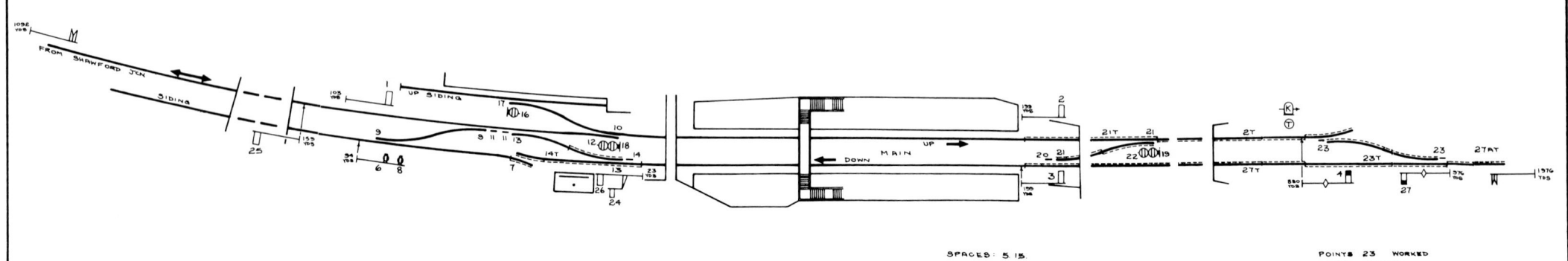

Plate 169: These are the four figures referred to in the *GWR Magazine* article which is reproduced overleaf. The quality is slightly below normal due to the direct reproduction from the magazine.

a) - The interior of the signal box.
b) - The lever route locking frame.
c) - The power switcboard (left) and contactor case.
d) - The layout for two facing points and one trailing point in close proximity, showing motors, detectors, new type of facing point bolts, and run-through safety springs.

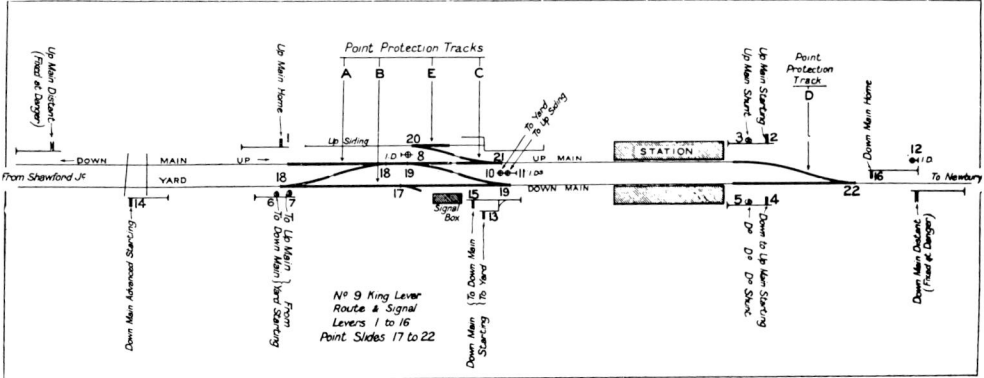

Fig. 1.—The Lay-Out of Winchester station.

New Signalling System at Winchester (GW) Station.

By H. D. Anderson. (Great Western Magazine)

An interesting and novel signalling installation has recently been brought into use at Winchester - a 'crossing' situated on the single line railway which runs from Newbury to Southampton. The layout of the station is as shown in the accompanying diagram (Fig. 1). The ordinary method under which each set of points or a signal is worked by hand, by means of a separate lever in the signal box, has, in this instance, given place to an electric power 'route' system, operated by miniature levers, and so arranged that the movement of each lever not only sets the points, but also lowers the signal controlling any particular route for the movement of trains.

In studying the working of the station it was found that fifteen different movements could be made by trains, and there are, therefore, fifteen 'signal and route' levers in the power locking frame which is illustrated in *Plates 169a and 169b*. It will also be seen in *Plate 169c* that underneath the lever frame are separate point slides, which have been provided for the independent working of the various points, in case of emergency.

The four sets of facing points which exist are fitted with a new pattern facing point bolt, but instead of the usual mechanical locking bars, short track circuits are provided to prevent the points being moved whilst vehicles are standing upon or passing over them. The trailing points are also controlled by similar track circuits. At each pair of points, semaphore signal, and disc signal, is a small 120 volt direct current electric motor, which works the points or signal.

An illustration is given in *Plate 169d* of the type of electric motor and mechanism provided at each facing point. It will be observed that 'run through' safety springs are fitted, in order to prevent damage to the motors, should by any chance a train run through the points. A friction clutch is also provided in the mechanism, to prevent damage to the motor, should any obstruction be between the switch tongues and the rail while the motors are being operated.

Plate 169c also shows the power switchboard in the signal box controlling the electric current supply, which is obtained from two batteries of stationary type accumulators, arranged in the under portion of the signal box. Each battery consists of 6 cells, giving a voltage of 120, and can be charged direct from the public current supply of the Winchester Corporation.

Next to the switchboard is a case holding the special contactor switches and detector relays, and a cupboard containing the track circuit relays. The method of working may now be described.

It will be seen from *Plate 169b* that behind each lever in the lever frame are four circular discs. These discs, when illuminated, give, respectively, the following indications:

Red = Signal at 'Danger'
Green = Signal at 'All right'
Orange = Route correctly set
White = Point protection track clear

The signal and route lever for the route required cannot be operated unless the white 'track' disc behind the lever is illuminated, to indicate that the point protection track or tracks concerned are clear of vehicles. Each lever moves through a four position quadrant, and in pulling a lever from the first or 'normal' position to the second or 'route-setting' position, the following operations take place in the sequence given:

1) The movement of the lever closes the 'route' slide contacts in the locking frame, and also moves the master contact slide, and current at 24 volts flows to the track circuit or circuits concerned.
2) If a track ciruit is occupied by a vehicle, no further movement can take place, as no current reaches the track relay.
3) Provided the track circuit is clear, the current passes along the rail and back to the track relay, which lifts and closes it contacts.
4) If any of the points for the desired route are in the wrong position, a current passes through the point contactor and the motor moves the points into the required position.
5) The points having moved, the point detectors operate the point detector relays, and a 24 volt current passes through the contacts and lifts the electrical check-lock holding the lever, and lights up the orange disc behind the lever, indicating that the route has been properly set.
6) The lever can now be moved right over to the fourth or 'signal off' position, and a current passes through the contacts on the point detector relays and through the master slide contacts to the signal motor, and the signal moves into the 'all right' position, which is indicated to the signal man by the illumination of the green disc and the extinguishing of the light in the red disc.

While a train is passing over any points operated by the lever, the light in the white disc is extinguished and, after the passage of the train, the replacement of the lever from the fourth to the third position restores the signal or disc to 'danger', the light in the green disc disappears and the red disc again becomes illuminated, but the lever cannot be restored to its No. 1, or normal, position until the white disc is once more illuminated, indicating that the train has passed clear of the point tracks, and the back lock is released. The replacement of the lever to its normal position does not reset the points, except those which act as trap points, in which case they are automatically restored to 'normal'.

In order to provide for emergencies, a 'king', or master, lever is provided in the centre of the frame for use in case of inability to establish a route by the proper route lever. Provided the whole of the route levers are in their normal positions, the 'king' lever can be pulled over, which releases the point slide, previously mentioned, and locks all the other levers. The point slides may then be operated to set the desired route. The position of the points is indicated over the point slides by two light indications, green (normal) above and red (reverse) below, for those points which are automatically restored to the 'normal' position by the reversing of the signal and route levers, and green above and orange below for those points which can be left in either position. In all cases, a correct alteration of the position of the points is indicated by a change from green to red or orange, or vice versa. The point slides have three positions, viz., normal, neutral, and reverse and, during ordinary working, they must be in the neutral position.

The 'king' lever can also be used for the purpose of releasing the back-lock on a route lever if the track or signal circuit fails to do so, but every occasion on which it is thus used is automatically registered on a recording instrument.

The lights in the coloured discs behind the route levers and point slides are illuminated by 24 volt lamps, energized from the accumulator batteries.

The installation comprises altogether eight point machines, eleven semphore signals with standard arms, two single disc signals, and one double disc, the latter operated by one motor fitted with a magnetic selective clutch.

For the benefit of technical readers, it may be stated that the two voltages required are obtained from the same batteries, one set of 60 cells being run all in series giving 120 volts, whilst the other set of 60 is working in five groups of 12 cells giving 24 volts and an amperage hour capacity five time as great.

The batteries can be used alternately at the different voltages, the change being made in one operation by means of a rotary switch which is usually changed over every 24 hours.

The battery which, for the time being, is giving 120 volts, is recharged about once a week, while in use, from the Winchester Corporation Electrical Supply, the recharging occupying about three hours.

The whole of the electrical apparatus was manufactured by Messrs Siemens Brothers & Co. Ltd., and installed by them under the supervision of the Great Western Railway Company's Signal Engineer, Mr A. T. Blackall.

Plate 170(above, top left): A GWR Collett 0-6-0 locomotive, No. 2232, heads the 10.50a.m. Didcot to Eastleigh three coach stopping train into Winchester Chesil on 14th September 1959.

J. N. Faulkner

Plate 171(above, top right): No. 2299, a GWR Collett 0-6-0, waits at the 'down' platform with a Southampton train in 1959.

Lens of Sutton

Plate 172(above, bottom left): Passing the nameboard Winchester Chesil a GWR Mogul, No. 6340, a mixed traffic engine, is seen in charge of a through freight. Note the sighting panel on the wall where the signal has been removed.

Author's Collection

Plate 173 (above, bottom right): A further view looking south from the tunnel mouth, with the signal box clearly visible in the distance, under the footbridge.

Author's Collection

Plate 174 (left): A fine view from the footbridge of No. 75071 with the 10.50a.m. Didcot to Eastleigh service, seen entering Winchester Chesil from the north tunnel on 2nd June 1956. This view shows the station roof and turrets, station awning and the stationmaster's house (overlooking the station) very distinctly. It is noticeable that both starter signals are still in position.

J. N. Faulkner

Plate 175 (below left): A 1930s view, with a three coach stopping train having just disgorged a large number of passengers, as can be seen from the footbridge and platform. Note the heavy shoring by the tunnel mouth as obviously a landslide had recently taken place, on to the 'down' platform. The building on the right is the gentlemen's toilet.

Lens of Sutton

Plate 176 (below): An inspection train at Winchester (Chesil) in 1932.

R. W. Kidner

After passing the station, there was a short section between the girder footbridge and Bar End Bridge. *Plate 177* is a reproduction taken from the *GWR Magazine* and shows this section of the track.

The signal box is on the left and the 'new' crossovers are clearly visible, as is the horse loading dock on the right. This was used greatly for the racehorse traffic in the 1920s, and strawberries were a regular commodity dispatched from here. This dock was also the official change-over place for the LSWR and GWR engines, and it is reported that the LSWR engine would wait here rather than use the shed facilities, to avoid paying fees to the GWR. After the bridge, the track entered Bar End goods yards (the Winchester Chesil goods yard). The yard had the only engine shed on the DN&SR and could only house two tank locomotives. The shed was 83ft. long and 20ft. wide and was of brick and stone construction. It had a 4,725 gallon water tank built over the northern end, feeding a stand-pipe at the south end on the coaling stage. Just past the engine shed was the goods shed, of GWR design, built of brick with slate roofing. Inside was a small wooden lock-up office and two 25cwt. platform cranes. The yard wall had three lorry loading platforms with extensive canopies over each, and windows spaced in between each bay down one side and all down the other. A substantial office was provided at the south end of the goods shed.

The same line that led to the shed also proceeded to the Ransomes & Rapier 42ft. turntable (a further 4ft. was added in August 1934 by use of extension bars). In 1946, after the war, the GWR decided to replace it with a new Cowans Sheldon vacuum 65ft. turntable and this finally came into service on 29th September 1947. The Southern Region took over the shed in April 1950 and then, in 1953, closed and removed the turntable to Nine Elms and demolished the shed building in 1955. A loading gauge stood alongside the entry to the yard, by the side of the shed. At the southern end of the yard stood an iron footbridge and the yard was controlled by a small wooden-hutted ground frame, which had to be unlocked by a token from the main signal box, before any movements could take place. The yard also contained a 15 ton weighbridge (No. 40) which had a 16ft. x 8ft. base plate. Cattle pens and a loading bay were also provided and a short headshunt, south of the iron footbridge, was also available.

Plate 177

After leaving Bar End, and with a sweeping curve, the track passed the base of St. Catherine's Hill, alongside the A34 bypass. Just before reaching the junction with the LSWR, a long viaduct (Shawford Viaduct) was crossed and the accompanying official drawing shows details of the structure. It was an impressive 32 brick arch structure over the River Itchen and still stands today (1984).

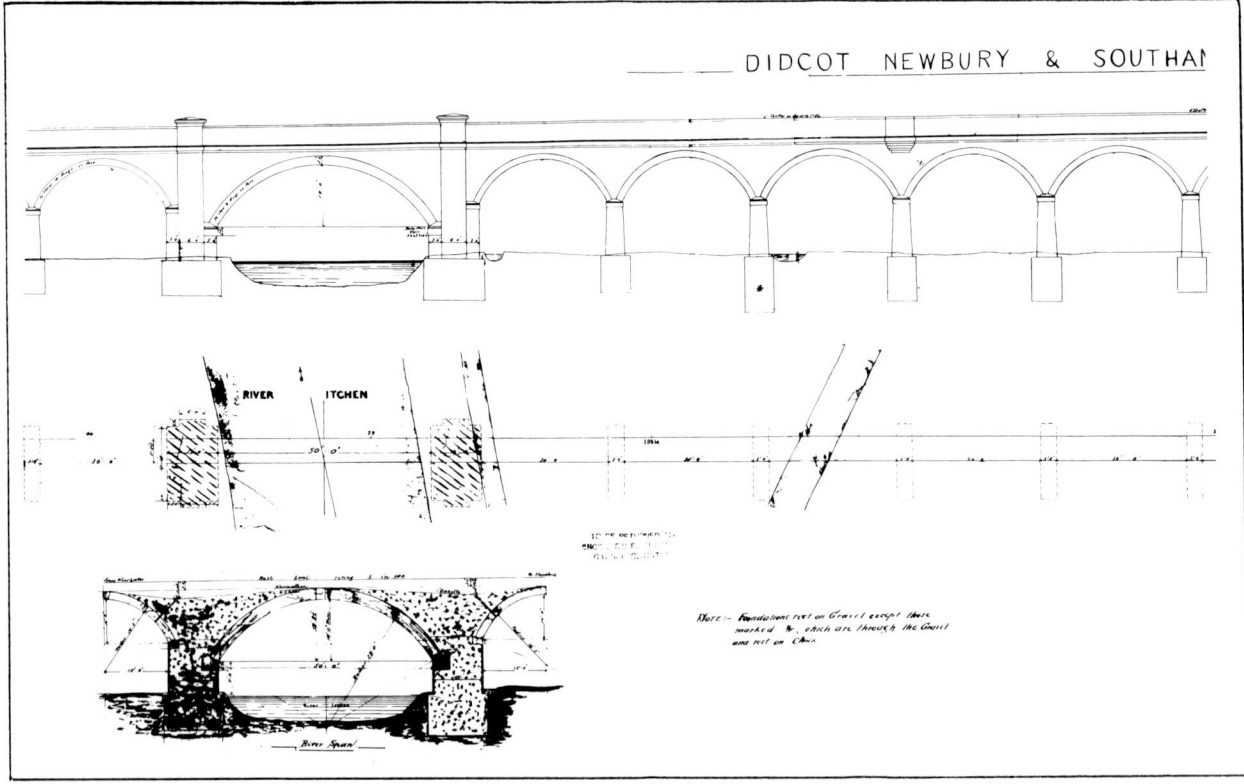

Shawford Junction

Plate 178: This view, taken in May 1961, shows Shawford Junction with the new third line. The signal box and set of steps, for the signalman to hand over the single line token, can be seen, as can a lamp alongside for night use. The signals were of Southern Railway construction and the length of loop junction into a single line is approximately the same as per the alteration in 1921. Shawford Viaduct can be seen to the extreme right of the picture. This view, taken from a bridge, is looking towards Winchester.

Michael Hale

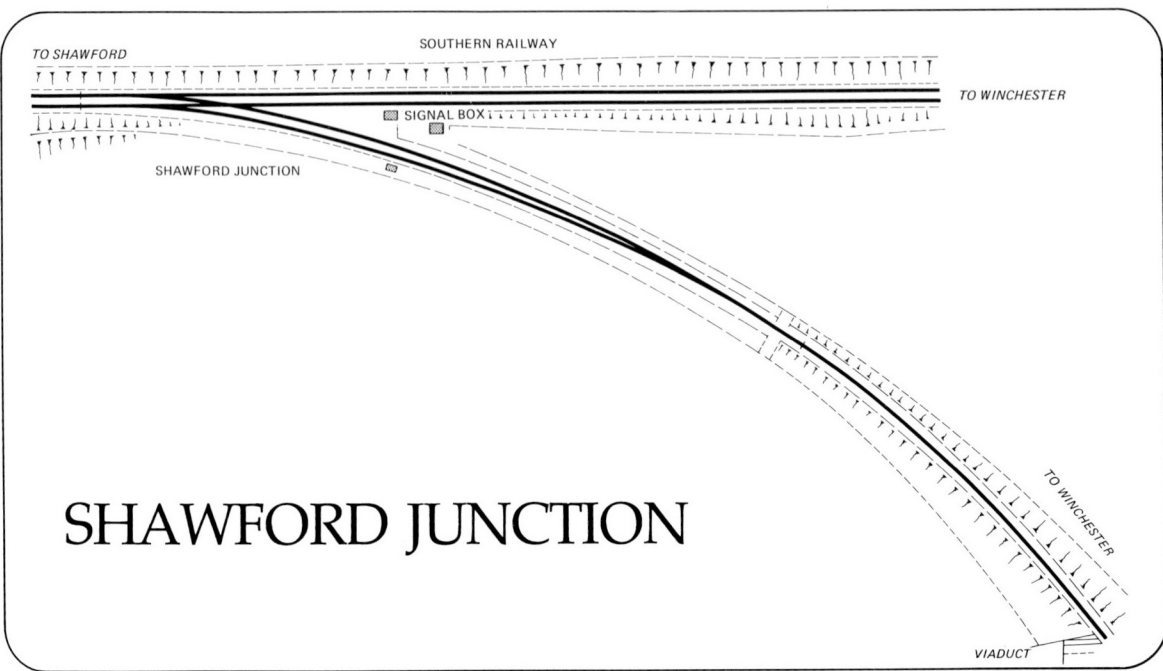

TO SHAWFORD

SOUTHERN RAILWAY

TO WINCHESTER

SIGNAL BOX

SHAWFORD JUNCTION

TO WINCHESTER

SHAWFORD JUNCTION

VIADUCT

The plan shows the original survey with just the two main LSWR lines and the single line of the DN&SR splitting into two (on the curve) and feeding into the main lines. The long approach loop was very seldom used so it was lifted and made much shorter in the winter of 1921/2.

Plate 179: Our old faithful GWR locomotive, No. 3440 *City of Truro*, comes off the DN&SR in 1957 on to Southern metals, having just dropped the token, and rides the 'slow' line towards Shawford.

L. Elsey

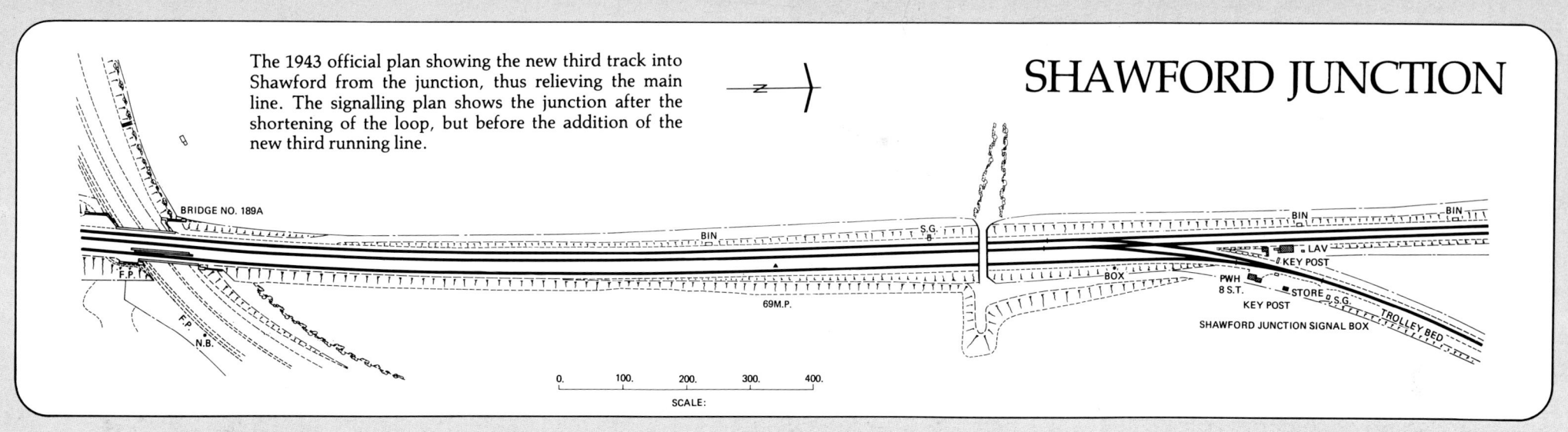

SHAWFORD JUNCTION

The 1943 official plan showing the new third track into Shawford from the junction, thus relieving the main line. The signalling plan shows the junction after the shortening of the loop, but before the addition of the new third running line.

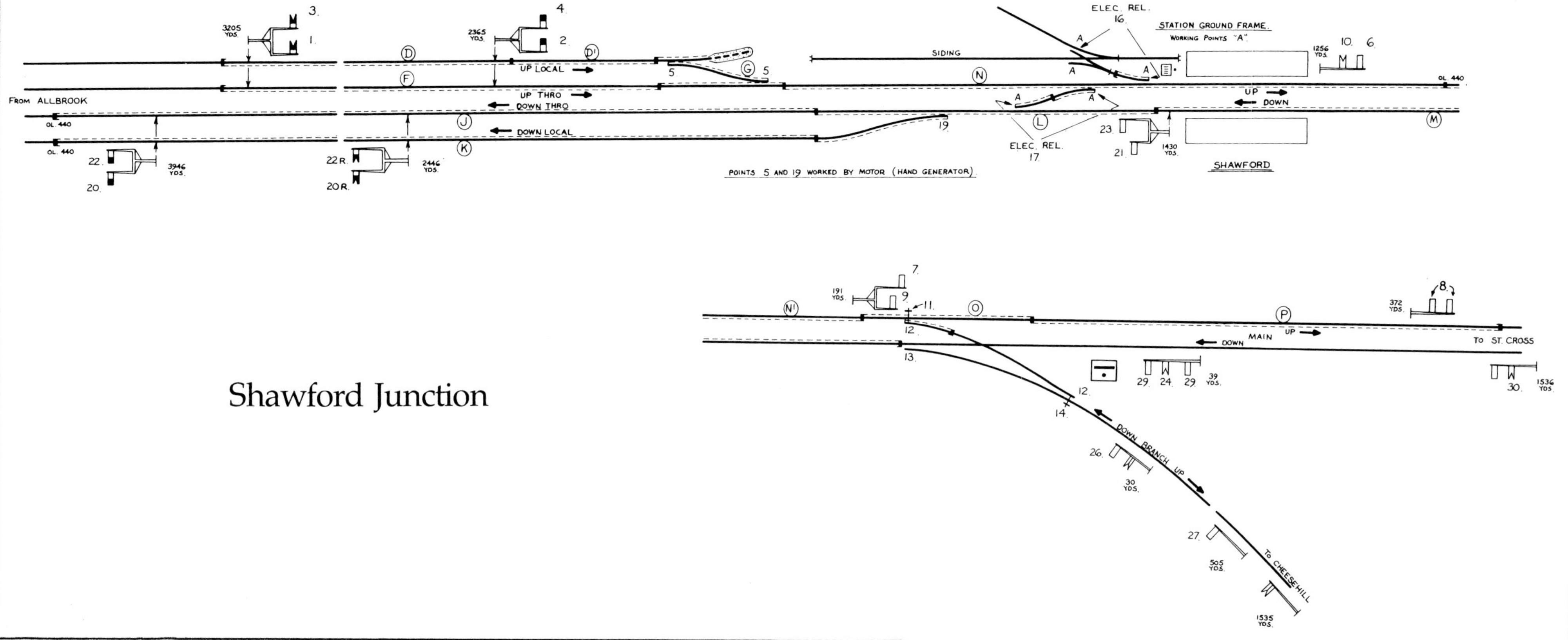

BRIDGE NO. 189A

F.P. "A"

F.P. N.B.

BIN

S.G.

69 M.P.

BIN

BIN

LAV

KEY POST

BOX

PWH 8 S.T. STORE S.S.G.

KEY POST

SHAWFORD JUNCTION SIGNAL BOX

TROLLEY BED

SCALE:

0.   100.   200.   300.   400.

FROM ALLBROOK

UP LOCAL

UP THRO
DOWN THRO

DOWN LOCAL

SIDING

ELEC. REL. 16

STATION GROUND FRAME
Working Points "A"

ELEC. REL. 17

POINTS 5 AND 19 WORKED BY MOTOR (HAND GENERATOR)

UP   DOWN

SHAWFORD

Shawford Junction

DOWN   MAIN   UP

TO ST. CROSS

DOWN BRANCH UP

TO CHESIL HILL

THROUGH TRAIN SERVICE
BY THE
DIDCOT AND NEWBURY ROUTE.
NOVEMBER, 1895.

	a.m.	a.m.	a.m.	p.m.	p.m.
Cowes (Boat) ......dep.	....	7 0	9 40	....	3 40
South'ton Docks „	7 8	9 8	11 50	2 10	5 35
St. Denys .... „	7 13	9 3	11 29	2 18	5 41
Eastleigh .... „	7 20	9 18	12 5	2 25	5 49
Winchester ...... „ (Cheeseh'l St.)	7 40	9 36 A	12 28 A	2 46	6 10
OXFORD ....arr.	10 53	11 32	2 36	5 33	8 28
WORCESTER (Shrub Hill),	12 47	2 10	4 27	7 43	10 25
GLOUCESTER .... „	12 9	1 46	6 3	8 35	10 41
CHELTENHAM .... „	12 30	2 8	6 25	8 55	10 19
BIRM'GHAM (Snow Hill) „	12 42	1 34	4 23	7 26	10 15
CHESTER .... „	3 33	4 33	7 20	9 43	
LIVERPOOL (Lan. Stg.) „	4 30	5 20	8 25	10 25	
MANCHESTER (Lon.Rd.),	5*3	5 16	8 0	11 28	

*Exchange Station.

	a.m.	a.m.	noon	a.m.
MANCHESTER (Lon. Rd.)....dep.	....	....	....	11 40
LIVERPOOL (Lan. Stage) .... „	....	6 0	....	11 50
CHESTER .... „	....	6 52	....	12 45
BIRMINGHAM (Snow Hill) .. „	7 30	10 20	.....	4 0
CHELTENHAM .... „	7 23	10 0	....	3 20
GLOUCESTER .... „	7 43	9 45	....	2 38
WORCESTER (Shrub Hill) .. „	6 50	10 5	....	3 20
OXFORD .... „	9 20	12 23 A	12 30	5 50 A
		p.m. 2 15	p.m. 3 33	
Winchester (Cheeseh'l St.) arr.	12 27	2 15	3 33	8 13
Eastleigh .... „	12 48	2 34	3 53	8 33
St. Denys .... „	12 59	3 15	4 3	8 44
Southampton............. „	1 7	2 48	4 10	8 52
Cowes (Boat) .... „	3 0	4 50	7 0	....

Passengers should be careful to ask for their tickets by the Didcot, Newbury, and Southampton (the shortest) Route.

A—Through trains between Southampton and Oxford.

GOODS TRAFFIC.

The Didcot, Newbury, and Southampton Railway forms the shortest route for Goods Traffic between

LIVERPOOL, BIRKENHEAD, MANCHESTER,

SOUTH STAFFORDSHIRE,

THE BIRMINGHAM DISTRICT, OXFORD, &c.

AND

WINCHESTER, SOUTHAMPTON,

PORTSMOUTH, and the ISLE OF WIGHT.

Goods intended for this route should be consigned " Via Great Western, and Didcot, Newbury and Southampton Railways."

SOUTHAMPTON STEAMER SAILINGS.

Steamers depart from SOUTHAMPTON as under:—

For WEST COWES and RYDE (Isle of Wight)—
Week-days at 8.30, 11.10 a.m., 2.0, 3.50, and *6.0 p.m.
Sundays—8.45 a.m., 2.45, and *5.15 p.m.
* To Cowes only.

„ HAVRE and PARIS, HONFLEUR, TROUVILLE, and CAEN every weeknight (at 12 midnight).

„ CHERBOURG, Tuesdays, Thursdays, and Saturdays.

„ ST. MALO, Mondays, Wednesdays, and Fridays.

For HAMBURG (North German Lloyd and Union Lines), every Thursday and alternate Saturdays.

„ NEW YORK (North German Lloyd), every Sunday and Wednesday.
„ „ „ (Hamburg-American Line), every Friday.
„ „ „ (American Line), every Saturday.

„ CANARY ISLANDS, MADEIRA, and CAPE OF GOOD HOPE (Union and Castle Lines), every Saturday.

„ EAST INDIES, every Tuesday.

„ WEST INDIES (Royal Mail Line), every alternate Wednesday.

„ SOUTH AMERICAN PORTS (River Plate, Monte Video, Buenos Ayres, &c.) every alternate Friday.

„ SUEZ CANAL, PORT SAID, ADEN, COLOMBO, &c., every alternate Sunday.

„ CHINA, JAPAN, and AUSTRALIAN PORTS (North German Lloyd), once Monthly.

For other sailings and full details, see the Sailing Bills of the respective Lines.

Didcot, Newbury, and Southampton Railway.

IMPROVED TRAIN SERVICE.

SHORTEST & MOST DIRECT ROUTE
BETWEEN
SOUTHAMPTON,
PORTSMOUTH,
The Isle of Wight and Winchester,
AND
OXFORD,
BANBURY, LEAMINGTON, STRATFORD-ON-AVON,
BIRMINGHAM,
LIVERPOOL, MANCHESTER,
And the NORTH.

TIME TABLE
FOR
NOVEMBER, 1895,
AND UNTIL FURTHER NOTICE.

Passengers should ask for tickets by the Didcot, Newbury, and Southampton Route.

Through Carriages are run:
Oxford to Winchester and Southampton Docks, 12.23 noon and 5.50 p.m.
Southampton Docks to Oxford, 9.8 a.m. and 11.50 a.m.
Winchester to Oxford, 9.36 a.m. and 12.28 noon.

Through Carriages between Southampton and Didcot by all trains.

Information as to trains and arrangements on the Didcot, Newbury, and Southampton Railway, may be obtained at the Stations on the Line; from CAPTAIN BINGHAM (Secretary), 11, Victoria Street, London, S.W.; or from Mr. W. H. H. M. GIPPS, 32, Queen's Terrace, Southampton.

COX & SHARLAND, Printers, High Street, Southampton.

UP TRAINS.	a.m	a.m	a.m	a.m A	a.m	a.m	a.m A	p.m.	p.m.	p.m. S
Ventnor ....dep.	..	..	..	..	8 5	..	8 5	..	2 10	4 15
Newport, I.W..... „	..	..	..	..	9 5	..	9 5	..	3 2	5 10
Cowes (Boat) .... „	..	..	..	7 0	9 40	..	9 40	..	3 40	5 45
South'ton D'ks. „	6 50	7 8	8 55	9 8	1050	1133	1150	2 10	5 35	7 55
Northam .... „	6 54	..	8 59	..	1054	1136	..	2 14	5 38	7 59
St. Denys .. .. „	6 58	7 13	9 3	..	1058	1139	..	2 18	5 41	8 3
Swaythling .... „	7 2	..	9 7	..	11 2	1143	..	..	..	8 7
Eastleigh ....arr.	7 7	7 19	9 12	9 17	11 8	1148	12 4	2 24	5 48	8 12
Bournemouth East ....dep.		..	..	7 20	9 25	..	10 0	1110	4 0	6 40
Brockenhurst .... „		..	..	8 5	9 54	..	1043	1148	4 35	7 7
Ryde (via Stokes B.) „		..	..	7b15	9 3	..	1010	1115	4 0	6 10
Southsea .... „		..	..	7 55	9 10	..	1030	1212	4 10	6 20
Portsmouth (Town).... „		6 15	..	8 0	9 25	..	1040	1225	4 18	6 45
Eastleigh ....dep.		7 20	╰──	9 18	11 9	╰──	12 5	2 25	5 49	8 13
Shawford.................. „		..	..	G	1118	..	..	2 34	5 57	8 22
Winchester ......arr.		7 35	..	9 32	1126	..	1220	2 42	6 5	8 28
(Cheesehill St.) ......dep.		7 40	..	9 36	●	..	1228	2 46	6 10	8 30
Sutton Scotney .... „		7 54	..	9 49	..	..	1241	2 59	6 24	8 44
Whitchurch .... „		8 5	..	9 59	..	..	1252	3 10	6 35	8 55
Litchfield .... „		8 14	..	10 8	..	..	1 1	3 19	6 44	9 4
Burghclere .... „		8 20	..	1014	..	..	1 8	3 25	6 50	9 10
Highclere .... „		8 25	..	1019	..	..	1 13	3 30	6 55	9 15
Woodhay .... „		8 31	..	1025	..	..	1 20	3 36	7 1	9 21
Newbury ....arr.		8 40	..	1033	..	..	1 29	3 45	7 10	9 30
Newbury ....dep.		8 49	..	1125	..	..	2 21	3d35	8 41	10 0
Reading ....arr.		9 13	..	12 7	..	..	3 0	4d35	9 25	1025
London (Paddington).. „		1015	..	1 30	..	..	4 7	5d35	10 55	1140
Newbury ....dep.		8 45	..	1057	..	..	2c22	3 52	7 13	● ☞ Saturdays only.
Hungerford ....arr.		9 6	..	1115	..	..	2c40	4 12	7 31	
Marlborough .... „		9 48	..	1H0	..	..	..	5 15	..	
Devizes .... „		10 2	..	1 8	..	..	..	5 9	9 55	
Trowbridge........... „		1031	..	1 33	..	..	..	5 35	10 20	
Devizes ....dep.		7 55	..	..	..	..	1233	1 8	4 18	
Hungerford .... „		8 57	..	..	.	..	11 3	2e 1	5 19	
Newbury ....arr.		9 14	..	..	.	..	1 24	2e18	5 36	
London (Paddington)..dep.		6 30	..	..	..	..	10 0	1 45	5 15	..
Reading............. „		7 55	..	..	..	..	11 8	3 5	6 20	..
Newbury ....arr.		8 39	..	..	..	..	1154	3 48	7 3	..
Newbury ....dep.		9 20	..	1035	..	..	1 31	3 53	7 13	..
Hermitage .... „		9 30	..	1044	..	..	1 40	4 3	7 23	..
Hampstead Norris ...... „		9 38	..	1051	..	..	1 47	4 11	7 31	..
Compton .... „		9 44	..	1058	..	§ Leave Didcot at 8.12 p.m. for Gloucester and Cheltenham.	1 54	4 17	7 37	..
Upton .... „		9 56	..	1110	..		2 6	4 29	7 49	..
Didcot ....arr.		10 2	..	1116	..		2 12	4 37	7 55	..
Didcot...............dep.		1025	..	12 3	..		3 10	4J49	8 50	..
Reading ....arr.		1110	..	1243	..		3 54	6 7	9 30	..
London (Paddington) .. „		1235	..	1 58	..		5 10	6 0	10 55	..
Didcot...............dep.		1017	..	1151	..		3 25	5 30	8 S21	..
Swindon..............arr.		1050	..	1224	..		4 0	6 40	8 52	..
Bath .... „		1134	..	1 35	..		5 12	7 44	9 35	..
Bristol.............. „		1157	..	1 57	..		5 35	8 10	9 57	..
Cheltenham .... „		1230	..	2 8	..		6 25	8 55	10§19	..
Gloucester .... „		12 9	..	1 46	..		6 3	8 35	10§41	..
Cardiff.............. „		1 46	..	3 33	..		6 59	10 5	2 10	..
Swansea .... „		3 45	..	5 25	..	..	8 30	1145	4 10	..
Didcot................dep.		1025	Manchester Exchange Station.	1118	..	..	2 20	5 10	8 12	..
Oxford .... arr.		1053		1132	..	..	2 36	5 33	8 28	..
Banbury.............. „		..		1222	..	..	4 17	7 27	9 5	..
Leamington .... „		12 5		1250	..	..	3 45	6K57	9 30	..
Stratford-on-Avon ..... „		1 15		3 17	..	..	5 3	8 5	10 40	..
Birming'm (Snow H.) „		1242		1 34	..	..	4 23	7 26	10 15	..
Wolverhampton .... „		1 8		2 0	..	..	4 48	7 49	10 45	..
Shrewsbury .... „		1 59		3 4	..	..	5 46	8 35	11 55	..
Chester .... „		3 33		4 33	..	..	7 20	9 43	●	..
Birkenhead (Woodside).. „		4 13		5 6	..	..	8 10	9 59	..	..
Liverpool (Lan. Stg.) „		4 30		5 20	..	..	8 25	1025	..	..
Manchester(Lon. R) „		5 * 3	*	5 16	..	..	8 0	1128	..	..

A Through trains between Southampton and Oxford.
B via Portsmouth.
C Wednesdays and Saturdays only.
D Wednesdays and Saturdays only. Other days leave Newbury 5.39, and arrive Reading 6.18, and Paddington 7.32.

DOWN TRAINS.	a.m.	a.m.	a.m.	a.m.	a.m.	noon	a.m.		
Manchest'r(Lon.R.) dep.	..	..	..	..	..	..	1140	..	..
Liverpool (Lan Stg.) „	..	..	..	6 0	..	..	1150	..	..
Birkenhead (Woodside).. „	..	..	..	6 15	..	..	12 5	..	..
Chester .... „	..	..	..	6 52	..	..	1245	..	..
Shrewsbury .... „	..	..	..	8 12	† Stapleton Road Station.	..	2 17	..	..
Wolverhampton .... „	..	..	6 55	9 52		..	3 32	..	..
Birming'm (Snow H.) „	..	..	7 30	1020		..	4 0	..	..
Stratford-on-Avon ...... „	..	..	7 10	9 43		..	3 30	..	..
Leamington .... „	..	..	8 2	11 4		..	4 37	..	..
Banbury .... „	..	..	8 30	1136		..	5 7	..	..
Oxford .... „	..	..	9 20	1223		1230	5 50	..	..
Didcot ....arr.	..	..	9 43	1242		1253	6 10	..	..
				A			A		
Swansea.............dep	..	..	..	6 53		..	1055	..	..
Cardiff............... „	..	..	6 15	8 17		..	1245	..	..
Gloucester .... „	..	..	7 43	9 45		..	2 38	..	..
Cheltenham .... „	..	..	7 23	10 0		..	3 20	..	..
Bristol............... „	..	..	7 50	9†47	†	..	3 0	..	..
Bath.................. „	..	..	8 7	10 8	..	..	3 17	..	..
Swindon .... „	..	..	9 15	1129	..	..	4 10	..	..
Didcot..............arr.	..	..	1020	1234	..	..	4 43	..	..
London (Paddington)..dep.	5 30	..	9 0	1032	..	12 0	5 0	..	..
Reading .... „	6 33	..	9 50	1145	..	1255	5 51	..	..
Didcot ....arr.	6 58	..	1012	1227	..	1k16	6 15	S	..
	a.m.	a.m.	a.m.	p.m.	.	p.m.	p.m.	p.m.	..
Didcot ....dep.	7 45	..	1035	1245	..	1 30	6 25	..	..
Upton .... „	7 55	..	1043	..	..	1 38	6 33	..	..
Compton .... „	8 9	..	1058	1 1	..	1 54	6 46	..	..
Hampstead Norris ...... „	8 14	..	11 3	..	..	1 59	6 51	..	..
Hermitage .... „	8 23	..	1111	1 11	..	2 7	6 59		..
Newbury ....arr.	8 33	..	1119	1 19	╭	2 15	7 8		..
Newbury ....dep	8 49	..	1125	1 25	..	2 21	8 41	Saturdays only.	..
Reading ....arr.	9 13	..	12 7	..	..	3 0	9 25		..
London (Paddington) .. „	1015	..	1 30	2 35	..	4 7	1055		..
Newbury ....dep.	8 45	..	1158	..	2 22	3 52	7 13	☞	..
Hungerford ....arr.	9 6	..	1219	..	2 40	4 12	7 31		..
Devizes .... „	10 2	..	1 8	..	●	5 9	9 55		..
Trowbridge ....dep.	7 29	..	9 33	..	Wednesdays and Saturdays only.	12 38	3 40	6 38	..
Devizes .... „	7 55	..	10 7	..		1 8	4 18	7 11	..
Marlborough.......... „	8 0	..	1022	..		1 20	4 15	7 0	..
Hungerford .... „	8 35	..	11 3	..		2 1	5 19	8 19	.
Newbury ....arr.	8 47	..	1120	..		2 18	5 36	8 36	..
London (Paddington)..dep.	6 30	..	9 0	10 0		12c25	5 15	7 0	..
Reading .... „	7 55	..	1010	11 8		1c30	6 20	8 0	..
Newbury ....arr.	8 39	..	1054	1154		2c20	7 3	8 43	..
Newbury ....dep.	8 58	..	1125	1 20	..	2 25	7 10	9 45	..
Woodhay................ „	9 7	..	1134	1 32	..	2 34	7 19	9 54	..
Highclere .... „	9 16	..	1143	..	..	2 43	7 28	10 3	* Via St. Denys.
Burghclere............. „	9 22	..	1149	..	..	2 49	7 34	10 9	
Litchfield .... „	9 29	..	1156	..	..	2 58	7 41	1016	
Whitchurch .... „	9 37	..	12 4	1 52	..	3 9	7 49	1024	
Sutton Scotney.......... „	9 49	..	1215	2 3	..	3 20	8 0	1035	
Winchester ....arr.	10 1	..	1227	2 15	..	3 33	8 13	1048	
(Cheesehill St.).......dep.	10 5	..	1233	2 20	..	3 38	8 18	11L29	
Shawford................ „	1013	..	1242	..	..	3 47	8 27	..	
Eastleigh ....arr.	1018	─╮	1248	2 34	─╮	3 53	8 33	1139	..
Portsmouth (Town)....arr.	1139	..	2 31	4 27	..	5*10	9 53	1236	..
Southsea............. „	1145	..	2 40	4 29	..	5 32	..	..	..
Ryde (via Stokes B.) „	12 0	..	2 55	5 15	..	5 15	..	3B10	..
Brockenhurst .... „	1124	..	2 19	..	..	4 53	..	1259	..
Bournemouth East .... „	1214	..	3 4	..	..	5 42	..	..	..
Eastleigh ....dep.	1019	1024	1250	2 35	3 6	3 54	8 35	1146	..
Swaythling .... „	..	1029	1255	..	3 11	3 59	8 40	..	..
St. Denys.............. „	..	1033	1259	..	3 15	4 [illegible]	8 44	..	..
Northam................ „	1028	1037	1 4	2 45	3 20	4 8	8 49	1156	..
Southampt'n D'ks.arr.	1031	1040	1 7	2 48	3 23	4 10	8 52	1158	..
Cowes (Boat) .... „	1210	..	3 0	4 50	..	7 0	..	..	..
Newport, I.W......... „	1250	..	3 55	5 10	..	7 35	..	..	..
Ventnor.............. „	1 51	..	4f52	6 6	..	8 30	..	..	..

E On Wednesdays and Saturdays, leaves Hungerford 3.33 p.m. and arrives Newbury 3.50 p.m.
F Saturdays only to Ventnor. **G** Stops at Shawford on Saturdays.

PASSENGER FARES.

WITH	SOUTHAMPTON. Single 1st	Single 2nd	Single 3rd	Return 1st	Return 2nd	Return 3rd	WINCHESTER. Single 1st	Single 2nd	Single 3rd	Return 1st	Return 2nd	Return 3rd
Abingdon	13/10	10/-	5/4½	23/3	17/3	10/9	10/-	7/9	4/4½	16/9	13/-	8/9
Aylesbury	17/10	12/6	7/-	30/-	21/6	14/-	15/6	11/7	6/6½	26/-	19/6	13/1
Banbury	18/1	13/4	7/5½	30/6	22/6	14/11	14/4	10/10	6/5½	24/-	18/-	12/11
Birkenhead ..	38/4	28/8	19/4	68/3	51/-	38/8	35/7	26/6	18/4	62/-	47/3	36/8
Birmingham ..	25/8	19/-	11/0½	44/-	32/6	22/1	22/-	16/7	10/0½	37/3	28/3	20/1
Burghclere....	5/11	4/7	2/7	9/6	7/3	5/-	3/7	2/10	1/7	6/-	4/9	3/2
Cardiff	31/2	22/10	14/3	52/-	38/6	28/6	26/6	19/6	11/8	42/9	31/6	23/4
Cheltenham ..	17/10	13/-	8/0½	28/1	21/9	16/-	17/2	12/6	7/10	26/10	19/9	15/8
Chester	37/2	28/5	18/1	64/-	47/9	36/2	34/5	26/3	17/1	57/9	44/-	34/2
Cirencester....	19/8	14/5	8/2½	33/6	25/-	16/3	16/-	12/2	7/2½	27/3	20/6	14/5
Compton......	9/1	7/-	4/-	14/9	11/3	7/10	6/9	5/3	3/-	11/3	8/9	6/-
Cork..........	53/-	39/6	23/9	87/-	64/-	42/8	53/-	39/6	23/9	87/-	64/-	42/8
Crewe	33/6	25/8	16/5	58/3	43/-	32/10	30/9	23/6	15/5	53/6	39/3	30/10
Didcot	10/10	8/4	4/8½	17/9	13/6	9/3	8/6	6/7	3/8½	14/3	11/-	7/5
Dudley........	27/-	20/-	11/8	45/3	33/9	23/4	23/4	17/8	10/8	39/3	29/9	21/4
Evesham ..	20/3	17/5	9/1½	32/11	26/7	18/3	20/-	15/4	8/1½	32/11	25/9	16/3
Gloucest'r	17/10	13/-	8/0½	28/1	21/9	16/-	17/2	12/6	7/10	28/-	21/9	15/8
Great Malvern	23/-	17/-	10/6½	37/3	29/9	21/1	22/5	16/11	10/-	37/3	29/9	20/-
Hamps'd Norris	8/9	6/9	3/10	14/3	11/-	7/6	6/5	5/-	2/10	10/9	8/6	5/8
Handsworth ..	26/1	19/5	11/3	44/10	33/3	22/6	22/4	17/-	10/3	38/3	29/-	20/6
Henley in Ar'n	24/2	17/8	10/4½	42/-	30/6	20/9	..	..	..	..	..	..
Hereford......	24/3	18/9	10/6½	39/5	30/6	21/1	23/7	18/9	11/8½	38/2	30/6	23/5
Hermitage	8/-	6/2	3/7	13/-	10/-	7/-	5/8	4/5	2/7	9/6	7/6	5/2
Highclere	6/4	4/9	2/9	10/3	7/9	5/4	4/-	3/-	1/9	6/9	5/3	3/6
Hungerford ..	8/10	6/11	3/10½	14/9	11/4	7/7	6/6	5/2	2/10½	11/3	9/-	5/9
Kidderm'r	26/10	20/-	11/5½	45/3	33/9	22/11	23/4	17/8	10/5½	39/3	29/9	20/11
Leam'ton	21/7	16/-	9/1½	37/-	27/-	18/3	17/9	13/6	8/1½	30/-	22/9	16/3
Litchfield	5/4	4/1	2/4	8/6	6/6	4/6	3/-	2/4	1/4	5/-	4/-	2/8
Liverpool	38/4	28/8	19/5	68/6	51/3	38/10	35/7	26/6	18/5	62/-	47/5	36/10
London (Pad.)	..	..	..	..	..	..	13/9	9/8	5/6	24/-	16/-	10/6
Maid'head	11/4	8/3	4/10	19/6	14/3	9/6	8/7	6/3	4/-	14/9	10/6	8/-
Malvern Wells	23/3	17/-	10/7½	37/8	29/9	21/3	..	..	..	..	..	..
Manchester ..	34/4	26/10	18/11½	66/-	49/9	37/11	31/7	24/8	17/11½	61/-	45/9	35/11
Marlboro'	11/1	8/1	5/0½	16/9	12/6	9/11	8/9	6/4	4/0½	13/3	10/-	8/1
Midgham	8/6	6/5	3/8½	14/3	10/6	7/3	6/2	4/8	2/8½	10/9	8/-	5/5
Newbury	7/4	5/9	3/2½	12/-	9/3	6/3	5/-	4/-	2/2½	8/6	6/9	4/5
Oswestry ..	37/6	27/8	16/3	62/9	46/6	32/6	33/10	25/7	15/3	56/6	42/9	30/6
Oxford	14/1	10/4	5/7	24/6	17/6	11/2	10/5	8/-	4/7	17/9	13/6	9/2
Reading ..	9/4	6/10	3/10½	16/-	11/9	7/7	6/7	4/8	2/10	11/3	8/-	5/8
Rock Ferry ..	38/4	28/8	19/2½	68/-	50/9	38/5	35/7	26/6	18/2½	61/9	47/-	36/5
Rossett	37/2	28/5	17/1[illegible]	64/-	47/9	34/3	..	..	..	..	..	..
Ruabon	37/2	28/5	17/0½	64/-	47/9	34/1	34/5	26/3	16/0½	57/9	44/-	32/1
Savernake	10/2	7/5	4/7	15/6	11/4	9/-	7/10	5/8	3/7	12/-	8/10	7/2
Shrewsbury ..	33/9	24/8	14/7	56/6	41/6	29/2	30/-	22/6	13/7	50/6	37/9	27/2
Slough........	12/5	8/11	5/4	21/6	16/-	10/6	11/-	7/11	4/7	18/9	13/6	9/2
Stourbridge Jc.	26/10	19/10	11/5½	45/3	33/9	22/11	23/4	17/8	10/5½	39/3	29/9	2[illegible]11
Stratf'd-on-A'n	24/2	17/2	10/0½	40/6	29/3	20/1	20/6	15/-	9/0½	34/3	25/3	18/1
Sutton Scotney	3/8	2/10	1/7	5/9	4/4	3/-	1/4	1/1	-/7	2/3	1/10	1/2
Swansea	40/2	29/6	18/3	67/-	49/9	36/6	35/6	26/3	15/5½	57/9	42/9	30/11
Swindon	15/6	11/7	6/8½	24/6	18/6	13/3	10/8	7/9	5/3	16/3	12/-	10/6
Twyford ..	10/2	7/3	4/3½	17/3	12/9	8/7	8/1	5/9	3/9	13/9	9/9	7/6
Upton......	10/4	7/11	4/5½	16/9	13/-	8/9	8/-	6/2	3/5½	13/3	10/6	6/11
Uxbridge	13/9	10/-	5/11½	23/6	17/3	11/9	11/-	8/-	5/1½	18/9	13/6	10/3
Warring'n	37/2	28/8	18/7½	64/6	48/6	37/3	34/5	26/5	17/7½	58/3	44/3	35/3
Warwick	21/10	16/2	9/3½	37/4	27/3	18/7	18/-	13/8	8/3½	30/4	23/-	16/7
Wednesbury ..	27/-	20/-	11/8	45/3	33/9	23/4	23/2	17/7	10/8	39/3	30/-	21/4
Wellington ..	31/9	23/5	13/8½	53/3	39/3	27/5	28/-	21/3	12/8½	47/-	35/6	25/5
Welshpool	37/6	27/5	16/2½	62/10	46/2	32/5	34/-	25/7	15/2½	57/-	42/9	30/5
Whitchurch ..	4/10	3/9	2/0½	7/9	5/9	3/11	2/6	2/-	1/0½	4/3	3/3	2/1
Winchester .	2/4	1/9	1/-	3/6	2/6	1/10	..	..	..	..	..	..
Wolverha'pton	27/9	20/5	12/1	46/6	34/3	24/2	24/-	18/3	11/1	40/9	30/6	22/2
Woodhay	6/8	5/2	2/11	10/9	8/3	5/8	4/4	3/5	1/11	7/3	5/9	3/10
Worcester	20/9	15/11	9/10	33/11	27/7	19/8	20/9	15/5	9/3½	33/11	27/7	18/7
Wrexham	37/2	28/5	17/0½	64/-	47/9	34/1	34/5	26/3	16/0½	57/9	44/-	32/1

PLEASURE PARTY TICKETS at a single fare and a quarter for the double journey will be issued to parties of not less than 6 first, or 10 second or third class passengers.

H Arr. Marlboro' 11.48 a.m. on Thursdays.
J Leave Didcot 5.27 p.m. for Reading. **K** Slip Coach.
L Leaves Winchester L. & S. W. Station. Passengers must find their own way across the City. **S** Saturdays only.

Didcot, Newbury, and Southampton Railway.

IMPROVED TRAIN SERVICE.

TIME TABLE FOR MAY, 1901,

AND UNTIL FURTHER NOTICE.

(Railway route map showing lines connecting Southampton, Winchester, Newbury, Didcot, Oxford, Reading, Birmingham, Manchester, Sheffield, Nottingham, and other destinations. Map labelled "TO CHESTER, NORTH WALES, LIVERPOOL & MANCHESTER", "NEW DIRECT NORTH AND SOUTH ROUTE", "LEICESTER AND NOTTINGHAM (GREAT CENTRAL) LINE", "DIDCOT & NEWBURY ROUTE", "LONDON (PADDINGTON)".)

Time Tables, Fares, Rates, and all information will be supplied at the Company's Offices, 11, Victoria Street, Westminster, London, and 11, Oxford Street (near Docks Station), Southampton.

COX & SHARLAND, PRINTERS, SOUTHAMPTON.

(Vertical text at right of first column:) GOODS TRAFFIC should be ordered by the DIDCOT & NEWBURY (the Best and Shortest) ROUTE.

(Vertical text:) Passengers should ask for Tickets VIA NEWBURY.

THROUGH TRAIN SERVICE.

SOUTHAMPTON, READING, & LONDON (Paddington)

	a.m. ▲	a.m.	a.m.	p.m.	p.m. T	p.m. S
Cowes (Boat) ...... dep.	....	7 0	9 40	....	3 40	8 0
SOUTHAMPT'N Dks „	7 5	9 8	11 48	2 10	5 35	8 5
Northam ...... „	6*49	9 11	11 51	2 14	5 39	8 9
St. Denys ...... „	7 10	9 15	11 55	2 18	5 43	8 12
Eastleigh ...... „	7 18	9 22	12 2	2 25	5 55	8 22
Winchester (Cheesehill) „	7 35	9 40	12 20	2 46	6 16	8 43
Newbury ...... arr.	8 32	10 27	1 17	3 45	7 16	9 42
Reading ...... „	9 9	10 54	2 25	4 50	8 10	10 30
MAIDENHEAD ...... „	11 34	11 41	2 51	5 37	8 58	....
SLOUGH ...... „	10 35	11 59	3 8	6 7	8 45	11 11
WINDSOR ...... „	10 45	12 10	3 40	5 55	9 2	11 35
EALING ...... „	12 16	12 26	3 39	6 55	9 0	....
LONDON (Paddington) .. „	10 10	11 45	2 47	5 50	9 10	11 45

	a.m.	a.m.	noon. T	p.m.	p.m.	p.m.
LONDON (Paddington) ..dep.	6 30	9 5	12 0	1 50	5 45	....
EALING ...... „	6 7	8 10	11 31	1 32	3 36	....
WINDSOR ...... „	6 30	8 30	11 30	1 40	4 35	....
SLOUGH ...... „	7 4	8 46	11 59	1 55	4 14	....
MAIDENHEAD ...... „	7 17	9 1	12 16	1 16	4 46	....
Reading ...... „	7 55	10 15	12 57	3 5	6 34	6 50
Newbury ...... „	8 55	11 40	1 40	3 55	7 0	8 11
Winchester (Cheesehill) arr.	10 4	12 46	2 38	4 53	7 49	9 9
Eastleigh ...... „	10 22	1 5	2 57	5 13	8 5	9 28
St. Denys ...... „	10*46	1 16	3*12	5 22	8 13	9 39
Northam ...... „	10 32	1 19	3 6	5 25	8 17	9 42
SOUTHAMPT'N Dks „	10 37	1 24	3 11	5 29	8 21	9 47
Cowes (Boat) ...... „	12 10	3 0	4 50	7 0	9§45	....

▲—Through Fast Trains Southampton, Reading and Paddington.
S—Saturdays only.   *—Change at Eastleigh.
T—Through Carriages between Southampton and Reading.

NOTTINGHAM, SHEFFIELD, & GREAT CENTRAL Ry.

	a.m. C	a.m.	a.m. C	p.m.	p.m.	p.m. S
Cowes (Boat) .... dep.	....	7 0	9 40	....	3 40	6 0
SOUTHAMPTON ...... „	7 5	9 8	11 48	2 10	5 35	8 5
Northam ...... „	6 49	9 11	11 51	2 14	5 39	8 9
St. Denys ...... „	7 10	9 15	11 55	2 18	5 43	8 12
PORTSMOUTH ...... „	6 10	8 10	10 50	12 40	4 20	6 58
Eastleigh ...... „	7 18	9 22	12 2	2 25	5 55	8 22
Winchester (Cheesehill).. „	7 35	9 40	12 20	2 46	6 16	8 43
Newbury ...... „	8 53	10 33	1 26	3 56	7 22	....
Didcot ...... arr.	9 33	11 13	2 7	4 37	8 0	....
OXFORD ...... „	10 3	11 29	2 30	5 13	8 29	1 51
BANBURY ...... „	10 40	12 20	3 58	6 40	9 14	....
RUGBY ...... „	11‡15	1 55	4‡30	....	....	Saturdays only
Leicester ...... „	11 40	2 19	4 57	....	....	
NOTTINGHAM ...... „	12 39	2 55	6 31	....	....	
Sheffield ...... „	1 33	8 50	7 58	....	....	
GRIMSBY ...... „	3 54	6 8	....	....	....	
HUDDERSFIELD ...... „	2 23	5 6	8 55	....	....	
Bradford ...... „	2 52	6 13	9 48	....	....	

	a.m.	a.m.	a.m.	a.m. C	p.m.	p.m.
Bradford ...... dep.	....	....	....	10 7	12 0	1 22
HUDDERSFIELD ...... „	....	....	....	10 33	12 30	2 17
GRIMSBY ...... „	....	....	....	8 21	....	11 15
Sheffield ...... „	....	4▯50	7 55	11 19	1 41	3 20
NOTTINGHAM ...... „	....	5▯50	8 52	12 16	2 37	4 25
Leicester ...... „	....	6 45	9 30	12 52	3 15	5 25
RUGBY ...... „	....	7 18	....	1‡11	3 42	6 27
BANBURY ...... „	....	8 30	11 35	1 51	5 10	6 27
OXFORD ...... „	7 15	9 25	12▯20	2 25	5 47	7 0
Didcot ...... „	7 45	10 33	12 50	2 57	5 30	7 20
Newbury ...... arr.	8 33	11 17	1 27	3 39	....	8 7
Winchester (Cheesehill).. „	10 4	12 46	2 38	4 53	7 49	9 9
Eastleigh ...... „	10 22	1 5	2 57	5 12	8 5	9 28
PORTSMOUTH ...... „	11 39	2 23	4 36	6 36	9 12	11 25
St. Denys ...... „	10 46	1 16	3 12	5 22	8 13	9 39
Northam ...... „	10 32	1 19	3 6	5 25	8 17	9 42
SOUTHAMPTON ...... „	10 37	1 24	3 11	5 29	8 21	9 47
Cowes (Boat) ...... „	....	....	....	....	....	9§45

B—Through Trains Oxford to Southampton.
C—Through Corridor Trains, Southampton, Oxford and Leicester.

DONNINGTON CASTLE, NEWBURY.

The Didcot, Newbury, and Southampton Railway.

The initial letters "**D. N. & S. R.**," which stand for the "Didcot, Newbury, and Southampton Railway," might equally well be read for "**Direct North and South Route**," this Line being, as reference to the map will show, by far the shortest means of communication between Southampton, the Isle of Wight, and Portsmouth and the Central and Northern Counties of England—shorter, indeed, by many miles than any other route by means of its connections with the **Great Western** and **Great Central** systems. And not only is it the shortest way to the North, but it also forms a most convenient means of access to **Paddington**, for **the West End and North of London**, via Newbury, Reading, and **Windsor Castle** (of which an excellent view is obtained on the way), as well as the best route to the various parts of "Gallant little Wales."

The places of interest, either on the Didcot, Newbury, and Southampton Line (which for the sake of brevity is usually spoken of locally as "the Didcot"), or reached by its route, are unexcelled by any other; and whilst it would be impossible, within the limits of space available, to give anything like an exhaustive description, it is hoped that a brief reference to a few of its principal attractions may indicate, if but faintly, its surpassing interest to the traveller and tourist.

SOUTHAMPTON TO LONDON (Paddington)

Via Winchester, Newbury, Reading, and Windsor Castle.

Starting from the Southampton terminus in a through train of the Great Western Company, the passenger travels for a short distance over the London

and South Western Railway, calling at

EASTLEIGH and BISHOPSTOKE,

where passengers from the **Portsmouth** and **Bournemouth** Lines join the train, and passing on to the Didcot and Newbury Line proper at Shawford Junction—10 miles from Southampton. From this point there is spread out on the left hand the City of Winchester and its environs—a splendid view being obtained of the ancient **Hospital of St. Cross,** founded in 1136 by Henry de Blois, where cake and ale are still given to the wayfarer, and William of Wykeham's old **College,** as well as the grey towers of the vast and venerable **Cathedral,** which, in its present form, dates from the year 1093, and is, next to St. Peter's at Rome, the largest in the world.

A few minutes after passing Shawford Junction, the train stops at

WINCHESTER

Station. In this Ancient and Royal City there are so many objects of interest that it is impossible to do more than give a passing reference to them. In **the Cathedral** lie the remains of many of our Saxon Kings — Ethelwulf, father of Alfred the Great; Egbert; the Great Canute and Queen Emma, Hardicanute, and William Rufus. Here also rest the remains of William of Wykeham, Izaak Walton, and many other men of note. In this Cathedral Queen Mary was married to Philip of Spain in 1554. Besides the other places already named, may be mentioned the Deanery, **Wolvesey,** the Castle (the principal residence of William the Conqueror, and his successors), numerous Churches, St. John's Hospital, the **Old Walls,** and **Ancient City Gates,** several of which are still standing. Here, too, was the last resting place of the remains of King Alfred the Great.

WINCHESTER CATHEDRAL.

Winchester, as is well known, was anciently the Capital, and is the oldest Incorporated City in the

5

Kingdom. Leaving Winchester, the next station is

SUTTON SCOTNEY,

from whence the Archæologist and Ecclesiologist may make a pleasant round, visiting the interesting churches of Barton Stacey and Longparish, also Wonston, Hunton, and Stoke Charity, on the banks of a tributary of the Test, and where the Artist will find no lack of subjects for his pencil. There is also good fishing in the neighbourhood, and accommodation for anglers is provided at the "Coach and Horses" Inn.

WHITCHURCH

is the next station on the route. It is an ancient little town, and formerly returned Members to Parliament. The Saxon Chronicle records a battle fought here in 1001 between the Saxons and Danish settlers. When the railway was made a large number of skulls, pronounced Anglo-Saxon, were found. The church contains a curious piece of sculpture, believed to be Roman stone, and appropriated to a thirteenth century monument. There is also a fine Jacobean monument to one of the Brooke family, in whose house Charles I. was entertained shortly before the Second Battle of Newbury. It was here that Cardinal Newman commenced the "Lyra Apostolica" with the line :—

"Are these the tracks of some unearthly friend?"

whilst waiting for the mail to Falmouth in December, 1832. Whitchurch is renowned for its famous trout fishing, and possesses an excellent inn, yclept the "White Hart," of old coaching fame, and once a favourite resort of Charles Kingsley.

Near here is **Hurstbourne Priors,** the beautiful seat of the Earl of Portsmouth, and two miles away, **St. Mary Bourne,** where the Church, with its Norman Arcades and remarkable font, calls for notice. At **Laverstoke,** a neighbouring village, the paper for the Bank of England notes is made. Coming next to

LITCHFIELD,

the traditional scene of a great battle, during the Saxon period, the line passes on the left a group of Ancient British tumuli, and soon afterwards, **Beacon Hill,** on the crest of which is a fine Celtic Entrenchment in excellent preservation.

BURGHCLERE

is the station for **Kingsclere,** distant three or four miles. The **Church** at Kingsclere is Norman, with central tower. On the top of the hill is the site of **Freemantle Park,** a favourite Hunting Lodge of King John and the Plantagenet Kings. Along the high land stretches the **Roman Road** from Old Sarum (Salisbury) to Silchester, known as the **Port Way.** At Kingsclere is also the famous Racing Stable of Mr. **John Porter**—noted for its Derby winners. Near

6

HIGHCLERE

Station is the **Park,** one of the finest in Hampshire, thirteen miles in circumference. **Highclere Castle,** by Barry, is the seat of the Earl of Carnarvon, and by

HIGHCLERE CASTLE.

his lordship's courtesy the grounds are open to the Public on Wednesdays and Saturdays during the Summer.

WOODHAY

boasted formerly a Palace of the Bishops of Winchester. Three of the Rectors of this parish—Ken, Hooper, and Lowth—became Bishops of London. **West Woodhay House** was erected temp. Charles I. from designs of Inigo Jones. On the summit of the range of hills is **Walbury Camp,** which occupies the highest position to which the chalk rises in England, nearly 1000 feet above sea level. Just North of Woodhay platform we pass over the Enborne stream from Hampshire into Berks.

NEWBURY

is an important Junction Station with the **Great Western,** and also with the **Lambourn Valley** Railway. The town is situated on the River Kennet, at its junction with the Kennet and Avon Canal, and on the celebrated **Bath Road** from London to Bath and Bristol. It has one of the largest Corn Markets in the country. Its Norman Castle formerly stood on the banks of the Kennet, and was invested by King Stephen in 1152, and after a siege of three weeks taken by storm. In the sixteenth century the town was a principal seat of the English Cloth Trade, and John Winchcombe, better known as **"Jack of Newbury,"** raised himself from a poor clothier to opulence, and kept 100 looms at work. When the Scots invaded England he was ordered to furnish four pikemen and two horse soldiers for the King's service, and answered the call by marching out at the head of fifty footmen with bow and pike and fifty mounted men—and an ancient ballad says of Flodden that—

> "None soe loude wythe fame dyd rynge
> "As the laddes of Newberrie."

The **Old Cloth Hall** is the last remnant of the once famous industry.

The **Parish Church** is a handsome structure. In Northbrook Street are the remains of Jack of Newbury's house. Newbury teems with memories of the civil wars. In Cheap Street is the house in which Lord Falkland received his last communion the night before the great battle in which he lost his life. The **First Battle** was fought on the 20th September, 1643, and a memorial to Falkland and the Royalist officers is erected on the battlefield. The **Second Engagement** was on the 27th October, 1644. In the neighbourhood is **Shaw House**, garrisoned for Charles I. In the wainscot of one window is a bullet hole, made by a shot fired at the King. **Donnington Castle**, built *circa* 1385, is renowned for its defence by the Royalist Governor, one of the most remarkable during the wars. **Donnington Hospital** was founded in 1393, and the **Priory**, a house of the Maturine friars, about the same time. Some ten miles from Newbury is the remarkable Roman city of **Silchester**—the English Pompeii.

From Newbury the traveller may diverge to visit

LAMBOURN

easily reached by a short branch railway—the site of a Palace of Alfred the Great—the Windsor of those days. Near here is also **Wayland Smith's Cave**, familiar to readers of "Kenilworth," and the famous "**Blowing Stone.**" Lambourn is also the best point from which to visit the well known **Vale of White Horse**, celebrated in history as the scene of English victories over the Danish invaders, perpetuated by the figure of a white horse cut out of the chalk downs. **Faringdon, where Alfred the Great died** (also his son, Edward the Elder), is within easy distance, as well as many other historic land marks in this "fairy land of Berkshire." Lambourn possesses a fine **Norman Church,** and some of the most noted **Racing Stables** in the country.

From Newbury also the Berks and Hants line of the Great Western Railway runs Westward to Hungerford, **Savernake, Marlborough,** Devizes, Bath and Bristol.

Leaving Newbury, the train proceeds on the Great Western Line, along the valley of the Kennet, to

READING,

sometimes known as "Biscuitopolis," from the world-famed business of Messrs. Huntley and Palmer. Here also is Sutton and Sons' great Seed Establishment, an **Old Abbey,** and a **Museum,** in which is a most interesting section devoted to the wonderful finds of

tools, pottery, jewellery, coins, &c., at Silchester, and dating from early Roman times.

TWYFORD

Junction for **Henley,** of Regatta fame, is passed, and

MAIDENHEAD,

picturesquely situated on the Thames, and soon after a magnificent view of **Windsor Castle** is obtained on the right, as the train rushes past, and after passing a number of smaller stations, and getting a good view

WINDSOR CASTLE.

of **Clieveden Woods,** the beautiful place of Mr. W. Waldorf Astor, and of the unbeautiful convict prison of Wormwood Scrubbs, the train pulls up in the Great Western Railway Company's splendid terminus at

PADDINGTON,

from whence by means of the Metropolitan and District (Underground) Railways, there is speedy and economical access to the City, and the other railway termini, and all the principal parts of the Metropolis.

SOUTHAMPTON to OXFORD, STRATFORD-ON-AVON, BIRMINGHAM and the NORTH.

From Southampton to the North the Didcot, Newbury and Southampton Railway forms by far the most direct route, whether to places served by the **Great Western** or **Great Central** systems. Starting from Southampton **in a through Great Western train,** the route is the same to Newbury as that already described. From Newbury, however, instead of going Eastward to London, we proceed directly North, and crossing the Kennet and Lambourn Rivers (noted for angling) arrive at

HERMITAGE.

Here is the primeval forest of Grimsbury, and within it the Celtic hill fortress called "**Grimsbury Castle,**" remarkable for its strength, extreme beauty of situation, and skill displayed in construction. Near the station a series of prehistoric pile dwellings were discovered a few years ago. **Marlstone,** the fine residence of Mr. George W. Palmer, M.P., is near. The next station is

HAMPSTEAD NORRIS.

Two miles from here is **Yattendon,** the seat of Alfred Waterhouse, R.A. Sir John Norreys, of Netherland war renown, and Carte, the historian, are buried in the **Church.** On the road to Pangbourne and the beautiful Thames Valley is **Ashampstead Common,** a lovely tract of forest scenery. Frilsham House, seat of Sir Cameron Gull, Bart., M.P., is in the neighbourhood. At

COMPTON

are interesting instances of Roman occupation. South of the village is a remarkable Celtic encampment, known as **Perborough Castle,** from whence, Eastward, a good view is obtained of **Lowbury,** another ancient military station, rising about 620 feet, and supposed to be the chief position held by the Danes the night before King Alfred's **Great Battle of Aescesdune** (Ashdown). This fortified post, with well defined traces of a Roman Camp, commands a view of a chain of no less than twelve military entrenchments.

Many racehorses are trained in this neighbourhood, the downs being eminently suited for the purpose.

Two miles away is **East Ilsley,** a small ancient market town, now known chiefly for its Sheep Fairs, which existed as early as Henry III., and are the largest in this part of England. Ilsley is described in the old rhyme as—

> "Far famed for sheep and wool, tho' not for spinners,
> "For sportsmen, doctors, publicans and sinners."

On the highest point of the Downs above East Ilsley is **Cwichelmslawe,** the reputed burial place of **Cwichelm,** King of the West Saxons. About two miles from Compton, high in the hills, is **Aldworth Church,** containing **nine very curious stone monuments**—six knights in armour, and two females, six of them under enriched decorated canopies. They represent the family of De la Beche, the last of them the tutor to the Black Prince. Leaving Compton we pass

CHURN,

which has of late years acquired importance as a military camp. On Chilton Downs here the celebrated racehorse "Eclipse," was bred. At **Churn Knob**, according to tradition, St. Birinus, the Apostle of Wessex, preached the Gospel to the pagan Saxons in the 7th century. Near here the railway crosses the **Ridgeway**, one of the four great Roman Ways which ran from end to end of the Kingdom. At

UPTON

is a curious small Norman Church. Not far away is **East Hendred**, a very picturesque village, at the entrance of which are the remains of the "**Jesus of Bethlehem**" **Monastery**, consisting of an old stone Chapel, with fine perpendicular windows. Attached to the Manor House is the **Chapel of St. Amand**, one of the only three in England which have always been devoted to the Roman Catholic Church. At

DIDCOT,

the terminus of the Didcot, Newbury and Southampton Railway, a junction is effected with the main line of the Great Western. Three miles from here is **Little Wittenham**, in the Church of which is an alabaster monument, bearing the effigies of Sir Wm. Dunch and his wife, the daughter of Sir Henry Cromwell and Aunt of the great Oliver. Here are the famed twin hills of **Sinodun**, and on the other side the Thames the remarkable artificial entrenchments called the **Dyke Hills**, at the junction of the Thame and Isis. An Anglo-Saxon Cemetery has been discovered in this parish, and also evidences of Roman-British occupation **Dorchester Abbey Church** is one of the most interesting structures in England, associated with the earliest English history. **East Hagbourne**, the "Hacca's Broc" of Alfred the Great's Charter, has a fine Church and many picturesque half-timbered houses. Lockinge, the seat of Lord Wantage, V.C., a Director of the Railway, and **Wantage**, the birthplace of King Alfred, are within easy reach.

From Didcot the traveller continues his journey on the Great Western Main Line, either Westward to **Swindon, Gloucester, Cheltenham, Bath, Bristol**, and **South Wales**, or, Northward, to **Abingdon** and

OXFORD,

the great seat of ancient and modern learning, with its picturesque old Colleges rising on every hand, its **Cathedral, Bodleian Library**, beautiful "High" Street, River, and places of interest too many to mention, greeting one on all sides. Going on from Oxford, **Blenheim**, the palace of the Duke of Marlborough,

and **Woodstock**, Fair Rosamond's Bower, and scene of Sir Walter Scott's well-known book, is passed, and

BANBURY,

well known to childhood's days for its "Banbury Cross" and Banbury Cakes, and now the junction for the **Great Central Co.'s new direct Line to Rugby, Leicester, Nottingham, Sheffield**, the Midlands and East Coast.

Then come **Leamington** (for **Kenilworth Castle** and **Coventry**), Warwick, Stratford-on-Avon, the home of our great Shakespeare, and

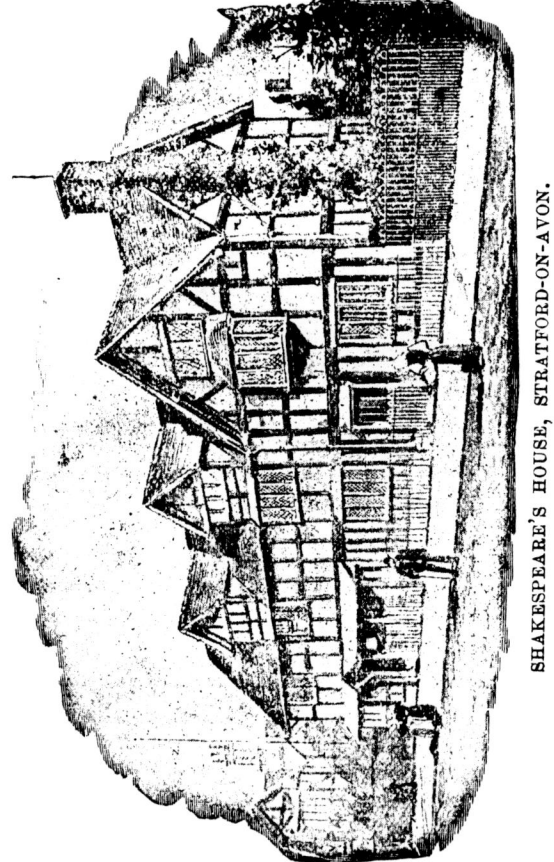

SHAKESPEARE'S HOUSE, STRATFORD-ON-AVON.

BIRMINGHAM.

Going further North, this is still the best route to **Wolverhampton, Shrewsbury, Crewe, Chester**, with its historic old walls, Cathedral, "Rows," ancient City Gates and Racecourse, to the beautiful watering places of the **North Wales Coast**, and to **Liverpool** and **Manchester**. In fact, the traveller journeying to or from the Isle of Wight, Southampton, or Portsmouth will find the "Didcot," in conjunction with the Great Western and Great Central Lines to be, in fact, **the Direct North and South Railway**.

12

TIME TABLE for MAY, 1901,

UP TRAINS.	a.m	a.m	a.m	a.m	a.m	a.m	p.m	p.m	p.m	p.m
Cowes (Boat) ......dep.	..	..	7 07	0 9 40	..	9 40	..	3 40	6 0	
Southampton Town & Docks St'n. "	6 45	7 5	8 20	9 8	1050	..	1148	2 10	5 35	8 5
Northam ......"	6 49	..	8 23	9 11	1054	..	1151	2 14	5 39	8 9
St. Denys ......"	6 54	7 10	8 27	9 15	1058	..	1155	2 18	5 43	8 12
Swaything ......"	6 58	..	8 31	0	11 2	..	0		5 47	8 16
Eastleigh ......arr.	7 37	7 16	8 36	9 20	11 8	..	12 0	2 24	5 52	8 21
Bournemouth Central ....dep.	..	..	7 10	9 26	..	9 54	1110	3 51	6 45	
Ryde (via Stokes Bay) "	..	..	7b15	9 3	..	1010	1115	4 0	..	
East Southsea "	..	..	7 50	9 10	..	1015	1212	4 06	6 20	
Portsmouth (Town) "	6 10	..	8g10	9 25	..	1050	1240	4 20	6 58	
Eastleigh ......dep.	7 18	8 37	9 22	11 9	..	12 2	2 51	5 55	8 22	
Shawford ......"	F	8 46	P	1119	..	F	2 34	6 4	8 30	
Winchester ......arr.	7 30	8 55	9 35	1127	..	1214	2 41	6 11	8 38	
(Cheesehill Street) ......dep.	7 35	9 15	9 40	..	..	1220	2 46	6 16	8 43	
Sutton Scotney ......"	7 48	9 28	9 52	..	..	1233	2 59	6 29	8 57	
Whitchurch ......"	7 58	9 38	P	..	..	1243	3 10	6 39	9 7	
Litchfield ......"	8 7	9 47		..	..	1252	3 19	6 48	9 16	
Burghclere ......"	8 13	9 53	P	..	..	1258	3 25	6 54	9 22	
Highclere ......"	8 18	9 58		..	..	1 3	3 30	6 59	9 27	
Woodhay ......"	8 24	10 4		..	..	1 9	3 36	7 9	9 33	
Newbury ......arr.	8 32	1013	1027	..	..	1 17	3 45	7 16	9 42	
Newbury ......dep.	8 42	—	1029	..	..	1 37	4 10	7 30	10 0	
Reading ......arr.	9 9	..	1054	..	..	2 25	4 50	8 10	1030	
London (Paddington) .. "	1010	..	1145	..	..	2 47	5 50	9 10	1145	
Newbury ......dep.	8 46	..	1059	..	..	2 39	3 52	7 34	..	
Hungerford ......arr.	9 6	..	1116	..	..	2 56	4 13	7 51	..	
Marlborough ......"	9 48	..	1121	..	..	..	5 15	..	..	
Devizes ......"	10 1	..	1132	..	..	..	5 12	10 19	..	
Trowbridge ......"	1028	..	1 57	..	..	..	5 38	10 44	..	
Devizes ......dep.	7 39	..	..	..	..	10 9	1E8	4 16	..	
Hungerford ......"	8 27	..	8 53	..	..	11 8	3 30	5 16	..	
Newbury ......arr.	8 39	..	9 10	..	..	1125	3 48	5 33	..	
London (Paddington) ...dep.	6 30	..	..	..	..	12 0	1 50	5 45	..	
Reading ......"	7 55	..	..	..	..	1257	3 4	..	..	
Newbury ......arr.	8 42	..	..	..	..	1 21	3 48	6 58	..	
Newbury ......dep.	8 53	..	1033	..	..	1 26	3 56	7 22	..	
Hermitage ......"	9 2	..	1042	..	..	1 35	4 5	7 31	..	
Hampstead Norris ......"	9 9	..	1049	..	..	1 42	4 12	7 39	..	
Compton ......"	9 15	..	1055	..	..	1 49	4 19	7 45	..	
Upton ......"	9 27	..	11 7	..	..	2 1	4 31	7 57	..	
Didcot ......arr.	9 33	..	1113	..	..	2 7	4 37	8 3	..	
Didcot ......dep.	10 0	..	12 0	..	..	3 19	4 46	8 40	..	
Reading ......arr.	1045	..	1241	..	..	3 59	6 13	9 38	..	
London (Paddington) "	1145	..	1 58	..	..	5 10	6 0	11 8	..	
Didcot ......dep.	1017	..	1150	..	..	3 20	5 38	8§36	..	
Swindon ......arr.	1049	..	1225	..	..	4 56	6 47	9 7	..	
Bath ......"	1134	..	1 58	..	..	5 12	8 3	9 51	..	
Bristol ......"	1157	..	2 22	..	..	5 35	8 25	10 13	..	
Cheltenham ......"	1230	..	2 10	..	..	4C30	9 22	10§40	..	
Gloucester ......"	12 9	..	1 46	..	..	5C37	8 32	11§45	..	
Didcot ......dep.	9 36	..	1115	..	..	2 15	5 3	8 14	..	
Oxford ......arr.	10 3	..	1129	..	..	2 30	5 31	8 29	..	
Banbury ......"	1040	..	1220	..	..	3 58	6 40	9 14	..	
Leamington ......"	12 5	..	1249	..	..	3 35	7 2	9 42	..	
Stratford-on-Avon ......"	..	..	3 20	..	..	5 8	8	11 20	..	
Birmingh'm (Snow H.) "	1245	..	1 34	..	..	4 26	7 50	10 25	..	
Chester ......"	3 51	..	4 33	..	..	7 10	9 42	..	..	
Birkenhead (Woodside) "	4 30	..	5 6	..	..	7 45	10 2	..	..	
Liverpool (Land. Stg.) "	4 30	..	5 20	..	..	8 0	1025	..	..	
Manchester (Lon. R.) "	5*11	..	5 35	..	..	8 5	1125	..	..	

Side notes: L. & S. W. Railway. — Great Western Railway. — Manch'ter Exch'ge Station. — § Leave Didcot at 8.14 p.m. for Gloucester and Cheltenham (via Chipping Norton). — Saturdays only.

A Through Fast Train between Southampton, Reading, and Paddington.
B via Portsmouth.
C via Chipping Norton Junction.
D Through Carriages between Oxford and Southampton by these trains.
E On Thursdays, leaves Devizes at 2.30 p.m. and Marlboro' 2.35 p.m.
F Stops when required to pick up for Newbury and beyond. **G** Via St. Denys.
H Arr Marlboro' 11.52 a.m. and Devizes at 12.10 noon on Thursdays.
J Leave Didcot 5.30 p.m. for Reading.
K Slip Coach.

and until further notice.

DOWN TRAINS.		a.m.	a.m.	a.m.	a.m.	p.m.	a.m.	a.m. ▲	a.m.	
Great Western Railway.										
Manchest'r (Lon. R.) dep.		..	..	..	..	..	8 35	1150	1150	S
Liverpool (Land Stg.) „		..	..	..	6 0	..	9 10	1140	1140	
Birkenhead (Woodside) .. „		..	..	..	6 15	..	9 30	12 0	12 0	..
Chester „		..	..	..	6 48	..	10 7	1240	1240	..
Birming'm (Snow H.) „		..	..	7 27	10 20	..	1220	4 0	4 0	..
Stratford-on-Avon „		..	..	7 5	9 45	..	1155	3 30	3 30	..
Leamington „		..	..	7 58	11 4	..	1255	4 40	5 5	..
Banbury „		..	..	8 30	11 35	..	1 51	5 10	6 27	..
Oxford „		7 15	..	9 25	12 20	..	2 25	5 47	7 0	..
Didcot arr.		7 38	..	9 49	12 43	..	2 49	..	7 16	..
					D		D		D	
Gloucester dep.		..	..	7 45	..	..	1145	Via Reading	3 20	..
Cheltenham „		..	..	7 20	..	.. C	1140		3c10	..
Bristol „		..	..	7 50	..	..	12 0		3 43	..
Bath „		..	..	8 9	..	..	1218		4 0	..
Swindon „		..	..	9 15	..	..	1 25		6 0	..
Didcot arr.		..	..	1021	..	..	1 54		7 5	..
London (Paddington) dep.		5 40	..	9 5	10 50	..	12 0		5 10	..
Reading „		6 42	..	10 0	11 58	..	1 7		6 0	..
Didcot arr.		7 5	..	1022	12 40	..	1 49		6 22	..
		a.m.		a.m.	p.m.		p.m.	p.m.	p.m.	
Didcot dep.		7 45	..	1033	12 50	.	2 57	..	7 20	..
Upton „		7 55	..	1041	..	..	3 5	..	7 30	..
Compton „		8 9	..	1056	1 6	..	3 18	..	7 46	..
Hampstead Norris .. „		8 14	..	11 1	P	..	3 23	..	7 51	..
Hermitage „		8 23	..	11 9	1 19	..	3 31	..	7 59	
Newbury arr.		8 33	..	1117	1 27	..	3 39	6 58	8 7	
Great Western Railway.										
Newbury dep		8 42	..	1130	1 37	..	4 10	..	8 40	Saturdays only
Reading arr.		9 9	..	1219	2n25	..	4 50	..	9 20	
London (Paddington) „		1010	..	1 40	2 47	..	5 50	..	11 5	
Newbury dep.		8 46	..	1217	2 39	..	3 52	..	9 5	
Hungerford arr.		9 6	..	1237	2 56	..	4 13	..	9 27	
Devizes „		10 1	..	1 32	..	..	5 12	..	1019	
										p.m.
Trowbridge dep.		7 15	..	9 35	1145	..	1238	3 40	3 40	6 43
Devizes „		7 39	..	10 9	1238	..	1e 8	4 16	4 16	7 17
Marlborough „		7 52	..	1025	1237	..	1e30	4 17	4 17	7 37
Hungerford „		8 27	..	11 8	..	..	3 30	5 16	5 16	9 42
Newbury arr.		8 39	..	1125	1 32	..	3 48	5 33	5 33	9 58
					T					
London (Paddington) ..dep.		6 30	..	9 5	12 0	..	1 50	5 45	..	7 15
Reading „		7 55	..	1015	1257	..	3 5	6 34	6 50	8 15
Newbury arr.		8 42	..	1056	1 21	..	3 48	6 58	7 31	9 0
Newbury dep.		8 55	..	1140	1 40	..	3 55	7 0	8 11	10 5
Woodhay „		9 5	..	1150	1 49	..	4 4	Q	8 20	1014
Highclere „		9 14	..	1159	1 57	..	4 12	Q	8 28	1023
Burghclere „		9 20	..	12 4	2 2	..	4 17	Q	8 33	1029
Litchfield „		9 27	..	1210	2 8	..	4 23	Q	8 39	1036
Whitchurch „		9 38	..	1219	2 15	..	4 30	Q	8 46	1044
Sutton Scotney „		9 52	..	1234	2 26	..	4 41	Q	8 57	1055
Winchester arr.	a.m.	10 4	..	1246	2 38	..	4 53	7 49	9 9	11 7
(Cheesehill Street) dep.	9 10	10 8	..	1252	2 43	..	4 57	7 53	9 14	11L35
L. & S. W. Railway.										
Shawford „	9 18	1016	..	1 0	2 51	..	5 5	..	9 22	..
Eastleigh arr.	9 24	1022	—	1 5	2 57	—	5 12	8 5	9 28	1145
Portsmouth (Town) arr.		1139	..	2 23	4 36	..	6 36	9 12	1125	1246
East Southsea „		1145	..	2 40	4 53	..	6 42	G	..	..
Ryde (via Stokes Bay) .. „		12 0	..	2 55	5 15	..	7 0	..	..	3B10
Bournemouth Central „		1244	..	3 10	5 52	..	7 9	9 32	1133	..
Eastleigh dep.	9 25	1023	1040	1 7	2 58	3 3	5 13	8 7	9 30	1152
Swaythling „	9 30	..	1050	1 12	..	3 9	5 18	..	9 35	..
St. Denys „	9 34	..	1046	1 16	..	3 13	5 22	8 13	9 39	..
Northam arr.	9 36	1032	..	1 19	3 6	3 16	5 25	8 17	9 42	12 0
Southampton (Town & Docks Stn.) „	9 40	1037	..	1 24	3 11	3 22	5 29	8 21	9 47	12 7
Cowes (Boat) arr.	..	1210	..	3 0	4 50	..	7 0	9S45	..	..

L Leaves Winchester L. & S. W. Station. Passengers must find their own way across the City.
N Leaves Newbury 2 p.m. for Reading
O Leave Swaythling 9.7 a.m. and 2.12 p.m. and change at Eastleigh.
P Calls when required, to pick up passengers for Paddington.
Q Calls when required, to set down passengers from London.
R Leaves Didcot 2.15 for Cheltenham via Chipping Norton.
S Saturdays only.
T Through Carriages, Southampton and Reading, by these trains.

For List of Through Carriages, see page 14.

THROUGH CARRIAGES

Are Run as under:—

Southampton to Oxford, Banbury, Rugby, and Leicester (Gt. Central), 7.5 and 11.48 a.m.
„ London (Paddington), 9.8 a.m.
„ Reading, 9.8 a.m. and 5.35 p.m.
Winchester to Oxford, Banbury, and Leicester, 7.35 a.m. and 12.20 p.m.
„ London (Paddington), 9.40 a.m.
„ Reading, 9.40 a.m. and 6.16 p.m.

Banbury to Winchester and Southampton, 1.51 and 6.27 p.m.
Leicester (Gt. Central) to Winchester and Southampton, 12.48 p.m. and 5.25 p.m.
Oxford to Winchester and Southampton, 12.20, 2.25 & 7 p.m.
Paddington to Winchester and Southampton, 5.45 p.m.
Reading to Winchester and Southampton, 12.57 and 6.34 p.m.
Rugby (Gt. Central) to Winchester and Southampton, 1.11 and 5.48 p.m.

GOODS TRAFFIC

TO AND FROM

SOUTHAMPTON AND WINCHESTER,

AND

READING, LONDON (Paddington & Smithfield), OXFORD, BIRMINGHAM DISTRICT, LEICESTER, NOTTINGHAM, and GREAT CENTRAL LINE.

THROUGH RATES

AND A

THROUGH SERVICE OF GOODS TRAINS

ARE NOW IN FORCE BY

THE DIDCOT, NEWBURY AND SOUTHAMPTON DIRECT ROUTE.

Goods intended for this route should be consigned "Via Didcot, Newbury and Southampton Railway."

Rates and Full Particulars can be obtained on application at the Company's Office, 11, Oxford Street (near Docks Station), Southampton.

Telegrams: "GIPPS, SOUTHAMPTON." **Telephone 380, Southampton.**

LAMBOURN VALLEY RAILWAY.

DOWN TRAINS.	T.S.O. a.m.	Mix'd T.S.X a.m.	T.S.O. a.m.	p.m.	p.m.	p.m.		SUNDAYS. p.m.	SUNDAYS. p.m.
Newbury	*9 15*	*9 30*	*11 30*	1 45	4 5	7 25	..	3 30	7 45
SPEEN	*9 23*	*9 39*	*11 38*	1 53	4 13	7 33	..	3 38	7 53
STOCKCROSS	†	†	..	†	†	7 38	..	†	7 58
BOXFORD	*9 32*	*9 50*	*11 47*	2 2	4 22	7 44	.	3 47	8 4
WELFORD PARK	*9 39*	*10 0*	*11 53*	2 9	4 29	7 51	..	3 54	8 11
GREAT SHEFFORD	*9 45*	*10 9*	*11 59*	2 15	4 35	7 57	..	4 0	8 17
EAST GARSTON	*9 51*	*10 19*	†	2 21	4 41	8 3	..	4 6	8 23
EASTBURY	*9 55*	*10 29*	..	2 25	4 45	8 7	..	4 10	8 27
Lambourn	*10 0*	*10 35*	*12 12*	2 30	4 50	8 12	..	4 15	8 32

UP TRAINS.	a.m.	T.S.O. a.m.	p.m.	p.m.	p.m.			SUNDAYS. p.m.	SUNDAYS. p.m.
Lambourn	7 45	*10 30*	12 35	3 0	6 5	..	..	2 15	6 5
EASTBURY	7 51	*10 36*	†	†	6 11	..	..	2 21	6 11
EAST GARSTON	7 55	*10 40*	12 43	3 8	6 15	..	..	2 25	6 15
GREAT SHEFFORD	8 1	*10 46*	12 49	3 14	6 21	..	..	2 31	6 21
WELFORD PARK	8 8	*10 53*	12 56	3 21	6 28	..	..	2 38	6 28
BOXFORD	8 14	*10 59*	1 2	3 27	6 34	..		2 44	6 34
STOCKCROSS	†	†	†	†	6 41	..	..	†	6 41
SPEEN	8 24	*11 9*	1 12	3 37	6 46	..	..	2 54	6 46
Newbury	8 30	*11 15*	1 18	3 43	6 52	..	..	3 0	6 52

† Stop if required. T.S.O.—Thursdays and Saturdays only.
T.S.X.—Thursdays and Saturdays excepted.

PASSENGER FARES.

WITH	SOUTHAMPTON. Single 1st	Single 2nd	Single 3rd	Return 1st	Return 2nd	Return 3rd	WINCHESTER. Single 1st	Single 2nd	Single 3rd	Return 1st	Return 2nd	Return 3rd
Abingdon	10/9	6/9	5/4½	18/10	11/11	10/9	8/9	5/6	4/4½	15/4	9/8	8/9
Aylesbury	14/-	8/9	7/-	24/6	15/7	14/-	13/-	8/3	6/6½	23/-	14/6	13/1
Banbury	15/-	9/3	7/5½	26/3	16/5	14/11	13/-	8/-	6/5½	22/9	14/2	12/11
Bath	13/10	8/9	6/11	24/3	15/3	13/10	11/10	7/6	5/11	20/9	13/-	11/10
Birkenhead	35/-	23/1	18/5½	64/7	40/6	36/11	33/-	21/10	17/5½	61/2	38/3	34/11
Birming'm	22/-	13/9	11/0½	38/8	24/3	22/1	20/-	12/6	10/0½	35/2	22/-	20/1
Bradford	35/3	..	19/2	66/9	..	38/4	33/3	..	18/2	63/3	..	36/4
Bristol	15/9	9/11	7/10½	27/6	17/5	15/9	13/9	8/8	6/10½	24/-	15/2	13/9
Burghclere	5/2	3/3	2/7	9/-	5/9	5/-	3/2	2/-	1/7	5/6	3/6	3/2
Cardiff	22/9	14/3	11/4½	38/6	25/0	22/7	20/9	13/-	10/4½	35/-	22/9	20/9
Cheltenham	16/-	10/3	8/-	28/1	17/11	16/-	15/8	9/10	7/10	26/10	17/3	15/8
Chester	33/10	21/7	17/2½	60/1	37/9	34/5	32/4	20/4	16/2½	56/9	35/6	32/5
Cirencester	13/-	8/-	6/5½	21/11	14/3	12/11	13/-	8/-	6/5½	20/8	14/2	12/11
Compton	8/-	5/-	4/-	14/-	8/9	7/10	6/-	3/9	3/-	10/6	6/6	6/-
Cork	50/7	35/6	23/9	84/4	60/2	42/8	50/9	35/8	23/9	86/-	60/8	42/8
Crewe	30/3	19/3	15/5	54/-	33/11	30/10	28/9	18/-	14/5	50/6	31/8	28/10
Didcot	9/6	5/11	4/8½	16/6	10/5	9/3	7/6	4/8	3/8½	13/-	8/2	7/5
Derby	..	..	..	..	..	..	25/0	14/4	12/4	43/3	27/0	24/8
Doncaster	31/9	..	17/3½	59/4	..	34/7	29/9	..	16/3½	55/10	..	32/7
Dudley	22/7	14/7	11/8	40/10	25/7	23/4	21/1	13/4	10/8	37/4	23/4	21/4
Evesham	18/3	11/5	9/1½	32/-	20/1	18/3	16/3	10/2	8/1½	28/6	17/10	16/3
Gloucest'r	16/-	10/3	8/-	28/1	17/11	16/-	15/8	9/10	7/10	26/10	17/3	15/8
Great Malvern	18/11	13/3	9/10	33/11	23/3	19/8	18/6	12/-	9/6½	32/6	21/-	19/1
Grimsby	34/8	..	19/3½	65/5	.	37/3	..	..	..	..	..	..
Hamps'd Norris	7/8	4/9	3/10	13/6	8/7	7/6	5/8	3/6	2/10	10/-	6/4	5/8
Henley in Ar'n	20/9	13/-	10/4½	36/4	22/9	20/9	18/9	11/9	9/4½	32/10	20/6	18/9
Hereford	21/-	14/3	10/6½	36/10	24/11	21/1	20/8	13/-	10/4	35/6	22/8	20/8
Hermitage	7/2	4/6	3/7	12/6	8/-	7/-	5/2	3/3	2/7	9/-	5/9	5/2
Highclere	5/6	3/6	2/9	9/8	6/3	5/4	3/6	2/3	1/9	6/2	4/-	3/6
Hull	35/1	..	19/5½	65/11	..	38/11	..	..	..	..	..	..
Hungerford	7/9	4/11	3/10½	13/6	8/9	7/7	5/9	8/8	2/10½	10/-	6/6	5/9
Leam'ton	18/3	11/5	9/1½	32/-	20/1	18/3	16/3	10/2	8/1½	28/6	17/10	16/3
Leeds	34/1	..	19/2	64/5	..	38/4	32/1	..	18/2	60/11	..	36/4
Leicester	21/4	..	11/2½	38/11	..	22/5	19/4	..	10/2½	35/5	..	20/5
Litchfield	4/8	2/11	2/4	8/2	5/3	4/6	2/8	1/8	1/4	4/8	3/-	2/8
Liverpool	35/-	23/3	18/6½	64/8	40/9	37/1	33/-	22/-	17/6½	61/2	38/6	35/1
Lond'n (Pad)	13/-	8/2	6/6	23/-	14/6	11/6	11/-	7/-	5/6	19/3	12/2	10/6
„ Ret. same dy.	or F	ri. to	Mon.	20/6	13/-	10/-	..	..	..	18/-*	12/-*	..
Maidenhead	9/6	6/-	4/9½	16/10	10/7	9/5	7/6	4/9	3/9½	13/4	8/4	7/7
Malvern Wells	18/11	13/3	9/10	33/11	23/3	19/8	18/2	11/9	9/4½	31/10	20/6	18/9
Manch'ter	32/10	22/6	18/-	63/-	39/6	36/-	30/10	21/3	17/-	59/6	37/3	34/-
Marlboro'	10/-	6/3	5/0½	16/9	11/3	9/11	8/-	5/-	4/-	13/3	8/9	8/-
Midgham	7/6	4/9	3/8½	13/-	8/3	7/3	5/6	3/6	2/8½	9/6	6/-	5/5
Newbury	6/6	4/1	3/2½	11/3	7/3	6/3	4/6	2/10	2/2½	7/9	5/-	4/5
Newport (Mon)	21/6	13/5	10/8½	37/6	23/7	21/3	19/6	12/2	9/8½	34/-	21/4	19/5
Nottingh'm	24/6	..	13/2	45/3	..	26/4	22/6	..	12/2	41/9	..	24/4
Oxford	11/2	7/-	5/7	19/6	12/3	11/2	9/2	5/9	4/7	16/-	10/-	9/2
Reading	7/8	4/9	3/10	13/6	8/7	7/6	5/8	3/6	2/10	10/-	6/4	5/8
Rock Ferry	35/-	22/11	18/3½	64/-	40/3	36/7	33/-	21/8	17/3½	60/6	38/-	34/7
Ruabon	31/8	20/9	16/2½	56/3	36/7	32/5	31/4	19/6	15/8	54/10	34/4	31/4
Rugby	18/8	..	9/6½	33/7	..	19/1	16/8	..	8/6½	30/1	..	17/1
Savernake	9/2	5/9	4/7	15/6	10/3	9/-	7/2	4/6	3/7	12/-	8/-	7/2
Sheffield	29/3	..	16/1	54/9	..	32/2	27/3	..	15/1	51/3	..	30/2
Shrewsb'y	27/5	17/11	14/1½	48/11	31/5	28/3	27/2	17/-	13/7	47/6	29/9	27/2
Slough	10/6	6/9	5/3½	18/6	11/9	10/5	8/6	5/6	4/3½	15/-	9/6	8/7
Stourbridge Jc.	22/7	14/3	11/5½	40/3	25/3	22/11	21/-	13/-	10/5½	36/9	23/-	20/11
Stratf'd-on-A'n	20/-	12/7	10/0½	35/2	22/1	20/1	18/-	11/4	9/0½	31/8	19/10	18/1
Sutton Scotney	3/2	2/-	1/7	5/6	3/7	3/-	1/2	9d.	7d.	2/-	1/4	1/2
Swansea	30/4	19/-	15/2	51/10	33/3	30/2	28/4	17/9	14/2	48/4	31/-	28/2
Swindon	10/6	6/6	5/3	17/6	11/6	10/6	10/6	6/6	5/3	16/3	11/6	10/6
Twyford	8/8	5/5	4/3½	15/-	9/7	8/7	7/2	4/6	3/7	12/6	8/-	7/2
Upton	9/-	5/7	4/5½	15/9	9/9	8/9	7/-	4/4	3/5½	12/3	7/6	6/11
Warring'n	33/10	21/9	17/5	61/-	38/3	34/10	32/4	20/6	16/5	57/6	36/-	32/10
Warwick	18/6	11/9	9/3½	32/6	20/6	18/7	16/6	10/6	8/3½	29/-	18/3	16/7
Wednesbury	22/7	14/7	11/8	40/10	25/7	23/4	21/4	13/4	10/8	37/4	23/4	21/4
Well'gton (Sal.)	27/-	17/3	13/8½	48/-	30/3	27/5	25/6	16/-	12/8½	44/6	28/-	25/5
Welshpool	31/-	20/-	15/9½	54/11	34/11	31/7	30/6	19/-	15/2½	53/3	33/6	30/5
Whitchurch	4/-	2/7	2/0½	7/2	4/7	3/11	2/-	1/4	1/0½	3/8	2/4	2/1
Winch'ter	2/-	1/3	1/-	3/6	2/3	1/10	..	..	..	..	..	..
Wolverha'pton	23/7	15/3	12/1	42/4	26/9	24/2	22/2	14/-	11/1	38/10	24/6	22/2
Woodhay	5/10	3/9	2/11	10/3	6/6	5/8	3/10	2/6	1/11	6/9	4/3	3/10
Worcester	18/11	12/11	9/10	33/11	22/9	19/8	18/6	11/8	9/3½	32/6	20/6	18/7
Wrexham	32/6	21/3	16/7½	57/9	37/5	33/3	32/-	20/-	16/0½	56/2	35/2	32/1

PLEASURE PARTY TICKETS at a single fare and a quarter for the double journey will be issued to parties of not less than 6 first, or 10 second or third class passengers. [*Friday or Saturday to Monday only.

THROUGH TRAIN SERVICE

Between The ISLE OF WIGHT, SOUTHAMPTON, PORTSMOUTH, WINCHESTER and NEWBURY, OXFORD, BIRMINGHAM, and the NORTH.

Passengers should ask for Tickets VIA NEWBURY.

	Station		a.m.	a.m. (C via Portsm'th)	a.m.	p.m.	p.m.	p.m. (Saturdays only)
I.W.C.R.	Ventnor (Town)	dep.	....		8 30	.. .	2 30	3 40
I.W.C.R.	Sandown	„	....		8 27	....	2 30	3 40
I.W.C.R.	Freshwater	„	....		....	....	2 20	4 20
I.W.C.R.	Yarmouth, I.W.	„	....		....	....	2 25	4 25
I.W.C.R.	Newport, I.W.	„	. ..		9 5	....	3 4	5 15
I.W.C.R.	Cowes (Boat)	„	....	7 0	9 40	....	3 40	6 0
	Southampton	dep.	7 5	9 8	11 48	2 10	5 35	8 5
I.W.R.	Ventnor	„	....	....	9 20	10 25	3 17	..
I.W.R.	Shanklin	„	....	....	9 32	10 38	3 30	..
I.W.R.	Sandown	„	....	....	9 38	10 45	3 37	..
I.W.R.	Ryde (via Stokes Bay)	„	....	7C15	10 10	11 15	4 0	..
	Portsmouth	„	6 10	8 10	10 50	12 40	4 20	6 58
	Eastleigh & Bishopstoke	„	7 18	9 22	12 2	2 25	5 55	8 22
	Winchester (Cheesehill)	„	7 35	9 40	12 20	2 46	6 16	8 43
	Newbury	arr.	8 32	10 27	1 17	3 45	7 16	9 42
	Didcot	„	9 33	11 13	2 7	4 37	8 3	....
G.W.R.	BATH	arr.	11 10N	1 58D	5 12D	6 42N	9 50D	....
G.W.R.	BRISTOL	„	11 35N	2 22D	5 35D	7 5N	10 12D	....
G.W.R.	NEWPORT (Mon.)	„	12 31	3 10	6 33	9 40	1 48	....
G.W.R.	CARDIFF	„	12 52	3 33	6 54	10 2	2 10	....
G.W.R.	SWANSEA	„	3 25	5 30	8 25	12 5	4 10	....
G.W.R.	OXFORD	„	10 3	11 29	2 30	5 31	8 29	1 51
G.W.R.	WORCESTER (Shrub Hill)	„	12 47	2 13	4 36	7 33	10 33	....
G.W.R.	MALVERN (Great)	„	1 20	2 47	5 3	8 7	11 13	....
G.W.R.	GLOUCESTER	„	12 9	1 46	5 37A	8 27	11 45 A	....
G.W.R.	CHELTENHAM	„	12 30	2 10	4 30A	9 16	10 40 A	....
G.W.R.	BIRM'GHAM (Snow Hill)	„	12 42	1 34	4 26	7 30	10 25	3 40
G.W.R.	WOLVERHAMPTON	„	1 8	2 0	5 0	7 53	10 55	4 7
G.W.R.	SHREWSBURY	„	1 59	3 3	5 45	8 33	12 8	4 55
G.W.R.	CREWE	„	3 34B	4 12	7 5	10 7	12 48B	....
G.W.R.	CHESTER	„	3 33	4 33	7 10	9 42		6 10
G.W.R.	LIVERPOOL (Lan. Stg.)	„	4 30	5 20	8 0	10 25	....	7 25
G.W.R.	MANCHESTER (Lon. Rd.)	„	5*11	5 35	8 5	11 25	....	9*35

	Station		a.m. (†Not on Mondays)	a.m.	a.m.	a.m.	a.m.	a.m.
G.W.R.	MANCHESTER (Lon. rd.)	dep.	..	....	....	8 35	11 50	....
G.W.R.	LIVERPOOL (Lan. Stg.)	„	..	....	6 0	9 10	11 40	....
G.W.R.	CHESTER	„	..	....	6 48	10 7	12 40	....
G.W.R.	CREWE	„	..	†4 32B	7 40B	9 40	1 5	....
G.W.R.	SHREWSBURY	„	..	....	8 9	11 7	2 15	....
G.W.R.	WOLVERHAMPTON	„	..	6 50	9 52	11 55	3 32	....
G.W.R.	BIRMINGH'M (Snow Hill)	„	..	7 27	10 20	12 20	4 0	....
G.W.R.	CHELTENHAM	„	..	7 20	....	11 40A	3 10A	....
G.W.R.	GLOUCESTER	„	..	7 45	....	11 45	2 38A	3 20
G.W.R.	MALVERN (Great)	„	....	6 19M	8 39	10 47	3 2	....
G.W.R.	WORCESTER (Shrub Hill)	„	....	8 45	9 12	11 30	3 0	....
G.W.R.	OXFORD	„	7 15	9 25	12 20	2 25	5 47	7 0
G.W.R.	SWANSEA	„	....	....	8 30	....	9 40	10 50
G.W.R.	CARDIFF	„	....	6 8	10 10	....	12 10	2 10
G.W.R.	NEWPORT (Mon.)	„	....	6 27	10 32	....	12 32	2 30
G.W.R.	BRISTOL	„	6 5N	8 12N	11 40N	12 0D	2 15N	3 42D
G.W.R.	BATH		6 23N	8 36N	11 56N	12 18D	2 37N	4 0D
	Didcot	dep.	7 45	10 33	12 50	2 57	...	†7 20
	Newbury	„	8 55	11 40	1 40	3 55	7 0	8 11
	Winchester	arr.	10 4	12 46	2 38	4 53	7 49	9 9
	Eastleigh	„	10 22	1 5	2 57	5 12	8 5	9 28
	Portsmouth	„	11 39	2 23	4 36	6 36	9 12	11 25
I.W.R.	Ryde (via Stokes Bay)	„	12 0	2 55	5 15	7 0	....	....
I.W.R.	Sandown	„	12 28	3 38	5 45	8 19	....	....
I.W.R.	Shanklin	„	12 36	3 45	5 50	8 25	....	....
I.W.R.	Ventnor	„	12 49	3 36	6 0	8 37	....	....
	Southampton	„	10 37	1 24	3 11	5 29	8 21	9 47
I.W.C.R.	Cowes (Boat)	arr.	12 10	3 0	4 50	7 0	9§45	....
I.W.C.R.	Newport, I.W.	„	12 55	3 55	5 15	7 40	....	....
I.W.C.R.	Yarmouth, I.W.	„	1 35	....	6 55S	9§25	....	....
I.W.C.R.	Freshwater (Alum Bay)	„	1 40	....	7 0S	9§30	....	....
I.W.C.R.	Sandown	„	1 28	....	5 43	8 15	....	....
I.W.C.R.	Ventnor (Town)	„	1 30	....	5 45	8 15	....	....

* Exchange Station. **A** via Chipping Norton Junction. **B** via Birmingham (New street). **D** via Didcot. **M** Mondays only (Bank Holidays excepted) from Great Malvern. **N** via Newbury. **S** Saturdays only.

For List of Through Carriages, see page 14.

The first timetable for 'up' and 'down' trains is reproduced below, and the 1902 timetable is also shown.

The line will be opened for public traffic on Monday, when the following time table will come into force:—

DOWN.						
Didcot	...	7 45	10 30	1 0	5 25	..
Upton	...	7 53	10 38	1 8	5 33	...
Compton	...	8 6	10 51	1 21	5 4[illegible]	...
Hampstead Norris	...	8 12	10 57	1 27	5 52	...
Hermitage	...	8 20	11 6	1 35	6 0	...
Newbury .... arr.	...	8 30	11 17	1 45	6 10	...
„ ...... dep.	...	9 0	11 22	2 15	6 15	...
Woodhay	...	9 10	11 32	2 25	6 25	...
Highclere	...	9 17	11 39	2 32	6 3[illegible]	...
Burghclere	...	9 23	11 45	2 38	6 38	...
Litchfield	...	9 30	11 52	2 45	6 45	...
Whitchurch	...	9 41	12 4	2 57	6 57	...
Sutton Scotney	..	9 53	12 17	3 10	7 10	...
Winchester	...	10 8	12 32	3 25	7 25	...

UP.						
Winchester	...	7 55	10 20	2 30	5 0	...
Sutton Scotney	...	8 11	10 36	2 46	5 16	...
Whitchurch	...	8 23	10 48	2 58	5 28	...
Litchfield	...	8 34	10 58	3 9	5 39	...
Burghclere	...	8 41	11 5	3 16	5 46	...
Highclere	...	8 48	11 12	3 23	5 53	...
Woodhay	...	8 55	11 19	3 30	6 0	...
Newbury .... arr.	...	9 5	11 28	3 40	6 10	...
„ ...... dep.	...	9 20	11 30	3 45	6 15	...
Hermitage	..	9 29	11 39	3 55	6 2[illegible]	...
Hampstead Norris	...	9 37	11 47	4 3	6 32	...
Compton	...	9 43	11 53	4 10	6 38	...
Upton	. .	9 57	12 7	4 26	6 52	...
Didcot	...	10 5	12 15	4 35	7 0	...

No Trains will run on Sundays.

DIDCOT, NEWBURY, WINCHESTER AND SOUTHAMPTON.

Down Trains. — Week Days only

	Down Trains.		a.m.	a.m.	a.m.	a.m.	a.m.	p.m.	pm	p.m.	p.m. (SATURDAYS ONLY)
	BIRMINGHAM (S. Hill)	dep	...	..	...	7 27	10 20	12 20	...	4 0	
	Leamington	„	.	.	.	7 58	11 4	12 55	.	5 5	
	Banbury	„	...	...	...	8 30	11 35	1 49	...	6 25	
	Oxford	„	.	7 15	.	9 25	12 20	2 25	.	7 0	
	Didcot	arr	...	7 38	...	9 49	12 43	2 49	...	7 16	
	Bristol (Temple Meads)	dep	.	.	.	7 50	9U35	12 0	.	3 45	
	Bath	„	...	...	...	8 9	9U52	12 18	...	4 2	
	Cheltenham	„	.	.	.	7 20	9U20	11V40	.	3V10	
	Gloucester	„	...	...	...	7 45	9U45	11 45	...	3 20	
	Didcot	arr	.	.	.	10 20	12 43	2 49	.	7 5	
	London (Paddington)	dep	...	5 40	...	9 5	10 50	12 0	...	5 10	
	Reading	„	.	6 42	.	10 0	11 58	1 7	.	6 0	
	Didcot	arr	..	7 5	...	10 22	12 40	1 49	...	6 22	
	DIDCOT	dep	Mixed.	7 45	.	10 33	12 50	2 57	.	7 20	
	Upton	„	Mixed.	7 55	...	10 41		3 5	...	7 30	
	Compton	„	Mixed.	8 9	.	10 56	1 6	3 18	.	7 46	
	Hampstead Norris	„	Mixed.	8 14	...	11 1	K	3 23	...	7 51	
	Hermitage	„	Mixed.	8 23	.	11 9	1 19	3 31	.	7 59	
	Newbury	arr	Mixed.	8 33	...	11 17	1 27	3 39	...	8 7	
	Newbury	dep	.	8 42	.	11 42	1 37	4 10	.	8 50	
	Reading	arr	...	9 10	...	12R28	2N25	4 50	...	9 30	
	London (Paddington)	„	.	10 10	.	12 45	2 47	5 50	.	11 8	
	LONDON (Paddington)	dep	...	6 30	9 35	...	12 35	1 50	5 45	...	7 15
	Reading	„	.	7 55	10 23	10 30	1 23	3 5	6 33	6 50	8 15
	Newbury	arr	...	8 42	10 46	11 11	1 46	3 48	6 58	7 31	9 0
	Newbury	dep	Mixed.	8 55	10 53	11 40	1 52	3 55	7 0	8 10	10 5
	Woodhay	„	Mixed.	9 5	...	11 50	2 1	4 4	M	8 20	10 14
	Highclere	„	Mixed.	9 14	.	11 59	2 9	4 12	M	8 28	10 23
	Burghclere	„	Mixed.	9 20	...	12 4	2 14	4 17	M	8 33	10 29
	Litchfield	„	Mixed.	9 27	.	12 10	2 20	4 23	M	8 39	10 36
	Whitchurch	„	Mixed.	9 38	11 17	12 19	2 27	4 30	M	8 46	10 44
	Sutton Scotney	„	Mixed.	9 52	.	12 34	2 37	4 41	M	8 57	10 55
	Winchester	arr	Mixed.	10 4	11 36	12 46	2 48	4 53	7 49	9 9	11 7
L. & S. W. R.	Winchester	dep	9 10	10 8	11 40	12 52	2 53	4 57	7 53	9 14	.
L. & S. W. R.	Shawford	arr	9 17	10 15	...	12 59	3 0	5 4	M	9 21	...
L. & S. W. R.	Eastleigh & Bishopstoke	„	9 24	10 22	11 51	1 5	3 6	5 12	8 5	9 28	.
L. & S. W. R.	Swaythling	„	9 29	..	...	1 11	...	5 17	...	9 34	...
L. & S. W. R.	St. Denys	„	9 33	.	11 59	1 15	3 16	5 22	8 13	9 38	.
L. & S. W. R.	Northam	„	9 36	10 32	12 3	1 19	3 20	5 25	8 17	9 42	...
L. & S. W. R.	**SOUTHAMPTON**	„	9 40	10 37	12 9	1 24	3 25	5 29	8 21	9 47	.

Up Trains. — Week Days only.

	Up Trains.		a.m.	a.m.	a.m.	a.m.	a.m.	p.m.	p m	p.m.	p.m. (SATURDAYS ONLY)
L. & S. W. R.	**STHAMPTON**	dep	7 5	8 20	9 8	10 50	11 48	2 13	5 28	...	8 5
L. & S. W. R.	Northam	„	.	8 23	9 11	10 54	11 51	2 17	5 31	.	8 9
L. & S. W. R.	St. Denys	„	7 10	8 27	9 15	10 58	11 55	2 21	5 35	...	8 12
L. & S. W. R.	Swaythling	„	.	8 31	.	11 2	.	.	5 39	.	8 16
L. & S. W. R.	Eastleigh & Bishpstke	„	7 18	8 37	9 22	11 9	12 2	2 28	5 45	...	8 22
L. & S. W. R.	Shawford	„	W	8 46	L	11 19	W	2 36	5 53	.	8 32
L. & S. W. R.	Winchester	arr	7 30	8 55	9 35	11 27	12 14	2 44	6 0	...	8 38
	Winchester	dep	7 35	9 15	9 40	.	12 20	2 50	6 5	6 18	8 43
	Sutton Scotney	„	7 48	9 28	9 52	...	12 33	3 3	6 17	6 31	8 57
	Whitchurch	„	7 58	9 38	L	.	12 43	3 13	6 27	6 41	9 7
	Litchfield	„	8 7	9 47	.	...	12 52	3 22	...	6 50	9 16
	Burghclere	„	8 13	9 53	L	.	12 58	3 28	.	6 56	9 22
	Highclere	„	8 18	9 58	...	...	1 3	3 33	...	7 1	9 27
	Woodhay	„	8 24	10 4	.	.	1 9	3 39	6 46	7 9	9 33
	Newbury	arr	8 32	10 13	10 27	...	1 17	3 46	6 53	7 16	9 42
	Newbury	dep	8 42	.	10 29	.	1 37	4 10	6 56	7 30	10 0
	Reading	arr	9 10	...	10 55	...	2N25	4 50	7 20	8 10	10 30
	LONDON (Pad'gton)	„	10 10	.	11 45	.	2 47	5 50	8 20	9 15	11 45
	London (Paddington)	dep	6 30	...	7 25	...	12 0	1 50		5 45	
	Reading	„	7 55	.	9 0	.	12 57	3 5	.	6 33	
	Newbury	arr	8 42	...	9 41	...	1 21	3 48	...	6 58	
	Newbury	dep	8 58	.	10 33	.	1 25	3 56	.	7 22	
	Hermitage	„	9 2	...	10 42	...	1 35	4 5	...	7 32	
	Hampstead Norris	„	9 9	.	10 49	.	1 42	4 12	.	7 39	
	Compton	„	9 15	...	10 55	...	1 49	4 19	...	7 45	
	Upton	„	9 27	.	11 7	.	2 1	4 31	.	7 57	
	DIDCOT	arr	9 33	...	11 13	...	2 7	4 37	...	8 3	
	Didcot	dep	10 0	.	12 0	.	3 17	4 46	.	8 40	
	Reading	arr	10 45	...	12 40	...	3 57	6T15	...	9 38	
	London (Padd'gton)	„	11 45	.	1 58	.	5 10	6 0	.	11 8	
	Didcot	dep	10 17	...	11 50	...	3 20	5 38	...	8 35	
	Gloucester	arr	12 9	.	1 46	.	5J37	8 32	.	11X46	
	Cheltenham	„	12 30	...	2 10	...	4J30	9 22	...	10X40	
	Bath	„	11 34	.	1 58	.	6 12	8 8	.	9 51	
	Bristol (T. Meads)	„	11 57	...	2 22	...	5 35	8 25	...	10 18	
	Didcot	dep	9 38	.	11 15	.	2 15	5 8	.	8 18	
	Oxford	arr	10 8	...	11 30	...	2 30	5 30	...	8 30	
	Banbury	„	10 40	.	12 20	.	3 58	6 40	.	9 14	
	Leamington	„	12 5	...	12 49	...	3 35	7 2	...	9 42	
	BIRM'GH'M (S. Hill)	„	12 42	.	1 34	.	4 26	7 30	.	10 25	

J—Via Chipping Norton Junction, leave Didcot at 2.15 p.m.
K—Calls at Hampstead Norris to pick up Passengers for London on notice being given at the Station not later than 12.30 p.m.
L—Calls to pick up Passengers for London, on notice being given at the Station.
M—Calls to set down Passengers from London, on notice being given by the Passenger to the Guard at Newbury.
N—Leave Newbury at 2.0 p.m.
R—Leave Newbury at 11.48 a.m.
T—Leave Didcot at 5.30 p.m.
U—Via Radley. **V**—Via Chipping Norton Junction,
W—Calls at Shawford to pick up Passengers for Newbury and beyond, on notice being given at the Station.
X—Via Chipping Norton Junction, leave Didcot at 8.18 p.m.

A 1902 timetable

An 1884 working timetable, showing the crossing arrangements

No. 1.

DIDCOT AND NEWBURY LINE.

SINGLE LINE WORKED BY TRAIN STAFF, ASSISTED BY DISC BLOCK TELEGRAP

(NARROW GAUGE.)

Distance	DOWN TRAINS. WEEK DAYS ONLY.	1 Goods & Passngr.		2 Oxford & Bristol Goods.		3 Passngr.		4		5 Goods & Passenger.		6 Passngr.		7 Passngr.		8 Passngr.	
	STATIONS.	arr.	dep.	arr.	dep.	arr.	dep.			arr.	dep.	arr.	dep.	arr.	dep.	arr.	dep.
		a.m.	a.m.	a.m.	a.m.	a.m.	a.m.			p.m.	p.m.	p.m.	p.m.	p.m.	p.m.	p.m.	p.m.
	DIDCOT	—	7 25	6 45	7 40	—	1030	...	...	—	12 25	—	3 0	—	5 25	—	7 25
2¼	Upton	7 33	7 37	—	—	10 37	10 38	...	..	12 35	12 40	3 7	3 8	5 32	5 33	7 32	7 33
8	Compton	7 51	7 55	8 13	8 15	10 49	10 51	..		12 57	X1 6	3 19	X3 21	5 44	5 46	7 44	7 46
10½	Hampstead Norris ...	8 2	8 5	—	—	10 56	10 57		...	1 15	1 23	3 26	3 27	5 51	5 52	7 51	7 52
12¼	Brick Yard Siding ...	—	—	C	R	—	—		...	C	R	—	—	—	—	—	—
13	Hermitage...	8 15	8 18	—	—	11 4	11 5	...	.	38	1 45	3 31	3 35	5 59	6 0	7 59	8 0
17	Greenham Junction ...	—	8 20	—	8 48	—	11 14	...	...	—	X1 55	—	3 41	—	6 9	—	8 9
17¾	NEWBURY	8 30	—	8X50	9 15	11 15	—	..	...	1 57	—	3 45	—	6 10	—	8 10	—

CR Call if required only.

Distance	UP TRAINS. WEEK DAYS ONLY.	1 Passngr.		2 Passngr.		3 A Bristol and Oxford.		4 B Bristol and Oxford.		5 Didcot Local Goods.		6 Passngr.		7 Passngr.		8 Goods & Passngrs	
	STATIONS.	arr.	dep.	arr.	dep.	arr.	dep.	arr.	dep.	arr.	dep.	arr.	dep.	arr.	dep.	arr.	dep.
		a.m.	a.m.	a.m.	a.m.	p.m.	p.m.	p.m.	p.m.	p.m.	p.m.	p.m.	p.m.	p.m.	p.m.	p.m.	p.m.
	NEWBURY	—	9X20	—	11 27	12 15	12 30	1 40	2 0	—	2 20	—	4 5	—	6 25	—	8 30
¾	Greenham Junction ...	—	9 21	—	11 28	—	12 32	—	2X2	—	2 22	—	4 6	—	6 26	—	8 31
4¼	Hermitage	9 28	9 29	11 35	11 36	—	—	—	—	2 34	2 45	4 13	4 14	6 33	6 34	8 40	8 43
6	Brick Yard Siding ...	—	—	—	—	—	—	—	—	—	—	—	—	—	—	—	—
7½	Hampstead Norris ..	9 36	9 37	11 43	11 44	—	—	—	—	2 53	3 0	4 21	4 22	6 41	6 42	8 50	8 53
9½	Compton	9 42	9 43	11 48	11 50	12 55	X1 10	2 36	3X20	3 7	X3 40	4 26	4 28	6 46	6 48	9 0	9 5
15	Upton	9 56	9 57	12 3	12 4	—	—	—	—	3 55	4 5	4 41	4 42	7 1	7 2	9 17	9 20
17¾	DIDCOT	10 5	—	12 12	—	1 45	2 40	3 50	4 15	4 15	—	4 50	—	7 10	—	9 30	—

A Not run on Thursdays. B Thursdays only.

CROSSING ARRANGEMENTS.

X Where this mark is shown one Train crosses another.

The 7.40 a.m. Goods from Didcot crosses the 9.20 a.m. Passenger Train from Newbury at Newbury.

The 12.25 p.m. Mixed from Didcot crosses the 12.30 p.m. Goods from Newbury at Compton, except on Thursdays. On Thursdays it crosses the 2.0 p.m. from Newbury at Greenham Junction.

The 3.0 p.m. Passenger Train from Didcot crosses the 2.20 p.m. Goods from Newbury at Compton.

On Thursdays only the 3.0 p.m. Passenger Train from Didcot crosses 2.0 p.m. Goods Train from Newbury at Compton

FORM AND COLOUR OF STAFF AND TICKET.

From	To	Colour of Staff and Ticket	Shape.
NEWBURY	COMPTON	BLUE	SQUARE.
COMPTON..	DIDCOT	RED	ROUND.

A 1933 timetable

DIDCOT, NEWBURY, WINCHESTER AND SOUTHAMPTON.

Miles.		Week Days a.m.	a.m.	a.m.	a.m.	p.m.	p.m.	p.m.	p.m. Saturdays only.	Sun. p.m.
...	London (Padd.) dep	.	5 30	8 40	11C15	1 45	3 35	5 15		12 45
...	Reading .... ,,	...	6 52	9 27	11 40	2 35	4 58	6 8		1 32
.	Oxford . . . ,,	.	7 10	9 50	11 35	2 50	4 58	6 5		1 0
...	Didcot .... dep	...	7 38	10 20	12 35	3 35	5 52	6 47		3 0
3	Upton & Blewbury ,,	.	7 46	10 30	12 42	3 43	5 59	6 54		3 8
6¾	Churn . . . . . ,,	...	7 53	X	X	X	X	X		...
8½	Compton . . ,,	.	7 58	10 42	12 56	3 55	6 13	7 7		3 21
10¾	Hampstead Norris ,,	...	8 3	10 47	1 1	4 0	6 19	7 12		3 27
12¾	Pinewood Halt ,,	.	8 9	10 53	1 7	4 6	6 25	7 18		3 33
13¾	Hermitage .. ,,	...	8 14	10 56	1 10	4 10	6 28	7 23		3 36
18	Newbury . arr	.	8 23	11 5	1 19	4 18	6 37	7 35		3 45
...	London (Padd.) dep	...	7 15	10 45	12 30	2 45	6 0	...	7 55	...
.	Reading . ,,	.	8 28	11 42	1 17	3 32	6 8	.	8 45	.
...	Newbury ... dep	7 45	9 5	12 25	2 0	4 28	7 18	...	10 20	...
21½	Woodhay . ,,	7 53	9 16	12 33	2 7	4 37	7 26	.	10 28	.
23¾	Highclere ... ,,	8 5	9 22	12 38	2 13	4 43	7 32	...	10 34	...
25¾	Burghclere D . ,,	8 10	9 27	12 43	2 18	4 48	7 37	.	10 39	.
28	Litchfield (Hants) ,,	8 16	9 33	12 48	2 23	4 54	7 43	...	10 45	...
31¾	Whitchurch (Hants) W	8 23	9 40	12 55	2 30	5 1	7 50	.	10 52	.
37¼	Sutton Scotney ,,	8 36	9 50	1 4	2 39	5 11	8 0	...	11 2	...
40¼	Worthy D'wn P'form ,,	8 42	9 56	1 10	2 45	5 17	8 6	.	.	.
42¼	King's Worthy ,,	8 47	10 1	1 15	2 52	5 22	8 11	...	11 12	...
44¼	Winchester¶ arr	8 51	10 5	1 19	2 56	5 26	8 15	.	11 16	.
...	Winchester¶ dep	8 58	10 14	1 22	3 2	5 31	8 25	...	...	...
47¼	Southern Rly. Shawford . arr	9 5	10 21	1 29	3 9	5 38	8 32	.	.	.
51¼	Eastleigh ... ,,	9 13	10 27	1 36	3 10	5 45	8 39	...	...	...
53¼	Swaythling ,,	9 20	10 34	2J 1	3 22	5 56	8 47	.	.	.
55	St. Denys ,,	9 24	10 38	2J 5	3 26	6 0	8 51	...	...	...
56	Northam . ,,	9 28	10 42	2J10	3 30	6 4	8 55	.	.	.
56¾	Southampton Terminus§ ..	9 32	10 46	2J14	3 34	6 8	8 59	...	...	...

	Week Days a.m.	a.m.	a.m.	a.m.	a.m.	p.m.	p.m.	p.m.	p.m. Sats. only.	Sun. p.m.
Southern Rly. Southampton Terminus§ dep	.	.	P 7 33	9 40	11 30	2 5	4 52	7 30		.
Northam ... ,,	...	...	7 36	9 43	11 33	2 8	4 55	7 33		...
St. Denys . ,,	.	.	7 40	9 47	11 37	2 12	4 59	7 37		.
Swaythling ,,	...	...	7 44	9 51	11 41	2 16	5 3	7 41		...
Eastleigh . ,,	.	.	7 51	9 58	11 48	2 25	5 10	7 48		.
Shawford ... ,,	...	...	8 0	10 5	11 56	2 34	5 18	7 56		...
Winchester¶ arr	.	.	8 8	10 13	12 4	2 41	5 26	8 4		.
Winchester¶ dep	...	7 5	8 16	10 23	12 10	2 46	5 33	STOP	8 50	...
King's Worthy . ,,	.	7 14	8 22	10 29	12 16	2 52	5 39	.	8 56	.
Worthy D'wn P'form ,,	...	7 19	8 27	10 34	12 21	2 57	5 44	...	R	...
Sutton Scotney ,,	.	7 27	8 35	10 42	12 28	3 3	5 51	.	9 8	.
Whitchurch (Hants) W	...	7 37	8 45	10 52	12 39	3 13	6 1	...	9 18	...
Litchfield (Hants) ,,	.	7 47	8 53	11 1	12 50	3 20	6 9	.	9 26	.
Burghclere D . . ,,	...	7 57	9 0	11 8	12 56	3 26	6 15	...	9 32	...
Highclere . ,,	.	8 4	9 7	11 13	1 1	3 31	6 20	.	9 37	.
Woodhay . . ,,	...	8 15	9 15	11 18	1 6	3 36	6 25	...	9 42	...
Newbury . arr	.	8 22	9 22	11 28	1 15	3 48	6 32	.	9 50	.
Reading ..... arr	...	9 12	10C13	12 7	2 3	4 43	7 18	...	...	...
London (Padd) ,,	.	10 0	10 50	12 55	2 55	5 50	8 10	p.m	.	.
Newbury ... dep	6 45	8 28	9 28	...	1 45	4 0	7 11	8 10	10 20	7 58
Hermitage . ,,	6 55	8 38	9 37	.	1 54	4 11	7 21	8 19	10 29	8 8
Pinewood Halt ,,	6 58	...	...	...	1 57	4 14	7 24	8 22	10 32	8 11
Hampstead Norris ,,	7 5	8 46	9 44	.	2 4	4 21	7 31	8 29	10 39	8 18
Compton ...... ,,	7 10	8 53	9 50	...	2 10	4 27	7 36	8 36	10 45	8 26
Churn . . ,,	.	K	K	.	K	K	K	K	.	.
Upton & Blewbury ,,	7 20	9 3	10 0	...	2 20	4 39	7 47	8 45	10 55	8 37
Didcot . . arr	7 26	9 10	10 6	.	2 26	4 48	7 53	8 51	11 1	8 43
Oxford ...... arr	8 35	10 9	10 37	...	3 22	5 25	8 30	9 16	11 30	9 39
Reading ,,	8 17	9C39	11 5	.	3 28	5 25		9 33	1‡48	9 14
London (Padd.) ,,	9 0	10 15	11 55	...	5 22	6 15	...	10 26	‡2 40	10 0

C—Slip Carriage. D—Station for Kingsclere (3¼ miles). J—Change at Eastleigh. K—Calls to pick up or set down Passengers on previous notice to the Station Master at Newbury. Evening trains call during daylight only. P—Through Train Southampton to York, Newcastle-on-Tyne, Edinburgh and Glasgow. R—Calls to set down on notice to the Guard at Winchester. W—About 1¼ miles from Southern Rly. Station. X—Calls to pick up or set down Passengers on previous notice to the Station Master at Didcot. Evening trains call during daylight only. ‡—Sunday morning. §—For Docks ¶—Cheesehill Station. About 1 mile from Southern Rly. Station.

A 1943 timetable

DIDCOT, NEWBURY AND WINCHESTER.

	Week Days a.m.	a.m.	p.m. Sats. only.	p.m. Saturdays only.	p.m.	p.m.	p.m.	p.m.	Suns. p.m.
Didcot .... dep.	...	7 37			12 45	3 35	5 52	6X30	3 0
Upton and Blewbury ,,	.	7 45			12 52	3 42	5 59	.	3 8
Churn .... ,,	...	7 52			R	R	R	...	...
Compton . . ,,	.	7 58			1 6	3 54	6 11	.	3 21
Hampstead Norris ,,	...	8 3			1 11	3 59	6 17	...	3 27
Pinewood Halt . ,,	.	8 9			1 17	4 5	6 24	.	3 33
Hermitage .... ,,	...	8 15			1 22	4 10	6 29	...	3 37
Newbury . arr.	.	8 25			1 30	4 18	6 38	7X20	3 45
Newbury dep.	7 45	9 5	12 35		2 0	4 25	7 18		
Woodhay . . ,,	7 53	9 16	12 42		2 10	4 33	7 28	.	.
Highclere ...... ,,	8 2	9 22	12 48		2 16	4 39	7 35	...	...
Burghclere . . ,,	8 8	9 27	1 0		2 21	4 44	7 40	.	.
Litchfield (Hants) ,,	8 14	9 33	1 6		2 27	4 50	7 46	...	...
Whitchurch (Hants) ,,	8 22	9 40	1 15	1 40	2 34	4 58	7 55	.	.
Sutton Scotney ... ,,	8 35	9 50		1 50	2 44	5 10	8 6	...	...
Worthy Down Plat. ,,	8 45	9 56	.	1 56	2 50	5 20	8 12	.	.
King's Worthy ... ,,	8 50	10 2	...	2 2	3 0	5 25	8 18	...	...
Winchester (¶) arr.	8 56	10 8	.	2 7	3 7	5 29	8 23	.	.

	Week Days a.m.	a.m.	a.m.	p.m.	p.m.	p.m.	p.m.	p.m.	Suns. p.m.
Winchester (¶) ... dep.	...	7 5	8 14	12 14	...	2 45	5 33	11 0	...
King's Worthy . . ,,	.	7 10	8 20	12 20	.	2 55	5 39	11 8	.
Worthy Down Platform ,,	...	7 16	8 25	12 25	...	3 2	5 44	11 18	...
Sutton Scotney . . ,,	.	7 25	8 35	12 31	.	3 12	5 50	11 26	.
Whitchurch (Hants) ,,	...	7 38	8 45	12 42	...	3 24	6 2		...
Litchfield (Hants) . ,,	.	7 48	8 53	12 52	.	3 32	6 10	STOP	.
Burghclere .... ,,	...	7 55	9 0	1 0	...	3 38	6 16	...	...
Highclere . . . . ,,	.	8 3	9 7	1 6	.	3 43	6 22	.	.
Woodhay .... ,,	...	8 12	9 15	1 12	...	3 48	6 28	...	...
Newbury . . arr.	.	8 21	9 22	1 22	.	3 58	6 36	p.m.	.
Newbury dep.	6 45		9 35		1 55	4 20		7 22	8 10
Hermitage . . . . ,,	6 55	.	9 45	.	2 4	4 30	.	7 32	8 20
Pinewood Halt ...... ,,	6 58	...	9 48	...	2 7	4 33	...	7 35	8 24
Hampstead Norris . ,,	7 3	.	9 56	.	2 15	4 42	.	7 43	8 32
Compton .... ,,	7 10	...	10 3	...	2 20	4 50	...	7 49	8 40
Churn . . . . ,,	.	.	Q	.	Q	Q	.	Q	.
Upton and Blewbury ,,	7 20	...	10 14	...	2 32	5 0	...	8 0	8 52
Didcot . . . . arr.	7 28	.	10 20	.	2 38	5 8	.	8 10	9 0

A 1947 timetable

DIDCOT, NEWBURY, WINCHESTER AND SOUTHAMPTON.

	Week Days a.m.	a.m.	a.m.	p.m.	p.m. Saturdays only.	p.m.	p.m.	p.m. Saturdays only.	Sun. p.m.
Didcot .... dep.	.	7 37	10 50	12 42	2 0	3 35	5 52	7 0	3 0
Upton and Blewbury ,,	.	7 45	10 56	12 48	2 7	3 42	6 0	7 7	3 8
Churn .... ,,	...	7 52	T	T	T	T	T	...	...
Compton . . ,,	.	7 58	11 7	12 59	2 18	3 54	6 12	7 19	3 21
Hampstead Norris ,,	...	8 3	11 13	1 4	2 25	3 59	6 18	7 24	3 27
Pinewood Halt . ,,	.	8 9	11 21	1 11	2 31	4 5	6 26	7 31	3 33
Hermitage ...... ,,	...	8 12	11 24	1 14	2 34	4 10	6 30	7 35	3 37
Newbury . arr.	.	8 20	11 33	1 25	2 50	4 18	6 41	7 45	3 46
Newbury dep.	7 45	9 5	12 25	2 0		4 25	7 12		
Woodhay . . ,,	7 53	9 16	12 32	2 8		4 33	7 21		.
Highclere ...... ,,	8 2	9 22	12 38	2 14		4 39	7 27		...
Burghclere . . ,,	8 8	9 27	12 43	2 19		4 44	7 33		.
Litchfield (Hants) ,,	8 14	9 33	12 49	2 25		4 50	7 39		...
Whitchurch (Hants) ,,	8 22	9 40	12 57	2 33		4 58	7 47		.
Sutton Scotney .. ,,	8 35	9 50	1 8	2 45		5 10	7 59		...
Worthy Down Plat. ,,	8 45	9 56	1 15	2 55		5 20	8 7		.
King's Worthy ... ,,	8 50	10 2	1 20	3 2		5 25	8 12		...
Winchester (¶) arr.	8 56	10 8	1 26	3 7		5 30	8 17		.
S.R. Eastleigh (D) arr.	9 21	10 28	1 41	3 37	...	5 54	8 39	...	...
Southampton Terminus (§) ,,	9 35	10 47	2 23	3 56	.	6 13	8 59		.

	Week Days a.m.	a.m.	a.m.	a.m.	a.m.	p.m.	p.m. Saturdays only.	p.m.	p.m. Saturdays only.	Sun. p.m.
S.R. Southampton Terminus (§) dep.	...	...	7 32	9 36	11 26	1 55	...	4 55	...	...
Eastleigh (D) ,,	.	.	7 50	9 56	11 45	2 20	.	5 12	.	.
Winchester (¶) dep.	...	7 5	8 14	10 25	12 7	2 45		5 33		...
King's Worthy . ,,	.	7 10	8 20	10 30	12 13	2 50		5 39		.
Worthy Down Plat. ,,	...	7 16	8 25	10 36	12 19	2 55		5 44		...
Sutton Scotney . ,,	.	7 25	8 35	10 43	12 25	3 3		5 50		.
Whitchurch (Hants ,,	...	7 38	8 45	10 54	12 38	3 14		6 2		...
Litchfield (Hants) ,,	.	7 48	8 55	11 4	12 52	3 23		6 10		.
Burghclere ...... ,,	...	7 55	9 0	11 10	12 58	3 29		6 16		...
Highclere . . ,,	.	8 3	9 7	11 15	1 3	3 34		6 22		.
Woodhay ...... ,,	...	8 12	9 15	11 22	1 10	3 39		6 28		...
Newbury . arr.	.	8 21	9 22	11 35	1 18	3 47		6 36		.
Newbury dep.	6 45		9 35		1 58	4 20	5 26	7 22	8 10	8 10
Hermitage . . ,,	6 55	.	9 45	.	2 7	4 30	5 36	7 32	8 20	8 20
Pinewood Halt ... ,,	6 58	...	9 48	...	2 10	4 33	5 38	7 35	8 24	8 24
Hampstead Norris ,,	7 3	.	9 56	.	2 16	4 42	5 46	7 43	8 32	8 32
Compton ...... ,,	7 10	...	10 3	...	2 21	4 50	5 52	7 49	8 40	8 40
Churn . . ,,	.	.	Q	.	Q	Q	Q	Q	Q	.
Upton and Blewbury ,,	7 20	...	10 14	...	2 32	5 0	6 3	8 0	8 52	8 52
Didcot . . arr.	7 28	.	10 20	.	2 38	5 8	6 9	8 10	9 0	9 0